£.80

GW00713244

FIRST OF THE SMALL NATIONS

OXFORD HISTORICAL MONOGRAPHS

The *Oxford Historical Monographs* series publishes some of the best Oxford University doctoral theses on historical topics, especially those likely to engage the interest of a broad academic readership.

First of the Small Nations

The Beginnings of Irish Foreign Policy in the Interwar Years, 1919–1932

GERARD KEOWN

OXFORD
UNIVERSITY PRESS

OXFORD
UNIVERSITY PRESS

Great Clarendon Street, Oxford, OX2 6DP,
United Kingdom

Oxford University Press is a department of the University of Oxford.
It furthers the University's objective of excellence in research, scholarship,
and education by publishing worldwide. Oxford is a registered trade mark of
Oxford University Press in the UK and in certain other countries

First Edition published in 2016

Impression: 1

Published in the United States of America by Oxford University Press
198 Madison Avenue, New York, NY 10016, United States of America

British Library Cataloguing in Publication Data
Data available

Library of Congress Control Number: 2015949832

ISBN 978–0–19–874512–9

Printed in Great Britain by
Clays Ltd, St Ives plc

For my parents,
Eamonn & Marie

Acknowledgements

This book began life many years ago, with a simple question: where did Ireland's foreign policy come from? Along the way, I have many people to thank.

My first attempt to answer my own question was as a D.Phil. student at the University of Oxford. I would like to thank Professor Roy Foster for setting me on a path that has led to this book, and for his friendship, support, and encouragement in the years since.

Thanks are due to the staffs of the National Archives of Ireland, the National Library of Ireland, the archives departments at University College Dublin and at Trinity College Dublin, the Bodleian Library in Oxford, the National Archives of the United Kingdom, and the Ministry of Foreign Affairs in Paris, as well as to the library at the Department of Foreign Affairs and Trade. I am grateful, in particular, to Seamus Helferty of UCD Archives, and Catriona Crowe and Aideen Ireland of the National Archives of Ireland. I am grateful, also, to Kathleen and Stephen MacWhite for permission to quote from the Michael MacWhite papers; to the late Louis le Brocquy for sharing memories of his father, Albert; and to the late Garrett FitzGerald for his insights and for his recollections of his father, Dermot.

Some of the ideas in this book were developed in a series of lectures at the Department of Foreign Affairs and Trade: I am grateful to Secretaries General David Cooney and Niall Burgess for their support, and to colleagues whose questions helped me to clarify my ideas. Thanks, also, to Professor Alvin Jackson and Dr Enda Delaney for an opportunity to present one of the chapters at Edinburgh University, to Owen Dudley Edwards for his thought-provoking comments, and to Susan Conlon for her warm hospitality.

Sincere thanks go to Enda Delaney and Dr Eibhlín Evans for comments on the completed manuscript, which were invariably on the mark. I owe a debt of gratitude to Haruko Onda for technical assistance at the outset; to Brian Glynn, Keith Moynes, and Martin Laflamme for reading chapters as they appeared and offering encouragement to keep going, and to Brian McElduff for his forensic ability to spot typos.

I would like to thank my editor, Professor Patricia Clavin, for her support and patience as I juggled writing with a busy day job. Thanks are due, also, to Professor R. J. Evans and Dr John Watts of Oxford

Historical Monographs, to Cathryn Steele of OUP for her patience, and to Dr Michael Kennedy and Professor Eunan O'Halpin for encouraging me to write this history.

I owe a particular debt of gratitude to my sister, Edwina, for her scholarly advice, her unflagging support, and for 'lit-proofing' the manuscript along the way.

Finally, thank you to my parents for encouraging me down the path of history, and to my partner, Stephen Donnelly, for putting up with my endless interest in Ireland's foreign relations, current and historical. The views expressed are in a personal capacity and any mistakes are my own.

Gerard Keown

Contents

Contents

List of Figures

Note on Names and Terminology

It was common at the time that is the focus of this book to use the Irish and English versions of names interchangeably, particularly in writing. For clarity, the version by which an individual is most commonly known is used: thus, Seán T. Ó Ceallaigh rather than O'Kelly; Diarmuid O'Hegarty, rather than Ó hEageartaigh; but Michael Collins and not Micheál Ó Coillean. Where an Irish language name or term is used, a translation is provided on the first appearance. A glossary of frequently used Irish terms is also provided.

Contemporary place names have been used throughout, except where the modern equivalent is more widely known, for example Ethiopia instead of Abyssinia, and Nanjing over Nanking. In some cases both are given, to provide clarity for the reader.

The use of acronyms—common in the world of diplomacy and its study—has been kept to a minimum, with an explanation provided to guide the reader where these may be unfamiliar. The French Foreign Ministry is referred to in places by its shorthand, the Quai d'Orsay, while its Italian and German counterparts are known as the Farnesina and the Wilhelmstrasse respectively; each derives from its address.

Irish Terms Used

Ard fheis	Party convention
Bean na hÉireann	Newspaper (lit. 'Woman of Ireland')
Clan na Gael	Irish-American nationalist organization (lit. family of the Gaels)
Conradh na Gaeilge	The Gaelic League
Cumann na nGaedheal	Political party, 1922–33 (lit. 'League of the Gaels')
Dáil Éireann	Lower House of the Irish Parliament (often abbreviated to Dáil)
Fianna Fáil	Political party, 1926– (lit. 'soldiers of destiny')
Fine Gaedheal	Proposed Irish race organization, 1922 (lit. 'family of the Gaels')
Inighidhna na hÉireann	Women's nationalist organization (lit. 'Daughters of Ireland')
Leabhair na hÉireann	The Irish Yearbook
Oireachtas	Houses of the Irish Parliament
Poblacht na hÉireann	Irish Republic
An Roinn Gnóthaí Coigriche	Department of External Affairs
Saor an Leanbh	Save the Children Committee
Saorstát Éireann	Irish Free State (often abbreviated to Saorstát)
Seanad Éireann	Upper House of the Irish Parliament (often abbreviated to Seanad)
Sinn Féin	Political party (lit. 'we, ourselves')
Taoiseach	The Irish prime minister after 1937
Teachta Dála (T.D.)	Member of Dáil Éireann

Abbreviations

CAI	Cork Archives Institute
Dáil Éireann deb.	Dáil Éireann Debates
DE	Dáil Éireann
DEA	Department of External Affairs
DF	Department of Finance
DFA	Department of Foreign Affairs
DT	Department of the Taoiseach
ES	Early Series, Department of Foreign Affairs archives
FO	Foreign Office
ILO	International Labour Organisation
IPP	Irish Parliamentary Party
IRA	Irish Republican Army
IRB	Irish Republican Brotherhood
ISDL	Irish Self-Determination League
LN	League of Nations
MA	Military Archives, Dublin
NAI	National Archives of Ireland
NLI	National Library of Ireland
PRO	The National Archives of the United Kingdom—Public Records Office, London
QO	Archives of the Ministry of Foreign Affairs, Paris
Seanad Éireann deb.	Seanad Éireann Debates
TCD	Trinity College Dublin
UCD	University College Dublin
UCDA	University College Dublin Archives

Introduction

Beginnings

In 1932, the German constitutional lawyer, Leo Kohn, published a lengthy tome on the Irish Free State's constitution. Kohn's study appeared in time for the tenth anniversary of both the country and its constitution. In its pages he dispassionately detailed the provisions by which independent Ireland was governed. While other areas were described at greater length, he singled out the existence of a foreign ministry as exemplifying most the changed political status of Ireland.[1] The Free State's first prime minister, William Cosgrave, had made a similar point the year before when describing the progress achieved in the Irish Free State in a cinema message to American audiences. Almost a decade had passed since the Anglo-Irish Treaty that gave birth to the Irish Free State. As he reflected on how Ireland had changed in the intervening years, Cosgrave chose the country's achievements in foreign policy to illustrate his message that 'the story of "Ireland amongst the Nations" has begun'.[2] Where that story begins—the beginnings of Irish foreign policy—and how it developed in the first decade of the Irish state is the subject of this history.

The ability to conduct a foreign policy and decide on matters of war and peace has long been regarded as one of the primary tests of independence. Indeed, foreign policy is still, largely, conducted by and between states, whether acting on their own, unilaterally; bilaterally with another state; or collectively as groups of states in a multilateral context. While there is much reflection and debate about the merits of a particular foreign policy or its implications, less often do we consider how the underlying tenets of a country's foreign policy were shaped, or the origins of the fundamental ideas and interests that underpin it.

---

[1] Leo Kohn, *The Constitution of the Irish Free State* (London, 1932).
[2] Copy of the text of cinema newsreel speeches made by William T. Cosgrave, 11 June 1931, NAI DFA DT S2366.

The legal establishment of the Irish Free State on 6 December 1922 is the date from which an Irish state was, in principle, able to engage in inter-state relations. In the decade that followed, the young Irish state took its first steps on the world stage, joining the League of Nations; engaging in Commonwealth affairs; creating a small network of diplomatic missions and espousing multilateralism as a cornerstone of Irish foreign policy. The following chapters will seek to explore how that first foreign policy was created.

As we shall see, the manner in which independence was achieved—not the independent republic called for in 1919 but as a dominion in the British Commonwealth—would render this a difficult undertaking at first. Overcoming the constraints on freedom of action on the international stage, imposed by the political settlement with Britain, is a well-told part of the story of early Irish foreign policy. Less well-told is the story of how Irish hopes and aspirations for an international voice developed.

The emergence of the Irish state coincided with the beginnings of global governance through the League of Nations, the first real attempt to establish the rule of law as the guiding principle in international relations. In the decades that followed, the course charted by the Irish state would closely follow the development and fortunes of the mechanisms of international governance. Like other states, a mixture of domestic and external considerations influenced policy-making. Ensuring and consolidating the new state's domestic security and external constitutional status were also early priorities.

If one were to sit down to design a foreign policy it is unlikely that one would start with a blank page. This book does not, therefore, take as its starting point the creation of an independent Irish state. The opening chapters in the story of Ireland among the nations had been written earlier; ironically, to look forward it is first necessary to look back.

A flowering of Irish nationalist thinking about foreign policy occurred at the turn of the twentieth century and during the two decades that followed. While the principal focus of political debate at the time was on home rule, advocates of an independent Irish state imagined how an Irish foreign policy might look, and attempted to put their imaginings into practice during the campaign for independence. It is the aim of this book to trace the development of these ideas and their impact on subsequent events during the campaign for independence and the establishment of the Irish state. Following independence, these ideas were tested by the challenge of creating the first Irish foreign policy, at times coming into conflict with the realities of statehood and international relations. How they shaped the new state's international identity and the consequences of this process for the framing and conduct of Irish foreign policy in the years after will also be explored.

This process did not take place in isolation, of course; the influence of ideas from outside Ireland on how the international order should be arranged and in whose interest it should be managed can be seen in some of the ideas circulating within the country at the time. Many of these ideas were radical then, some were hopelessly utopian, others simply naive. The claim was even advanced to be the first of the small nations. This conversation within nationalism, between the men and women who set out to create an Irish state and those who were caught up in the process, has not received as much historical attention as other aspects of the pre-independence period. To understand the course of Irish foreign policy it is necessary to uncover this conversation; in effect, to piece together the intellectual origins of early Irish foreign policy. In doing so, we will find echoes of ideas about Ireland's place and role in the world today.

This work began life as an attempt to find answers to these questions. In the course of fifteen years working for the Irish foreign ministry, it has become clear to me that many of the premises of Irish foreign policy and the external projection of the Irish state—small state and European country; honest broker and international good citizen; mother-country with a diaspora and bridge between Europe and America—have roots in the period 1900–1930. This is not to argue that policy or identity remained constant or immutable in the years since then. At times, differing emphases and priorities were adopted and pursued by governments of the day in response to external developments. But, when formulating the country's place on the world stage in the decades that followed, politicians and diplomats frequently drew upon a vocabulary and a palette of imagery to describe the Irish state and its place in the world that was first assembled in the period that saw the birth of the independent Irish state. The aim of this book is to trace the development and evolution of these ideas; in effect, to show how an Irish foreign policy identity was forged from a broad range of ideas and threads.

This history also aims to examine how these ideas were translated into policy once statehood had been achieved in 1922, the extent to which initial aspirations were realized or discarded, and how the reality of statecraft and navigating the turbulent waters of the international scene shaped policy in the years immediately after independence. As in other areas, there would be a need for compromise between the aspirations of an independence movement and the realities of government. It is, therefore, as much a book about the nature and process of creating a foreign policy, as it is the story of how the first Irish foreign policy emerged.

A brief word about sources: for the reader interested in Irish foreign policy, there is a broad range of source material, in particular, the archives of the Department of Foreign Affairs and Trade and the private papers of the politicians, diplomats, and commentators who were involved in shaping and articulating policy. There is also a rich vein of ideas and aspirations in the journals and newspapers of the day that provided a forum for an, at times lively, if limited, conversation about international affairs and Ireland's role abroad. The availability of this material has transformed the way Irish foreign policy can be seen, analysed, and understood.

There has been a renaissance in the study of Irish foreign policy and its history in recent years, prompted in part by publication of the excellent *Documents in Irish Foreign Policy* series.[3] There is a growing body of work, building on the work of Dermot Keogh, Eunan O'Halpin, Ronan Fanning, and Michael Kennedy. This has been complemented from a political science perspective by the work of Patrick Keatinge and Ben Tonra.[4] The pioneers of the study of Ireland's external relations from the Commonwealth perspective remain David Harkness and Nicholas Mansergh, whose works retain their insight despite the intervening years and have been wonderfully complemented by the work of Deirdre McMahon. A number of detailed monographs and studies have looked at individual aspects of Ireland's foreign policy history—for example, Bernadette Whelan on the United States; Mervyn O'Driscoll on interwar Germany; and Kate O'Malley on India—which have added to our store of knowledge, while there is a growing literature on Ireland and empire. We lack, however, a comprehensive picture of Ireland's foreign policy during the formative years of the Irish state, a lacuna this history seeks to fill.

This growing corpus of work has yet to find a reflection in surveys of European foreign policy, which overlook or relegate to the status of curiosity the Irish Free State. Sally Marks and Zara Steiner in their magisterial surveys of interwar diplomacy make only passing reference to Ireland despite a focus on other small states while others overlook the country entirely; unsure whether to categorize it as a small European state or Commonwealth member, it falls between both stools.[5] It is not until the Second World War and the policy of neutrality that Irish policy receives detailed historical attention.

[3] *Documents in Irish Foreign Policy* series (Dublin, 1998–).
[4] The bibliography contains details of these works.
[5] Zara Steiner, *The Lights that Failed, European International History 1919–1933* (Oxford, 2005); Sally Marks, *The Ebbing of European Ascendancy, an International History of the World 1914–1945* (London, 2002).

For the student of interwar European international relations, there is value in looking at the Irish experience, just as there is for those with an interest in how small states establish and manage their foreign relations in a world system dominated by their larger neighbours. In common with other states at the time, the Irish Free State recognized the value of multilateral fora in asserting and consolidating its own existence. As we have noted, the modern international order was being shaped in this period, a time of transition from old to new ways of conducting inter-state relations. Like other small and newly independent states, the Irish had to accommodate themselves to the emerging new order, with its attendant challenges and opportunities.

It is also interesting to look at what, for the time, were 'modern' characteristics of Irish nationalists' approach to the international arena: their aspiration to a foreign policy based on values and beliefs rather than the pure pursuit of interests associated with the foreign policy of the existing powers is one example. This idea has become commonplace in today's world but, at the start of the twentieth century it was novel. Equally modern was the attempt to create an international rationale for Irish independence and appeal to the international community, itself a concept then in its infancy. There was also a keen appreciation of the value of harnessing the power of public opinion in international affairs, again a relatively new commodity at the time.

These aspects of Ireland's early foreign policy will be examined in the pages that follow, including the aspiration to be 'first of the small nations'. It will become apparent that a set of ideas and aspirations that took shape in the first two decades of the twentieth century shaped the development of the Irish Free State's early foreign policy. Before we can look at Ireland's first steps as a recognized state on the world stage, therefore, we must look at the period that preceded independence to identify the raw material from which the first generation of Irish diplomats would attempt to craft a foreign policy.

1

The Story of Ireland in the World

In the summer of 1865, the cable-laying ship the *Great Eastern*, the largest vessel on the seas in its day, left the western coast of Ireland paying out the first underwater cable as it crossed the Atlantic, its aim to establish a telegraph link between Europe and North America. Its route traced the same path ploughed by emigrant ships carrying Irish and other Europeans from the old world to the new. The North Atlantic cable was completed in 1866 and, in the following years, the machinery of global communications was laid. By the end of the nineteenth century, cable networks spanning the globe reduced the time it took information to cross oceans and continents and this developing communications infrastructure fed the growth of news agencies transmitting news from the four corners of the globe in close to real time. The same cables provided a means for Irish emigrants passing over them on their westward journey to keep in touch with both family and news from Ireland. Faster trans-Atlantic crossing times as sail gave way to steam and wooden ships to steel also facilitated increased communication between Ireland and North America.

The ability of emigrant communities to keep in touch with the home countries they had left behind would have wide-ranging implications over time for the nature of politics within their adoptive countries and for relations between these countries and the former metropolis. In the Irish case, as the nineteenth century drew to a close, the Atlantic gradually ceased to be a barrier to become a channel of communication and interaction. In the same year that the *Great Eastern* began laying its underwater cable, the first nationalist Fenian Congress was held in Philadelphia. The Fenian Brotherhood had been established in 1858 as a sister organization to the Irish Republican Brotherhood (IRB) founded in Ireland in the same year. Both organizations were pledged to securing Irish independence from Britain, through violent means if necessary. In 1862, the IRB adopted a constitution for an independent Irish republic, which included a foreign minister and powers to make war and peace, and a secret 'provisional government' was proclaimed in the United States.[1] By the 1870s the Fenian Brotherhood had been succeeded by Clan na Gael as the IRB front organization in America which, together with its newspaper, the *Gaelic American,* would play an important and, at times, controversial role in the emergence of separatist nationalism as a political force in Ireland.

The combination of these developments—cheap and immediate global communications and a growing involvement by Irish communities abroad in Irish politics at home—over time introduced a new factor into the Irish equation: international public opinion. Fed by international wire services and the explosion of newspapers and printing presses made possible by strides in literacy, it became an increasingly important factor in international relations as the twentieth century dawned. Reports by British diplomats in the United States and other countries in which the Irish had settled in large numbers reveal the growing importance attached to public opinion, and the influence that this was believed to have on political decision-making in foreign capitals. The reality and extent of this influence was less important than the perception.

For Irish nationalism, the second half of the nineteenth century was a period of relative stability and strength, but not in pursuit of a separate Irish state. From the 1880s until the First World War, the Irish Parliamentary Party (IPP) and its objective of home rule within the United Kingdom shaped the path of Irish politics. Internal autonomy was envisaged, with a separate parliament and administration for Ireland within a federal United Kingdom to whose government was reserved a broad range of powers including foreign policy and defence. Though frequently divided, the IPP was a party with a project, and groups such as the IRB existed outside the political mainstream. Lacking popular support and rejecting involvement in the political process, they strove to pursue their goal of an Irish state from the fringes and saw in the ebb and flow of international relations a means to advance that end.

FENIANISM AND FOREIGN AFFAIRS

Physical force Irish nationalism has a long record of seeking to forge links with the rising European power of the day, be it Spain in the seventeenth century, France in the eighteenth century or, in the nineteenth century, France followed by Russia and then Germany. Indeed, Ireland's external

---

[1] James Stephens, *On the Capacity of Ireland to Exist as an Independent State* (Dublin, 1862), pp. xiii, 3.

environment played an important role in shaping both the path of political developments and the actions of those who sought to respond to them. Not least of these was the failed French invasion of 1798, timed to coincide with the uprising of the same year: 'the French are on the seas' would echo in both nationalist folklore and in the memory of British policy-makers for long after. It was this intervention which convinced the British that full legislative and political union was the best defence against future foreign attack through the Irish backdoor and it was that union which advanced nationalists sought to overthrow through the enlistment of further help from outside.

While it is a stretch to speak of a Fenian foreign policy, two broad themes run through advanced nationalist attitudes to the international environment in the nineteenth century. The first was a reactive approach, which sought to exploit situations of heightened international tension to attract foreign assistance or even intervention from abroad. The second was more proactive, aspiring to foment trouble and unrest against Britain wherever its interests were under pressure around the globe and thereby contribute to a heightening of international tension in the hope of bringing about the desired intervention from abroad. The relationship between these two strands was often characterized more by its contradictions than its harmonies.

The first trend was predominant simply because the benefits which might accrue were the most easily grasped. Approaches by republicans to foreign powers usually occurred against a backdrop of mounting international tension with the aim of securing armed assistance for a rising in Ireland. In the nineteenth century, it was the French followed by the Russians who were believed to pose the greater challenge to Britain and, accordingly, the Fenians courted each in turn. For the Fenian John Devoy, the need to consort with overseas governments was clear: to entice any would-be rival of Britain to include in its calculations the possibility of insurrection and intervention in Ireland. To this end, Irish republicans aimed to be 'an ally worth dealing with in England's next big war', even if their achievements in this regard often fell short of their ambition. John Mitchel described in his *Jail Journal* unsuccessful overtures to the Russian embassy in Washington to secure arms during the Crimean war.[2] The Russo-Turkish war of 1877 provided another pretext to involve a foreign government although, as before, the approaches came to nothing, the Russians seeing little gain in becoming involved in Irish affairs.

---

[2] John Mitchel, *Jail Journal* (Dublin, 1915), pp. 397–9.

The proactive strand was not confined to periods of international tension or warfare. Characterized by armed publicity stunts, it aimed to gain publicity both at home and abroad for the nationalist cause by simply embarrassing Britain. At different times the Fenians drew up plans for action around the globe, launching ill-fated raids on British Canada from across the American border in 1866, abortive plans to arm the Zulus in 1879, and successfully rescuing prisoners from a penal colony in Australia in 1876. The heterodox nature of the schemes tended to reflect the personalities and experiences of their sponsors rather than a coherent or consistent strategy and few had any discernible chance of success, although the rescue aboard the *Catalpa* caused a sensation at the time. A continental critic of Fenianism put it less charitably: Ireland 'has for centuries hungrily awaited the arrival of the Prince Charming, who is to raise her to the dignity of a Queen; but alas! the days of fairy princes are over'.[3]

Both themes can be traced back to the oft-repeated mantra that Ireland's opportunity would be found in Britain's hour of difficulty. This unsophisticated doctrine provided little by way of specific guidelines for action beyond seeking to derive advantage of the domestic consequences that might result from rivalry among the European powers. The rationale for becoming involved in others' struggles, however far-flung the field, was clear: as the Fenian, James O'Kelly, put it, 'we help ourselves by promoting the long wished for "opportunity"'.[4] There was a gradual shift in nationalist thinking towards a more sanguine appraisal of the international arena and its consequences for Ireland. Hopes of foreign troops landing on Irish shores gave way in nationalist imaginings to more achievable objectives, such as the supply of arms, funding, and training expertise but the objective remained the same. The experience gained by Irish soldiers fighting in the American civil war and in other Irish brigades that fought elsewhere provided military expertise that could be put to use in IRB and Fenian activities. This was the prism through which revolutionary Irish nationalism viewed the outside world and assessed the prospects for engaging with it.

It was a colonial war in Africa rather than a European conflagration that provided the catalyst for a chain of events that would ultimately give rise to the Sinn Féin party ('We Ourselves'). Popular memory in Ireland recalls the more recent Irish support for the struggle against apartheid in South

[3] Emile Montégut, *John Mitchel, A Study of Irish nationalism* (Dublin, 1915), p. 11, originally published as 'An exile of Young Ireland' in *Revue des Deux Mondes*, (Paris, 1855).

[4] James O'Kelly to Michael Davitt, 10 Mar. 1879, in *Devoy's Post Bag* (Dublin, 1953), vol. 1, p. 408.

Africa but, paradoxically, it was the fate of the Afrikaners and their defiance of British rule which caught the imagination of nationalist Ireland as the nineteenth century drew to a close. Celebrations in Ireland and by Irish communities around the world for the centenary of the 1798 rebellion provided a powerful reminder of the global network of expatriates that had developed over the course of the nineteenth century. Parades and festivities were held in places as far apart as the United States, France, and South Africa. Thus the shock waves of the Anglo-Boer war reached an Ireland that had just witnessed an international celebration of nationalist identity never before experienced. The organizing committees that sprung up to arrange the centenary events drew much of their membership from groups formed the previous year to protest at the marking of Queen Victoria's diamond jubilee in Ireland. It was this succession of activist groupings that provided a nucleus for opposition to the war in South Africa.

The Anglo-Boer war provoked strong sentiments around the world. Hostilities broke out in late 1899 as Britain tightened its grip on the Afrikaans-speaking colonies. The ensuing guerrilla war aroused great indignation and sympathy amongst broad sections of the Irish population. In nationalist Ireland, reaction against the war was felt in almost all areas of the political spectrum. Demonstrations were held in Dublin, including one in October 1899 at which an estimated 20,000 people were said to have been present. Posters appeared around the capital declaring it treasonous to Ireland to join the British forces. The women's nationalist organization, *Inghinidhe na hÉireann* ('Daughters of Ireland'), attempted to sabotage recruitment to the British army and its founder, the poet Yeats' muse, Maud Gonne, conceived a fantastic plan to sink troop ships bound for South Africa with grenades disguised as coal.[5] The dispatch of an armed, if poorly trained, brigade under Major John MacBride to fight alongside the Boers was seen by many at the time as a consummation of the link between the two peoples.

The plight of the Boers caught the imagination of a number of individuals who would later feature prominently in the development of Irish nationalism. Among them was Arthur Griffith, subsequent founder of Sinn Féin. Griffith worked for a while as a journalist in South Africa where, like Gandhi, he witnessed British colonial rule at first hand. He returned to Dublin in 1898 and was involved the following year in the activities of the Irish Transvaal Committee. Ostensibly set up to organize

---

[5] Elizabeth Coxhead, *Daughters of Erin* (London, 1965), p. 48. For an account of nationalist activities at the time of the second Anglo-Boer war, see Mark Ryan *Fenian Memoires* (Dublin, 1945), p. 179 *passim*.

medical supplies and an ambulance for the Boers, in reality it was an IRB facade for the Irish Brigade that travelled to South Africa to fight alongside the Afrikaners. The Committee, with financial assistance from Clan na Gael in the United States, also sent Maud Gonne, and her future husband John MacBride, on pro-Boer speaking tours to the USA in 1900 and 1901.

But it was through the pages of the nationalist press in Ireland that most was done to demonstrate support for the Boers. By the end of 1899, Arthur Griffith was editing a new nationalist newspaper, the *United Irishman*. Its overseas correspondents read like a role call of future Irish revolutionaries, including John MacBride in Paris and Tom Clarke in New York. Established with the help of his friend and fellow journalist, the language revivalist and poet William Rooney, and funds from the IRB, the broadsheet became influential as a forum for the discussion of nationalist ideas. The newspaper survived until 1906 when a libel suit forced its closure, but was quickly resurrected under the title *Sinn Féin*, serving as Griffith's mouthpiece until its eventual suppression by the British authorities at the outbreak of war in 1914 (it would reappear sporadically under the title *Nationality*). Griffith cast himself in the role of teacher to the Irish nation and his influence lay in his pen and in the columns of newsprint and editorials that were his classroom. As the poet and future foreign minister, Desmond FitzGerald, later observed, he 'read a national moral into everything that he commented on'.[6] Circulation figures may have been small, perhaps no more than 8,000 copies a week, but this was large enough to alarm the British authorities, who monitored his movements closely. They were right to do so, as Griffith's readership comprised many of those who would rise to prominence in nationalist politics and in the national movement more generally in the decades that followed, and who learnt their political lexicon from his writings.

SINN FEIN'S FOREIGN POLICIES

The *United Irishman* was not the Anglo-Boer War's only legacy to Irish nationalism. Queen Victoria's visit to Ireland in 1900 provided nationalists with a new cause against which to organize as hostilities in South Africa were drawing to a close. Griffith was instrumental in founding Cumann na nGaedheal ('League of the Gaels') in September 1900 out of, among other nationalist and Irish Ireland organizations, the Irish

[6] Desmond FitzGerald, *Memoirs of Desmond FitzGerald 1913–1916* (London, 1968), p. 4.

Figure 1. Arthur Griffith, founder of Sinn Féin (Image courtesy of UCD Archives P194/730)

Transvaal Committee. Another IRB front but this time a broader church, it incorporated both constitutional nationalists and separatists and its aims ranged from de-Anglicization to consumer protection for Irish industries. It was Cumann na nGaedheal which would be reconstructed in 1905–08 to form the Sinn Féin party. The fundamental principles on which Sinn Féin was initially founded were outlined by Griffith in a series of articles carried by the *United Irishman* in 1904 and subsequently published under the title *The Resurrection of Hungary: a parallel for Ireland*. These ideas were further fleshed out in a speech the following year and published under the title *The 'Sinn Féin' Policy* as a kind of manifesto showing how the ideas of 1904 might be implemented.[7] Taken together, they amounted to a manifesto for withdrawal from the British parliament and the creation of a separate government in Ireland.

Griffith's *Resurrection* is a rambling history of Hungary arranged as a prospectus for his ideas on abstention from Westminster, the establishment

---

[7] Arthur Griffith, *The Resurrection of Hungary: A Parallel for Ireland* (Dublin, 1904 & 1918), hereafter *Resurrection*; Arthur Griffith, *The 'Sinn Féin' Policy* (Dublin, 1905).

of a national administration in Ireland and the development of a national consciousness. He saw in the Austro-Hungarian dual monarchy a model for Ireland, and in the Hungarians' success in achieving it, a parable for Irish nationalists. There were both flaws and gaps in Griffith's reading of Hungarian history. He misread some of the factors that made possible the Hungarian success, talking-up the role of passive resistance, while discounting others, such as the threat of force. He overlooked entirely the plight of the minorities making up almost half the population of Hungary. But in its advocacy of abstention from Westminster and the pursuit of Irish interests organized along the lines of a state, its influence would prove lasting even if, at the time, few supported either idea.

Griffith's primary aim was to establish that separatists and constitutionalists could cooperate in a common framework. He succeeded in forging an unlikely nationalist platform drawn from the overlapping worlds of politics, literature, journalism, and cultural revivalism and his writings contained something that would find resonance with each.[8] These ideas would percolate over a generation and, in doing so, would gradually move from the fringe towards the mainstream. But as he wrote, the Irish Parliamentary Party dominated Irish politics and the advent of a Liberal government in London in 1910, dependent on Irish votes for power, seemed to confirm the policy of parliamentarianism Griffith dismissed.

Griffith also strove to cultivate an interest in international events from an Irish perspective and his proposal for an Irish consular network to promote Irish trade abroad marked a step towards a qualitatively different approach to matters beyond Ireland's shores. It was better, he argued, to send 'capable and patriotic men of business . . . to act as consuls in foreign countries, instead of sending them to orate in the British parliament'.[9] William Rooney had suggested funding an Irish consular service from money spent sending MPs to Westminster in 1900.[10] His sudden death in 1902 left Griffith to develop the idea as part of his *Resurrection* thesis, arguing that 'a country's consuls are its most valuable civil servants' and returned to the idea on many occasions, fleshing out his proposed network with details of work, location, and cost. *The 'Sinn Féin' Policy* included a section on the proposed consular network. Offices were envisaged in nine European states (Austria-Hungary, Belgium, Denmark, France, Germany, Italy, the Netherlands, Russia, and Spain), three in the Americas

---

[8] Richard Davies, *Arthur Griffith and Non-Violent Sinn Féin* (Dublin, 1974); Michael Laffan, *The Resurrection of Ireland: Sinn Féin Party, 1916–1923* (Cambridge, 1999).
[9] Griffith, *The 'Sinn Féin' Policy*, p. 17.
[10] *The United Irishman*, 17 Feb. 1900.

(Argentina, Chile, and the United States), and four others (Australia, Canada, South Africa, and Japan).

A fuller account appeared three years later, in the 1908 edition of the *Irish Year Book*, published by the National Council, in which Griffith was a leading figure. It devoted a whole chapter to a discussion on Irish trade and the positive impact separate commercial representation abroad would have on exports.[11] It was argued that possession of a network of representatives abroad would be a concrete manifestation of Ireland's distinctiveness from Britain. Griffith envisaged his consuls performing the same tasks as those of other countries 'save those which require the special exequatur granted to consuls of independent nations'. This was an open challenge to those who denied that Ireland was a separate entity, both at home and abroad. There were obvious obstacles in the way of such a scheme without lending it an overtly political colour and he accepted that they 'could obtain no official recognition, and should seek none'. As Griffith commented, 'to control our relations we should require the Irish equivalent, not of the British Foreign Office, but of the London Board of Trade'.[12]

Griffith also envisaged overseas representatives raising the general profile of Ireland in the capitals of the world. Information about Ireland was scarce in Europe and information from a nationalist viewpoint even harder to come by. As the French reviewer of Mitchel's *Jail Journal* perceptively observed, 'all Europe reads English newspapers; but who reads Irish journals or pamphlets?' while Griffith himself lamented, 'it is Europe that addresses itself to me at Dublin, Angleterre'.[13] A perennial preoccupation for many nationalists, this prompted attempts on a number of occasions to establish a press agency to feed news with a nationalist slant to the wire services for syndication abroad. Lack of resources meant these plans would come to nothing but efforts to influence the foreign press and international opinion more generally would take centre stage in 1919.

The problem with the consular scheme, as the *Irish Year Book* conceded, was that it could only be implemented if a governing authority existed to propose and fund it. Neither prospect seemed to hand. Indeed, without access to the levers of state it is difficult to see how it could have been implemented. Although he proposed remedies (a 'Council of Three Hundred' to be drawn from local authorities) they were neither feasible nor practical. But this was Griffith's point: to properly promote and protect Irish interests an Irish administration would be required in which Irish hands were on the levers. But there was little support for a

[11] National Council, *Leabhar na hÉireann* (Dublin, 1908), pp. 81–95.
[12] Griffith, *The 'Sinn Féin' Policy*, pp. 17–18.
[13] Montegut, *John Mitchel*, p. 94; *The United Irishman*, 4. Nov. 1905.

scheme that was beyond the capabilities of any nationalist organization at the time. Nonetheless, the connection between the economy, internal development, and external representation constituted an important development in Irish thinking on international affairs.

A closer parallel for Griffith's consular scheme was Norway, where Stockholm's reluctance to concede separate consular representation abroad for Norwegian business eventually precipitated the country's separation from Sweden in 1905. Griffith envisaged an Irish consular service supplying commercial intelligence and support for Irish business and the establishment of a mercantile marine that would enable Ireland to emulate the commercial success of Norway. The two countries shared a similar size of population and a similar lack of natural resources, but a separate government existed in Norway to promote and protect Norwegian economic interests. The separation confirmed Griffith in his belief that, if the economic arguments conducive to Irish independence could be demonstrated, political support would follow. He could only take the Norwegian example so far, however. While he naturally welcomed the country's independence, the Norwegians had opted out of the kind of dual monarchy on which he had based his Hungarian analogy.

Commenting on the velvet divorce of Norway and Sweden, Griffith declared the day of the 'little nations' had arrived and he believed the twentieth century would see the small state come into its own. Comparison with other small states such as Belgium, Denmark, and Switzerland became a regular feature of nationalist propaganda. The inference was simple: if they could survive as independent states Ireland could too. 'The world is measuring greatness,' he argued, 'not by the number of heads in a country, but by the spirit of its people.'[14] The analogies favoured by nationalists were not only small states, they were predominantly European; there was little comparison with the republics of South America or the kingdom of Siam. Griffith argued 'we must, if we are to be reckoned amongst the nations of Europe, get into closer communion with Europe', while the playwright J. M. Synge dreamed of a day when the young would 'teach Ireland again that she is part of Europe'.[15]

The traditional nationalist sympathy towards France remained strong, if more so in the collective consciousness than in fact. There was also a certain ideological affinity with the home of republicanism; the IRB's constitution for a future Irish state envisaged a 'perpetual alliance' between Dublin and Paris and many Fenians, including Mitchel and Stephens, spent time in the French capital. For those looking for an outside

[14] *The United Irishman*, 17 June 1905.   [15] *Sinn Féin*, 4 Aug. 1908.

intervention, Franco-British naval and colonial rivalry in the latter decades of the nineteenth century offered some cause for hope. Romantic notions and a lazy reading of the past resulted in an exaggerated sense of French interest in Ireland that was never as deep or as disinterested as the popular ballads of the day allowed.

By the early twentieth century, shifts in the geopolitical situation conspired to deny nationalists this traditional crutch as Britain and France progressed from détente to alliance in 1904, and French interest in Irish affairs declined rapidly after. Paris exploited this willing suspension of disbelief when it suited its interest to do so, such as during efforts to encourage enrolment as war in the trenches took its toll on allied manpower. While Francophiles lamented this state of affairs, others took a less sentimental approach. If sympathy for France derived from a common hostility to Britain, this could be reconsidered if that hostility was no longer shared. For similar reasons, but with different objectives in mind, German interest in Ireland increased following the Franco-British alliance and the Anglo-Russian alliance three years later.

In comparisons with other European countries, issues of demography inevitably arose. Griffith claimed in 1911 that the Irish population would have reached twenty million had the Union not taken place, and elsewhere argued that a restored government would pave the way for a recovery in population figures. At one stage he estimated a future population of ten to eleven million, while on another argued that implementing his economic programme would soon bring the Irish population back up to its pre-famine level of eight million. Griffith's take on demography may seem extreme to contemporary ears, and probably was for many at the time. Not everyone shared his hopes for a re-populated and industrialized Ireland. It was important to establish, in psychologically reassuring terms, the reason and the blame for the population collapse after the famine, which marked the country out compared with other European countries that had seen their populations grow over the course of the nineteenth century. By imagining an alternative past in which the famine and other disasters had not occurred, it also became easier to project a different future as somehow being the natural course of events.

The preoccupation with population figures sat uncomfortably alongside an insistence that headcounts were irrelevant when it came to the claims of nations, but then Griffith was an accomplished polemicist and consistency was not always his forte. The confused nature of much nationalist thinking on demography and economics allowed many to believe that the establishment of a separate government in Dublin would bring about a change in fortunes on both counts. Above all, the preoccupation with population was about how nationalists saw Ireland's place in the world. In an era of labour-intensive industry, population was as much an index of economic potential as it was national virility. Whether or not the day of the small nation had come, Sinn Féin aspired to the rank of a middle-sized nation, with population estimates placing Ireland above countries such as Sweden and the Netherlands in the European league table.

At the same time as emphasizing the viability of small states (whilst laying out the conditions under which a more populous Ireland might be achieved), commentators looked to the millions of Irish and their off-spring who had settled around the world. Griffith and others were conscious of Ireland's status as a 'mother-country' and contemporaries of all persuasions took pride in the Irish abroad and their achievements in the dominions and the United States. Griffith believed the diaspora, and Irish-Americans in particular, had a duty to invest their money in Ireland.[16] Noting an Australian reference to the 'Empire of Great Britain and Ireland' in 1913, he commented 'I thought the expression was a good one and I often wondered why it was not more extensively used.'[17] This was not so far removed from ideas for a federal parliament for the empire put forward by the Parliamentary Party leader, John Redmond (as a context in which to advance home rule rather than an end in itself), or imperial federalist ideas in vogue at the time in British liberal circles. There was also the expectation that their number would give Ireland a claim upon the attention of foreign governments.

The size of the Irish population in the United States was of particular importance. In 1920, just over four million Americans had been born in Ireland or had one Irish-born parent. Irish American organizations claimed the figure rose to twenty million if all those of Irish descent were included, almost 19 per cent of the population at the time.[18] The growth of Irish-American political and cultural organizations in the clos-ing decades of the nineteenth century allowed the illusion of a lever on American policy to develop in the minds of nationalists in Ireland. Belief in an ability to frustrate attempts at a closer Anglo-American understand-ing became one of the mainstays of nationalist propaganda. Griffith believed Irish organizations in the United States could be used not only to influence American politics but also its foreign policy, urging 'the leaders of the Irish, the German and the American patriotic societies to unite in a common policy' to improve relations between the three

---

[16] Ibid., 13 April–17 Aug. 1907; *The 'Sinn Féin' Policy*, op cit, p. 14.
[17] Ibid., 27 Dec. 1913; 'Pitt's Policy' in *Resurrection* (1918 edition).
[18] The report of the United States Federal Census, 1920, indicates that there were 1,037,233 Irish born residents, 7.6% of the total foreign-born population.

countries.[19] Irish-American agitation was an irritant in relations between London and Washington—reports from British diplomats in America amply bear this out—and President Wilson would confide to his Irish-American secretary Joseph Tumulty that 'there never can be real comradeship between America and England until this [Irish] issue is definitely settled'.[20]

A belief existed that the Irish overseas could be used as the cement in an agreement between the United States and other countries as well as a means to bring about a settlement in Ireland. This was an idea with a long pedigree in nationalist thinking. The Cork nationalist MP J. F. Maguire elaborated this idea in his 1868 book on the Irish in America, and it would subsequently become a tenet of the Irish Parliamentary Party, with Parnell touring the United States in 1880 and the party conscious of the potential to draw on émigré support for its work.[21] The Parliamentary Party was an early proponent of diasporic nationalism, grasping the opportunity presented by the Irish in the United States in particular to bolster, both financially and politically, the party's activities at home and at Westminster. In establishing a connection between overseas funding ('diaspora dollars' in F. H. O'Donnell's disapproving phrase) and the party's domestic fortunes, the Irish Parliamentary Party created a template that its successors would follow. There was a deep well from which to draw on the potential role that America and the diaspora might play in Irish affairs and this would also be a prominent aspect of Sinn Féin's foreign policy thinking in 1919–21.

Thus, on the one hand Griffith and others encouraged the idea of action within the empire, and asked why Irish nationalism 'could not find interests in common with the bureaucratised West Indians, the plundered Egyptians, and a dozen other constituents of the "empire"'. Surveying the position in 1905, Griffith advised his readers: 'the place of Ireland in the Empire is at the head of a combination of its oppressed peoples against British rule'. This he believed would form the contours of the 'foreign policy' that an abstentionist Irish administration would pursue.[22] Eamon de Valera would briefly suggest a similar approach in 1919. Assessing the implications for British power in Asia after the Japanese defeat of Russia in 1905, he concluded that 'England could not withstand for any period the Sinn Féin policy if carried out simultaneously in Ireland and in India.' The Irish socialist James Connolly's *Worker's Republic* can also be found

[19] *The United Irishman*, 8 April 1905.
[20] Francis M. Carroll, *American Opinion and the Irish Question* (Dublin, 1978), p. 18.
[21] John Francis Maguire, *The Irish in America* (London, 1868).
[22] *The United Irishman*, 13 May 1905.

encouraging Egyptian and Indian nationalists, as did Maud Gonne's *Bean na hÉireann*, which urged its readers to make common cause with them and develop a distinct Irish foreign policy.[23]

A common language facilitated interaction however much an Irish language revival might be wished for in some quarters. Griffith's newspaper might publish the Slovak nationalist song, but it was English speaking Indians who wrote letters of support to Irish newspapers. There was certainly a wide constituency for Irish nationalist ideas. Nationalist newspapers such as the *Gaelic American* claimed to have Indian readers, Griffith's writings were translated into several Indian languages as early as 1906 and Gandhi found them instructive when formulating his own policy of non-cooperation. The Irish socialist journalist Frederick Ryan published extracts from *Sinn Féin* in the pages of the *Egyptian Standard*, which he edited from Cairo in 1908–09. Political contacts were also facilitated by geographical proximity to London, where nationalists from around the empire could meet. The young Jawaharal Nehru visited Ireland in 1906 and attended Sinn Féin meetings in 1907 and 1910, while a student at Cambridge and the deported Punjabi nationalist Lala Lajpat Rai addressed the organization in London. This early interest in Sinn Féin ideas would provide the basis for both Egyptian and Indian contacts with the Dáil regime a decade later.

These contrasting identities—European island, mother country, victim of empire—were not mutually exclusive. There were two empires: that of the self-governing dominions, peopled as much by Irish emigrants as by English, Scots, Welsh, and others, and the colonial empire of territories and peoples ruled without their assent and, in the nationalist lexicon, against their interests. It was possible to take pride in the former while remaining critical of the latter, and many contemporaries did. A further juxtaposition of identities—European and imperial—was also possible insofar as notions of being a mother country and European-ness were complementary and reinforcing. But a conflict arose in nationalist dealings with Indians, Egyptians, and others in which pragmatic considerations of common agitation against a common foe conflicted with a wish to avoid being considered in the same category as other colonial peoples. This was an unresolved tension running through nationalism, reflecting a broader confusion in Irish attitudes towards empire. Where the tension resolved itself was by asserting Irish leadership in the hierarchy of subject peoples; the nationalist approach towards cooperation within the Empire was in

---

[23] Virginia F. Glandon, *Arthur Griffith and the Advanced Nationalist Press in Ireland, 1900–1922* (New York, 1985), pp. 20 & 128.

some respects framed in the reflexes of the very imperialism which it sought to subvert.

There was thus no inconsistency in welcoming any of the foregoing whilst at the same time lamenting the fact that the Irish were the only white race within the British Empire that were not self-governing. In a similar vein, Griffith's proposal for a dual monarchy was not incompatible with imperialism in all its guises. He saw in the Dutch empire an example of Sinn Féin-style self-reliance and praised the modernization of Japan while remaining silent on its colonial policy in East Asia. He overlooked the position of other nationalities within Hungary. In an age when imperialism was the status quo and empires still expanding, the extent to which a forthright opposition to imperialism might be expected is questionable. This reticence was a long way from the clear-cut views expressed during the heady days of the Boer war when the *United Irishman* had called upon Ireland to take its place 'leading the world against the bloody, rapacious and soul-shivering imperialism of England'.[24]

This was not true across the board. Republicans such as the Belfast Quaker and IRB member, Bulmer Hobson, took a more principled line on the subject. A fiery and proper republican, Hobson had split with Griffith and Sinn Féin in 1910 over what he viewed as their ambiguous support for a republic, and began editing the IRB organ *Irish Freedom* together with Patrick McCartan the following year.[25] Denouncing the Italian annexation of Libya in 1911, Hobson urged his readers to heed 'a warning to us to be careful how we build, to quench this smouldering Empire business lest it become a flame'.[26] *Irish Freedom* was even more forthright in its opposition to British imperialism, declaring in 1910 'we should rather remain a nation of political serfs than become a nation of political parasites'.[27] This was language that Griffith had used at the turn of the century and to which he would return at the start of the First World War.

Of course, there were sources of inspiration from within constitutional nationalism, such as Daniel O'Connell's opposition to slavery, which represented a global outlook: a political tradition based on the acquisition of rights, be they religious, electoral, or related to property, was not deaf to their denial elsewhere. The Parliamentary Party also took an interest in international parallels, citing the examples of Russian-ruled Finland and

---

[24] *The United Irishman*, 15 Mar. 1899.
[25] For more on Bulmer Hobson, see Marnie Hay, *Bulmer Hobson and the Nationalist Movement in Twentieth-Century Ireland* (Manchester, 2009).
[26] *Irish Freedom*, Nov. 1911.   [27] Ibid., Dec. 1910.

German-ruled Alsace-Lorraine in support of home rule for Ireland.[28] It is likely that this served to confuse, particularly when Griffith and others used the same examples in support of their own arguments. Desmond FitzGerald recalled in the run-up to the third Home Rule Bill 'when we made speeches about a new free Ireland with her own army, and with international recognition, somebody else would make a speech in support of us in which the Home Rule Bill was spoken of as fulfilling all our national aspirations'.[29]

Irish Parliamentary Party MPs had a respectable tradition of calling to account the British government for its actions in India in particular, but also elsewhere in the empire. In common with many at the time, the party took pride in the contribution which Irish men and women had made to the dominions and to the development of the United States. The party position was that such matters, along with foreign policy questions in general, should remain a matter for the Westminster parliament, where its members would ensure an Irish input to the formulation of British or imperial foreign policy, as foreseen under the home rule settlement. As John Redmond explained in 1910, 'we don't want, when we get Home Rule, to have a foreign diplomatic service . . . our ambition is a much more humble and humdrum one . . . to manage our purely Irish affairs'.[30] The parliament that would have been established under home rule provided for no foreign policy functions to be exercised in Dublin, the IPP did not argue that there should be and, with the exception of a small minority, there was little public interest or expectation that this should not be the case. Whether such expectations would have developed over time had home rule been implemented, one can only speculate.

By accepting that foreign policy should remain a matter for the government in London, home rule advocates left it to those who argued for separation to consider what an Irish foreign policy might look like. With the prospect of home rule becoming a reality, the imaginings of Griffith and company must have seemed an amusing if not particularly relevant parlour game to the leadership of the IPP. Electoral arithmetic suggested such ideas would remain a minority interest as the Parliamentary Party's dominance of Irish politics looked set to carry it into government in a home rule Ireland. The belief in a distinct Irish foreign policy conducted through exclusively Irish means would remain a concern of the few as minds focused on matters nearer home. Griffith criticized the

---

[28] John Redmond, *The Justice of Home Rule* (London, 1912), p. 28.

[29] FitzGerald, *Memoires*, p. 34.

[30] *The Freeman's Journal*, 22 Jan. 1910. Quoted in Dermot Meleady, *John Redmond, the National Leader* (Dublin, 2014), p. 179.

Parliamentary Party in 1911 for not seeking Irish control over foreign policy and defence, yet in his comments on the Home Rule Bill in 1912 he conceded that these would remain a Westminster competence.[31] His political views had shifted towards an accommodation with constitutional nationalism. The country looked set for a home rule future in which Griffith and others like him contemplated a possible opposition role. Perhaps had he been able to secure election in this alternative future he might have pressed a home rule administration to appoint consuls along Norwegian lines.

If *Resurrection* and *The 'Sinn Féin' Policy* did not provide a specific blueprint for a future Irish foreign policy, this was provided elsewhere in the general tone of nationalist comment on current affairs. Essentially, Griffith asked himself what would a national government do and he knew the answers before he asked the question. While claims that 'an Ireland with a foreign policy would cause every Chancellery in Europe to revise its own' reverberate with exaggeration and are typical of Griffith at his bombastic best, he was realistic about the prospects for securing foreign assistance. 'No nation in the world is going to aid Ireland to regain her independence,' he wrote in 1905, 'unless it be made the interest of that nation to do so.' It is here that the outward and inward looking aspects of Sinn Féin policy converged: 'a certain traditional sympathy exists between Ireland and some countries of the Continent which can be made a basis on which to build up a foreign commerce and a foreign policy, if those nations first behold her helping herself'. It was also the point of departure from Fenian ideas of external intervention. Griffith questioned the lack of Fenian forward planning, which left decisions about the shape and nature of an Irish state and its policies until after independence had been achieved. His approach was to imagine that state and what its policies would look like.

Columns of newsprint were taken up analysing the implications of the Japanese defeat of Russia in 1905, the naval alliance between London and Tokyo that followed, and the growing alliance between Britain and France. As the European powers retreated into rival blocs in the first decade of the twentieth century, hopes transferred to Germany as it assumed the role of chief rival to Britain. Not everyone agreed with the traditional embrace of whoever posed the greatest challenge to Britain. Bulmer Hobson warned in October 1911 that 'Ireland must play her own game' or end up 'the blind and unhappy tool of whichever power is

---

[31] *Sinn Féin*, 27 April 1912.

strongest'. This question would grow in significance with the advent of war in 1914.

IRELAND AND A EUROPE AT WAR, 1914–1918

Nationalist thinking would change under the pressure of world war. While the extent of support for the war would subsequently become an issue of contention in nationalist Ireland, the initial response to the British call to arms was positive, some 200,000 Irishmen enlisting to fight. The Parliamentary Party endorsed the war effort in the expectation that the British government, fighting to guarantee the freedom of small nations such as Belgium and Serbia, would honour its pledge to implement home rule once hostilities were over (the legislation was suspended when hostilities began). The link between the two in many minds was clear: 'the name of Ireland must now or never be written on the scroll of nations' declared the Irish Volunteers in August 1914.

Recruitment tapered off before the sea change in popular opinion that occurred after the British response to the Easter Rising in 1916 and the conscription scares of the following year when London sought to enforce conscription in Ireland. The start of the war saw both Griffith and republicans revert to an earlier mode of defining Irishness in negative terms. Griffith's editorial at the start of hostilities argued 'Ireland is not at war with Germany. She has no quarrel with any continental power. Our prime concern,' he argued, 'is what the Belgian prime concern is—our own country.' The republican *Irish Freedom* put it more bluntly: 'Germany is not Ireland's enemy.'[32] The Sinn Féin activist and historian, P. S. O'Hegarty, attempted to justify Griffith's wartime position in 1917 on grounds of expediency: 'abstract right and wrong in continental matters are luxuries Ireland cannot afford'.[33] The ends would justify the means. As Roger Casement put it, 'I didn't choose the Germans—it was England. If she had attacked France—I'd have gone to France.' A short-lived Irish Neutrality League was established in October 1914 with James Connolly as president and Griffith a committee member.

For a time it seemed as if nationalist thinking on the international environment had reset to the default position of my enemy's enemy is my friend. Yet, as Desmond FitzGerald later recalled, 'at the back of our minds was an awareness that a mere condition of war did not attain our promised land for us'. But this does not account for Griffith's remarkable reduction of the war to 'a battle of the free states under an Imperial head against the Imperial states which have blotted out the local self-governing communities, and seek to rule the world from the great city-centres of London, Paris and St Petersburg.'[34] Viewing the international context exclusively through a nationalist lens had a distorting effect and such unambiguous statements resulted in the suppression of *Sinn Féin* and the imprisonment of Griffith himself in the aftermath of the 1916 Rising despite his non-involvement.

With Britain at war, Ireland became of interest to the belligerents. The supply of German arms to nationalists and unionists on the eve of war in July 1914 signalled a degree of German interest in exploiting developments in Ireland and the German government issued a statement of support for Irish claims for self-rule at the start of the war. German industrial strength and pre-war naval scares inclined many to consider a German victory possible and the rapid early progress of the Kaiser's armies through Belgium and France seemed to confirm this prognosis. For those who saw in the shape of the war the long-awaited hour of opportunity, the prospect of securing military aid from Berlin was alluring. Casement initiated contact with the Germans in August 1914 through their Washington embassy, availing of introductions from senior Clan na Gael figures while on a fund-raising mission for the Irish Volunteers. The former British consul celebrated for uncovering human rights abuses in the Belgian Congo and Peru, Casement had helped organize the gun running in July and travelled to Berlin the following year on a quixotic mission to secure German aid for a rebellion in Ireland. Like many at the time, he had become convinced that Germany would prevail in a conflict with Britain, arguing in a 1913 publication that a neutral Ireland under German protection represented the best opportunity for independence in the event of war with Britain.[35] He hoped to realize this by negotiating a treaty with the Germans that would provide for arms, a political commitment to post-war independence, and the establishment of an Irish brigade of captured prisoners of war.

Casement's mission ended in failure. German interest waned when it became clear that the rebels could provide neither the numbers nor the degree of organization expected by Berlin. Only fifty prisoners signed up for the proposed brigade. The IRB was more interested in German guns than Casement's treaty but the Germans were unwilling to ship the amount desired. Casement returned to Ireland disappointed on the eve

---

[34] *Sinn Féin*, 15 Aug. 1914.
[35] Roger Casement (pseud. Sean Bhean Bhocht), *Ireland, Germany and the Next War* (Belfast, 1913), p. xx.

of the Easter rising in April 1916 and was arrested; the arms shipment was intercepted and sunk. The rising went ahead in Dublin and the rebels' *Proclamation of Independence* spoke of 'gallant allies in Europe', generally understood to be a reference to Germany. Desmond FitzGerald recalled talk among the rebels of placing a German prince on an Irish throne. Before the slaughter of the Somme later that year, nationalists might still assume a German victory was possible. The insurgents also hoped to benefit from a post-war reorganization of national boundaries. Beyond this, little consideration was given to Ireland's place in a future German hegemony.

TAPPING INTO NATIONALIST NETWORKS

The First World War would sweep away much of the old dynastic order of inter-state relations in Europe, but even before the liberal internationalism that would take its place had been conceived, aspects of the old way of doing things had given way to something new. The emergence of a global communications infrastructure gave rise to standing international organizations established to regulate these new, cross-border means of intercourse. The International Telegraph Union was established in 1865, followed by the Universal Postal Union in 1874. As the nineteenth century progressed, standing processes and mechanisms were established to regulate international shipping, rail, and road traffic, giving birth to a new form of rules-based diplomacy. In parallel, transnational networks of citizens such as the International Committee of the Red Cross, created in 1863, emerged to campaign on a range of humanitarian issues while political networks, such as the first Socialist International of 1864 and its successor the Second International of 1889, arose in response to the social and economic changes fuelled by deepening industrialization in the developed economies of the world. The birth of the Olympic movement in 1896 saw a similar process at work in the world of sport. As the twentieth century began, the first standing court of international arbitration had been established in The Hague and a series of conferences in the city regulated the laws of war and peace. A process of codifying what would soon become known as international law was getting under way. The fabric of a rules-based international order was beginning to emerge and, although it remained an age of empires, very gradually conditions were beginning to take shape that, over time, would prove conducive to the existence of smaller states.

The way governments were arranging their international business was not without effect on the way those who sought to unseat them went about theirs. This included a growing number of nationalist movements first in Europe, then in the colonial possessions of the major powers. The emergence of the international congress as a feature of political life at an unofficial as well as governmental level enabled nationalists to meet and exchange ideas. Meetings occurred in Paris at the turn of the century between John MacBride, Maud Gonne, and John O'Leary and activists from India, Egypt, and Morocco.

In the same year as The Hague conferences met to codify the laws of war, a gathering of subject peoples met in the Dutch capital to call for recognition of their right to independence by their ruling powers. Amongst the various delegates from disgruntled national groups across Europe was the barrister and future Irish foreign minister, George Gavan Duffy, representing the Sinn Féin precursor body, the National Council. Son of the Young Ireland leader Charles Gavan Duffy, he was married to Margaret Sullivan, whose father, A. M. Sullivan, had penned the influential history book *The Story of Ireland* in 1880. (In the overlapping worlds of nationalist Ireland, Sullivan had taken over the editorship of the Irish Ireland newspaper *The Nation* from Gavan Duffy's father.) The couple was akin to nationalist aristocracy and their London home served as a base for cultural nationalists and political activists alike. Urbane and French-educated, Gavan Duffy would later defend Roger Casement in his trial for treason in 1916, and moved back to Dublin to enter active politics in its aftermath. His ideas about how to win independence for Ireland and the shape an Irish foreign policy should take would prove both far-sighted and influential, but their impact was blunted by an austere manner and an inability to compromise that would win him few friends.

At The Hague conference in August 1907, Gavan Duffy's proposition that 'every subject nation whose representatives in national assembly demand independence shall have the support of all sovereign powers' was enthusiastically adopted.[36] He can hardly have imagined that little more than a decade later he would find himself making just such an appeal for international support. Looking for help beyond Ireland's shores did not mean abandonment of the Sinn Féin policy which, 'failing the intervention of the nations', was to be steadily pursued at home. The conference was organized by the International Subject Races Committee, of which the National Council was one of seven founding members; other members included Friends of Russian Freedom, the Egyptian Committee as well as international associations such as the International, Arbitration and Peace Association and the Anti-Slavery and Aborigines Protection

---

[36] *Sinn Féin*, 17 Aug. 1907.

Society. Members of the Committee committed themselves to the defence of 'the principle of Nationality, to maintain for each nation the management of its internal affairs, to protect subject races from oppression and exploitation'.

The Committee's first conference was held in London on 28–30 June 1910 and included demands for home rule for Ireland and India as well as independence for Finland, Georgia, Persia, and Poland. It was an eclectic gathering. George Gavan Duffy again presented the Irish case together with the Anglo-Irish language enthusiast Hon. William Gibson, Baron Ashbourne (Gibson sporting a saffron kilt and mantle) while Lala Lajpat Rai was among the Indian representatives present. Other speakers included the economist John Hobson, the author G. K. Chesterton and the editor of the *Positivist Review*, S. H. Swinny. The Labour MP Keir Hardie addressed the gathering on the subject of slavery. The honorary secretary of the Nationalities and Subject Races Committee, as the grouping had become known, was the Dublin-born Irish anarchist Nanny Florence Dryhurst, who would later translate Kropotkin's history of the French revolution. Its proceedings were published a year later, with Robert Lynd contributing a preface on nationalism and nationality.[37]

Largely a London-based grouping, the Committee's activities petered out, its thunder stolen by the establishment-endorsed Universal Race Conference of 1911, although Dryhurst popped up in Dublin in January the same year to lecture Sinn Féin members on 'a foreign policy for Ireland'.[38] It was through its meetings that Gavan Duffy came into contact with the Egyptian National Party and its leader, Mohammad Farid, contacts that would be renewed a decade later on the margins of the Paris peace conference. It was also at these gatherings that he came to appreciate both the impact that public opinion could have in advancing the nationalist cause and the limitations of banding together with other subject peoples: 'public opinion has to be created,' he wrote in a conference post mortem, but 'the pious aspirations of a handful of enthusiasts do not easily revolutionise the popular mind'.[39] It was a conundrum that would influence nationalist calculations in the years to come.

As in so many other areas, the war accelerated the development of nationalist thinking and exposure to ideas. Sinn Féin was represented at a further conference held in Paris in the summer of 1915 by the Union des Nationalités to propose guidelines for the treatment of small nationalities after the war. The conference was attended by Czechs and Belgians, Serbs

[37] N. F. Dryhurst (ed.), *Nationalities and Subject Races, Report of a Conference held in Caxton Hall, Westminster, June 28–30, 1910* (London, 1911).
[38] *Sinn Féin*, 15 Jan. 1911.   [39] *Sinn Féin*, 16 July 1910.

and Catalans, Danes and Finns, Latvians and Lithuanians, Romanians and Bulgarians as well as Germans from Alsace-Lorraine, Jewish representatives, Armenians, and Lebanese. Unsurprisingly, it endorsed the right of self-determination for all.[40] The Irish case was presented to the international Labour conference in Berne and at the Stockholm meeting in 1917, and at a number of nationalist gatherings in New York in the final year of the war. The step of making an appeal to international opinion was not without precedent.

INTERNATIONALIZING THE IRISH QUESTION

A redrawing of the European map was a goal shared by both sides during the war and it was generally recognized that, whichever side triumphed, a peace conference would be necessary to re-draw borders once hostilities were over. The prospect of a peace conference transformed nationalist thinking at the international level. As early as June 1915, Griffith's newspaper *Nationality* argued 'when the Congress meets let Ireland knock at the door and demand in the name of the small nationalities free admittance'.[41] Patrick McCartan recounted how, at the last meeting of the IRB supreme council before the Easter Rising, Pádraig Pearse and Tom Clarke urged that appeal be made to a peace conference when the war was over.[42] Pragmatism dictated that the vocabulary of the allies be used to seek admittance to the conference when it met. As Griffith wrote from prison at the end of 1916, 'we are going to the Peace Conference. We are going there as a small nationality, precisely the personage for whom England fought.'[43] This was supported by a belief in many quarters that Britain would be pressured into acceding to an Irish hearing.

American entry into the war in April 1917, a month after the first revolution in Russia that year, shifted the balance of power away from the Central Powers and introduced the idea of a more ambitious and altruistic reordering of the international system. For US president Woodrow Wilson, the idea of a more equitable ordering of international relations had been an idea in germination long before American troops crossed the Atlantic to fight in France. In his first major address on a post-war settlement in May 1916, he sketched out his thoughts for a mechanism for international cooperation based on principles of equality between states and consent of the governed. In his 'peace without victory' address

---

[40] *Nationality*, 14 Aug. 1915.   [41] Ibid., 26 June 1915.

[42] Patrick McCartan, *With de Valera in America* (Dublin, 1932), p. 2.

[43] Arthur Griffith to Lily Williams, 29 Nov. 1916, NLI mss 5942.

to the US Senate in January the following year, he called for a reordering of the international system based on a 'community of power' to replace the discredited balance of power which had failed to avert war in Europe. 'No right anywhere exists' he declared, 'to hand peoples about from sovereignty to sovereignty as if they were property.'[44] American war aims included a re-ordering of international relations based on equality among legitimate polities governed by popular consent. By mid-1917, Wilson had emerged as the champion of liberal internationalism and the 'new diplomacy'.

The collapse of the Tsarist regime in the March revolution, just days after the US entered the war, produced a new Russian government, which published a revised set of war aims containing the term 'self-determination' for the first time. Influential in the provisional government even before they overthrew it, the Bolsheviks insisted on including the term, correctly guessing at its explosive nature. Lenin had declared as early as March 1917 that, in power, the Bolsheviks would work to bring about the liberation of all colonial peoples. When they seized control of the revolution in November they threw open the archives of the Tsarist foreign ministry to publish a raft of secret treaties concluded by the European allies dividing between them the future spoils of war. The move was as dramatic as it was unprecedented and as embarrassing as it was intended to be. The Bolshevik revelations were reprinted in newspapers around the world, causing consternation, as they contradicted the aims for which the allies claimed to be prosecuting the war.

The secret treaties were viewed in Ireland as further proof that British undertakings could not be trusted, with an obvious read-across to the domestic arena where home rule continued to languish unimplemented on the statute book. Those who viewed the very conduct of international relations and diplomacy with suspicion and distaste felt vindicated in their belief. The Bolsheviks turned the screw again in late December, publishing a peace programme in which they provocatively asked if the allies would allow self-determination for the Irish, Egyptians, and Indians, or for the peoples of Madagascar and Indochina. Trotsky's programme was reprinted in the *Freeman's Journal*. Thus, as the war entered its last year, voices advocating a reworking of the international system and a new kind of diplomacy were heard from both east and west.

It might be easy to dismiss the Bolsheviks as dangerous radicals; less so an American president.[45] Rattled by both Bolshevik revelations and

[44] Woodrow Wilson speech to the United States Senate, 8 January 1918.
[45] Erez Manela, *The Wilsonian Moment, Self-determination and the International Origins of Anticolonial Nationalism* (Oxford, 2007), p. 38.

Wilson's growing influence, on 5 January 1918 the British issued revised war aims more in line with both public expectations and their own previously stated objectives. Not wishing to be outflanked on the moral high ground, these were now also based on principles of self-determination and consent of the governed. Three days later, President Wilson published his famous Fourteen Points, a distillation of his thoughts on how the international system should be re-cast to make the world safe for peace. The word self-determination did not appear in any of the points; Wilson would use the term for the first time a month later in an address to Congress. The text did contain, at point five however, the first specific reference to colonial questions, which were to be resolved taking into account the interest of their populations.

It was Wilson's fourteenth point, his proposal to create a world league of nations, that generated the greatest interest and much ink would be spilled debating what the president meant. As elsewhere, there was confusion in Ireland about what the proposed League would look like or what membership in it might entail. An Irish League of Nations Society sprang up in 1917 to promote Irish participation even before the contours of Wilson's grand scheme had taken full shape in the president's mind. Its founding members included three nationalist MPs and the future governor general, James McNeill. The Irish Dominion League, established by progressive southern unionists to promote a political settlement along dominion lines, argued that the country should take its place as a League member. John Redmond's nephew and biographer, L. G. Redmond-Howard, put the cart before the horse when he argued for membership in a League of Nations as a means to establish Ireland's status as a separate nation before the issue of whether it should also be a separate state might be addressed.[46] The fact was that Wilson did not fully know himself, elaborating his ideas during the sea passage to Europe. His anglophile Secretary of State, Robert Lansing, whom Wilson would sideline throughout the conference, confided to his diary that the president's ideas for self-determination were 'loaded with dynamite'.[47] And so they would prove to be.

Pledges by the allies to recognize Polish and Czech claims to independence after the war established the outlines of the post-war order. Irish nationalists now had to decide how they would seek a place in it. Sinn Féin canvassed at the Roscommon by-election in February 1917 on a platform

---

[46] L. G. Redmond-Howard, *Ireland, the Peace Conference and the League of Nations* (Dublin, 1818).
[47] Lansing diary, 30 Dec. 1918, quoted in Bernadette Whelan, *United States Foreign and Ireland, From Empire to Independence, 1913–29* (Dublin, 2006), p. 188.

of seeking a hearing at the peace conference. The following month, an editorial in *Nationality* declared

> The political objective of Ireland today is admission to the Peace Conference. Nothing else political now matters. Mr O'Connor's Free Institutions, Mr Redmond's Home Rule on the Statute Book and their Masters' Imperial Conference are of no account to Ireland. Ireland is out of the corner where for generations she had been hidden away from the world. She is no longer an island lying behind England—she is again politically, as well as geographically, part of Europe.[48]

The party set up a foreign affairs sub-committee to consider how to respond to the changing political landscape following American entry into the war. At the same time, the IRB drafted a statement of Ireland's case for independence to be presented to the peace conference that was expected to meet once the war was over. Following his victory in the Clare by-election in July, Eamon de Valera asserted 'to be heard at the peace conference, Ireland must first claim absolute independence'. This position was incorporated into article two of the party's constitution at a convention in October 1917. It was decided at the same meeting to campaign for an independent republic; the debate about the constitutional form of government would follow afterwards. Delegates also endorsed Arthur Griffith's plans to send representatives abroad. Though a commercial role was outlined for these envoys, the decision to opt for a republic made political activity inevitable. The party manifesto for the December 1918 general election reaffirmed these points. Ideas that, ten years earlier, had been part of the political margins now assumed greater importance as Sinn Féin grew in strength.

On the eve of the armistice in November 1918, the Sinn Féin organ *New Ireland* presented the case for the peace conference: 'Sinn Féin has always advocated going to the Peace Congress as the concrete application of the general principle that Ireland, as a nation, equal in status to any nation, is in duty bound to take her place in all international affairs.'[49] The party wrote to Wilson following the October convention, urging him to support Irish independence and a hearing at the conference. A delegation of party members unsuccessfully sought a meeting with him in December to press their case, while the President stopped off in London en route to Paris.

The peace conference offered an unprecedented opportunity to publicize the Irish case, canvass international opinion, and benefit from the general questioning of international borders and the political rationales upon which they were based. It offered a means to internationalize the Irish question and

---

[48] *Nationality*, 3 Mar. 1917.   [49] *New Ireland*, 9 Nov. 1918.

a device to exert pressure on Britain. The decision to seek a hearing at the peace process reflected a belief that Wilson would be able to deliver, combined with a cold-headed assessment that a refusal would be equally beneficial in propaganda terms. It was also a logical outcome of the decision to pursue the goal of independence in the form of a republic.

If appeal was to be made to a peace conference, the question of how this would be done arose. It was important to link the Irish case with those nationalities whose claims the allies had chosen to recognize. The party argued that 'among the Small Nations of Europe, Ireland holds a front place in extent, population, and wealth, and her claim to be heard at a Peace Conference is sustained by this fact'.[50] In keeping with Griffith's liking for charts and tables, an election pamphlet called 'First of the Small Nations' methodically compared Ireland to the other small nations of Europe. Of eleven that were independent (his slide rule extended from tiny Montenegro to colonial Belgium and the Netherlands), Ireland exceeded five in extent, four in population, and all except one in per capita revenue. Compared to Poland, Finland, and Bohemia, he claimed Ireland was second in revenue and third in both extent and population. Yet Ireland remained un-free, despite a longer record of suffering and a better-founded claim than many of the new states of Europe, such as Latvia and Czechoslovakia.[51] There was even an election song:

> The Spaniards, Bulgars, Swedes, and Danes
> Have claims less high than we,
> Yet suffer they no foeman's chains—
> Those nations can be free![52]

It was difficult to speak of the plight of other subject peoples without admitting that their claims to self-government were framed in much the same terms as those of the Irish. Yet Griffith was unwilling to accept that the situation of other nationalities was analogous to that of the Irish, fearing any connection might retard hopes of a settlement to Irish aspirations. In his introduction to a new edition of John Mitchel's *Jail Journal*, published in 1918, he argued that 'the right of the Irish to political independence never was, is not, and never can be dependent on the admission of equal rights in all other peoples'.[53] With the prospect of a post-war peace conference it was important to stress that Ireland demanded admittance as a small nation rather than as a subject people

[50] Sinn Féin Tract No. 5, *The Small Nations* (Dublin, 1917).
[51] See, also *Nationality*, 3 May 1919.
[52] Latest Ballads of Sinn Féin (pamphlet), pp. 7–8, quoted in Laffan, *The Resurrection of Ireland, The Sinn Féin Party, 1916–1923* (Cambridge, 1999) p. 265.
[53] John Mitchel, *Jail Journal* (Dublin, 1918).

of the British Empire. The Irish did not want to be bracketed with the Indians, Egyptians, and others. Not everyone agreed with this approach. Those whose nationalism was inseparable from their belief in self-determination for all were unhappy at this pragmatic approach. The Ulster-born Quaker and essayist Robert Lynd argued that Ireland did not demand any liberty that should not be accorded to all nations 'in equal measure'.[54] Quite apart from the difficulties this posed in the face of unionist opposition to an all-Ireland state, it also led Lynd to support the allied war effort in 1914, an issue on which he and Griffith parted company acrimoniously.

With the end of hostilities, hopes were high around the world that the peacemakers, when they met, would usher in a new era of peace and stability in place of the dynastic rivalries and competing blocs that had produced the war. Central to these hopes was the figure of Woodrow Wilson and his 'Fourteen Points' which provided the framework for a post-war settlement based on principles of equity, rule of law and self-determination. The scope and extent of Wilson's famous points were much debated at the time and after. His proposal for an international body to oversee relations between states and adjudicate in cases of conflict was revolutionary in its day and laid the basis for the modern international order. His prescription of self-determination as the basis for dismantling the defeated multi-ethnic empires was also unprecedented. Crucially, the president considered his principles should be applied only in the territories of the defeated powers, a position agreed among the allies at the time of the Armistice. Wilson believed that the claims of other subject peoples could be considered by his League of Nations once it had been established, a formula that would enable him to sidestep a number of thorny issues the British and French did not wish to see brought into the peace conference.

The nationalist advocate, Hanna Sheehy Skeffington, met Wilson in Washington as part of a suffragist delegation three days after his Fourteen Points speech. By her own tally the first Sinn Feiner to visit the White House, she used the opportunity to press the president to take action on Ireland, and came away convinced that he would do so for reasons of 'enlightened expediency' as well as honour and integrity.[55] A pacifist who had been radicalized by the murder of her husband by a British soldier during the Rising in Dublin, Sheehy Skeffington had been selected to represent the Irishwomen's International League at the international

---

[54] Robert Lynd, *If the Germans Conquered England and Other Essays* (Dublin, 1917), p. ix.
[55] Hanna Sheehy Skeffington, *Impressions of Sinn Féin in America* (Dublin, 1919). See, also, Maria Luddy, *Hanna Sheehy Skeffington* (Dundalk, 1995).

women's congress held in The Hague in 1915 that gave birth to the Women's International League for Peace and Freedom. Blocked from travelling by the British on account of her anti-war propaganda, the Irishwomen's International League put forward its secretary, the suffragist and trade union leader Louie Bennett (who would become the first woman president of the Irish Trades Union Congress), whose less forthright views were deemed more acceptable in London (the two would subsequently differ publicly on whether violence was justifiable to secure Irish independence). In the end the government prevented any Irish or British women from making the crossing to the Dutch capital. An Irish section of the Women's International League was quickly set up, combining calls for a just post-war international order and an Irish state. Its members hoped Wilson would intervene to ensure both would become a reality, a conviction shared by many in nationalist Ireland at the time.

As elsewhere, there were those in Ireland who were caught up in the wave of enthusiasm and expectation generated by Wilson's project that Erez Manela has called the 'Wilsonian moment'.[56] Louie Bennett was one, seeing Ireland as a test case of the new order many hoped would emerge from the war. Bennett used the Irishwomen's International League to lobby for a hearing for Ireland at the Paris peace conference and secured recognition as a separate Irish section by the International Committee of Women for Permanent Peace. She also travelled to the socialist meeting in Berne in 1919 to press the Irish case. The home rule advocate, Rosamund Spedding, was another. With the convening of the peace conference, the Irish Parliamentary Party commentator John J. Horgan believed Wilson's agenda of democracy and international peace had reached its 'testing time'.[57]

The president's words were seized upon in Ireland where they were quoted, as the nationalist and one of the drafters of the Free State constitution, Darrell Figgis recalled, 'as though they had been devised to meet her case' even though there was no reference to Ireland in any of his speeches.[58] Nationalists adapted the language of liberal internationalism to lobby for representation at the peace conference, and speeches and claims for recognition quoted from his Fourteen Points. Sinn Féin updated its political lexicon, going so far as to claim that 'self-determination' was a translation of Sinn Féin.[59] Irish nationalists might

[56] Manela, *The Wilsonian Moment*.

[57] Louie Bennett, *Ireland and a People's Peace* (Dublin & London, 1918); Rosamund Spedding, *The Call of Democracy: A Study of the Irish Question* (Dublin, 1919); John J. Horgan, 'The world policy of President Wilson', *Studies*, vol. 7, Dec 1919, pp. 553–63.

[58] Darrell Figgis, *Recollections of the War in Ireland* (London, 1927), p. 230.

[59] *Nationality*, 2 Dec. 1918.

share with counterparts elsewhere a mixture of hope and entitlement which Wilson's pronouncements evoked, but their aspirations for self government and the language and imagery used to claim it are from a different and older vocabulary of nationhood which Irish nationalism could draw on. For some national groups, in particular those in the colonial possessions of the European powers, Wilson's words were a catalyst for aspirations towards autonomy, independence or self-rule that had previously been couched in much vaguer terms, but in Ireland they were greeted by nationalists as confirmation of the justice of their claims and an assurance that the president would act to uphold them.

Sinn Féin and similarly minded Irish nationalists were able to draw on an older vocabulary of statist ambitions and imagery in their statements and claims, even if these ambitions were not necessarily part of the political mainstream at the time or before. The IRB's nineteenth-century constitution had proclaimed its executive the government of the republic pending its *de jure* establishment. Its appeal to Wilson in 1917 was couched in these terms, as was its authorization to Patrick McCartan in May of the same year to travel to Russia on behalf of the 'provisional government of the Republic of Ireland'.[60] Unable to reach his destination, he instead travelled to America to set up office in Washington as envoy of this virtual republic that had been renewed by the republic proclaimed at Easter 1916 (the Dáil would later confirm his appointment as its representative in America).[61] With the end of war in Europe in November 1918, he addressed memoranda to the American government describing the case for international recognition and admission to the forthcoming peace conference.

With the success of Sinn Féin at the general election on 14 December, documents drew legitimacy from describing the vote as an act of self-determination, in keeping with the allies' programme of self-determination for the peace conference. The legitimacy, in republican eyes, of this act was consolidated the following month with the establishment of the Dáil and the declaration of an independent republic. It was in the name of this republic that admission would be sought to the peace conference. But as 1918 drew to a close, an unsympathetic *Irish Times* confidently predicted that Sinn Féin stood not the slightest chance of gaining admission to the peace conference.

---

[60] Patrick McCartan, *With de Valera in America* (Dublin, 1932), p. 2.
[61] *Ireland's Appeal to America*, 1917 (Dublin, 1917).

2

'Apostles of Liberty'

The Republic's Quest for Recognition, 1919–1921

The general election of December 1918 transformed the political landscape in Ireland. Sinn Féin won seventy-three of the 105 Irish seats at the Westminster parliament. With six seats, the Irish Parliamentary Party's dominance of nationalist politics was over, another victim of the war. Having supported a war fought ostensibly on behalf of small nations, its policy of home rule within the United Kingdom was out of step with the new language of self-determination, the changing political landscape in Europe and a truculent mood at home. As voters had gone to the polls in Ireland, the map of Europe was being remade even before the peacemakers had started work in Paris. Movements that looked and sounded like Sinn Féin were carving out states amid the ruins of Europe's fallen empires, whose demise made possible the fulfilment of nineteenth-century national-ist aspirations for Poles, Finns, and Czechs among others. In keeping with the party's abstentionist manifesto, those Sinn Féin MPs who were not in prison or on the run gathered in Dublin a month after the election, on 21 January 1919, to establish an Irish parliament, Dáil Éireann ('Assembly of Ireland'), and declare a republic independent of British rule. The same day the opening shots were fired in what would be a protracted war of independence, that would last until the start of negotiations with the British in the summer of 1921 for an independent Irish state.

The republican regime recognized early on the value of international opinion and the potential to wield it in its favour. At its first sitting, the Dáil appointed a foreign minister, Count Plunkett, father of an executed 1916 rebel, and voted to despatch envoys abroad to plead its case for recognition. Plans were ambitious at first: information offices and what was hoped would soon become embassies were to be opened in the principal capitals of Europe, Scandinavia, and the newly independent states of Eastern Europe. A special envoy would be sent to India and one to Moscow, to cooperate with the Russians, Turks, and Persians. A 'foreign ministry' would later be created to support this work. Even the country's poets were to be pressed into service to petition Wilson in verse, Arthur Griffith wondering whether 'Yeats would use his muse for Ireland now'.[1] In a *Message to the free nations of the world*, the Dáil pledged to 'resume that intercourse with other peoples which befits us as a separate nation'.[2] The message was addressed to the Irish people, the British government and the word at large. Three days earlier, the peace conference had begun its work in Paris, its task a remaking of the European map and a division of the spoils of war. Action on the international stage had become possible in a way that had never before been the case.

Woodrow Wilson had never intended his words to encompass self-determination for all and would ultimately be dismayed at the tumult his vision provoked, describing it as 'the metaphysical tragedy' of the day.[3] But reports of his speeches reverberated around the world, finding a ready audience not only among stateless national groups in Europe but also among restive populations in the old world's colonial possessions. Taking the president's words at face value, they converged on the French capital in the hope of securing a hearing for their claims to self-determination, autonomy, or independence. Nationalists from Egypt and India, African countries under the colonial yoke and French Indo-China (including a young Ho Chi Minh) rubbed shoulders in the cafés and hotel lobbies of Paris. The president's rousing rhetoric raised expectations it would prove impossible to meet.

But as the tide of war was turning in the summer of 1918, Wilson had reverted to a non-interventionist path regarding Ireland, largely as a result of British pressure. He would need London's support if he were to implement his ambitious agenda at the conference and assured Prime Minister Lloyd George that he would not allow the Irish question to be raised. From January to June 1919, American labour organizations, religious and political figures, state senators, and the US Congress petitioned Wilson to accommodate Irish demands in the post-war settlement; but he had determined not to take action and, having made up his mind, was not to be dissuaded. Thus was set in motion a clash of expectations: the premise on which nationalist hopes for a hearing were unfounded from the outset. On the day the peace conference opened, de Valera accused Wilson in a public statement of hypocrisy if he did not deliver

---

[1] Extract from a memo on Dáil Éireann policy attached to a letter by Arthur Griffith, 23 Jan. 1919, NAI ms 1125/15.

[2] *Dáil Éireann Official Record*, p. 26, 21 Jan. 1919.

[3] Wilson meeting with American Commission on Irish Independence, 11 June 1919, quoted in Whelan, *United States Foreign Policy and Ireland*, p. 214.

self-determination for Ireland. But, on the whole, nationalist hopes were invested in the American president and the movement refrained from criticizing him while efforts were underway to secure a hearing in Paris.

The person entrusted by the Dáil with the task of securing a hearing at the conference was Seán T. Ó Ceallaigh, speaker of the Dáil and a founding member of Sinn Féin. A week before the first meeting of the Dáil, the Sinn Féin executive selected Eamon de Valera, Arthur Griffith, and Count Plunkett to present the case for independence in Paris. Ó Ceallaigh's task was to get them there and to persuade the conference to grant a hearing. He was a shrewd political operator who would enjoy a long political career culminating in his election as the second president of Ireland in 1945. But as he unpacked his bags in Paris in February 1919, the British Lord Lieutenant was still ensconced in the mansion in Dublin's Phoenix Park that would eventually become his official residence as president. What he lacked in sophistication or foreign experience Ó Ceallaigh made up for by force of personality and a relentless appetite for work that would take its toll on his health over the three years of the Dáil's campaign for recognition.

The need to get visas endorsed by British military authorities and the difficulty in obtaining a passport, at that time issued for a specific journey, meant that it was in his capacity as a Dublin councillor that he travelled to France as part of a delegation to confer on Wilson the freedom of the city. Upon his arrival on 8 February, Ó Ceallaigh opened an office in the Grand Hotel beside the Opera and announced his presence as the official representative of the Irish Republic to the peace conference. Tipped off by the British, the French police were instructed to prevent him from gaining access to any meetings of the peace conference and to keep a close eye on his activities.

On arrival, he found the city's hotels over-flowing with official delegations, international media, lobbyists and petitioners, the great, the good, and the just curious. Its salons and cafés were filled with speculation about how the assembled powers would reshape a continent ravaged by four years of war. As president, prime ministers, and plenipotentiaries took up residence, for a while the French capital was the centre of world opinion. This was the first modern peace conference played out before the world's press, its proceedings followed on a daily basis by millions around the world. It was also the first peace conference at which public opinion would play a part, made possible by the growth in coverage that resulted from the global penetration of news and other communications infrastructure of the day. The world's press took a keen interest in the Irish case and there was considerable speculation about what would happen in Paris if the Irish attempted to present their case. It would not be as simple, however, as knocking on the door and asking for admission.

Ó Ceallaigh's first act was not to seek a meeting with Wilson as a Dublin counsellor, but to deliver a petition to the American delegation at its base in the Hotel Crillon requesting a hearing for the Sinn Féin delegates. Aware of these overtures, Wilson had instructed his secretary to dissuade the Irish from sending a formal delegation to Paris. Two days later, Ó Ceallaigh succeeded in meeting his confidante and gatekeeper, 'Colonel' Edward Mandell House. The meeting did not go well, the American describing hopes to secure a hearing for Ireland as 'an unfortunate misunderstanding'; there was no question of the president intervening in an internal British matter. Wilson set sail for Washington a few days later and would not return to Paris until the end of March.

With the American president out of the frame, Ó Ceallaigh wrote to the chairman of the peace conference, French premier Georges Clemenceau, requesting a hearing and safe-conducts for the Irish delegates. He then turned his attention to the other delegates to the conference, delivering petitions to each of the seventy-one representatives as well as to the sizeable press corps assembled in Paris for the proceedings. His actions did not go unnoticed; George Creel, head of the US propaganda effort during the war and a member of the American delegation, described the Irish as the 'most clamorous of all the national groups'.[4] But by the end of March, he had not been received by a single delegation. It was dispiriting work. Ó Ceallaigh despairingly observed 'all these delegates great and small are solely interested in grabbing all they can of the spoils for themselves', accounting for his inability to get anyone to intervene on the Irish side by the fact that 'they have no time to listen to anyone like myself who wants justice and right to prevail'.[5] In Dublin, *Nationality* pictured the assembled dignitaries labouring hard to 'make the world safe for hypocrisy'.[6]

Arthur Griffith had predicted as early as 1916 'if we don't get in—which I suspect is possible—we shall stand on the stairs and harangue the world outside', and this is now what happened.[7] The Irish presence in Paris was reinforced in mid March with the arrival of George Gavan Duffy. Patrician and schooled in France, he both looked and sounded the part and moved with ease in the social milieu of Paris salon life. Ó Ceallaigh resented his appointment from the outset and the two enjoyed an awkward relationship that would ultimately deteriorate to the point where Gavan Duffy, by then serving as foreign minister,

---

[4] Ó Ceallaigh letter, 23 Feb. 1919, NAI DFA ES Paris 1919.
[5] Ó Ceallaigh to Cathal Brugha, 7 Mar. 1919, NAI, DFA ES, Paris 1919–21, original file 1919.
[6] *Nationality*, 19 April 1919.   [7] Laffan, *The Resurrection of Ireland*, p. 251.

would dismiss Ó Ceallaigh from the Dáil service in 1922 for campaigning against the peace treaty with Britain. But in the spring of 1919, Gavan Duffy's presence was a boost to publicity work in the French capital. Attempts were made to make contact in the corridors with influential delegates, such as the Japanese representative, Nobuaki Makino, but these were chance encounters, eliciting little more than non-committal expressions of sympathy. There was little contact with the representatives of what the peacemakers dubbed 'states in progress of formation', those whose claims the allies had chosen to recognize. Nor was there much contact with the neutrals, who came late to the conference having been excluded from the initial group of participants. Parties to the talks were primarily motivated by self-interest, be it winning recognition for new states, grabbing colonial spoils or the elusive quest for security guarantees to forestall a return of hostilities. All but a few were preoccupied with maximizing territorial or financial gain. It was unrealistic to expect governments would expend political capital to challenge Britain, the predominant power of the day, or lend support to separatists at a time when social and political unrest threatened states large and small. If the Americans were unwilling to do so what hope was there that others would? The idealism of the Irish collided with the *realpolitik* of the peace conference.

The most senior American delegate Ó Ceallaigh managed to meet was the future president, Herbert Hoover. The meeting on 14 February with Hoover, who was American relief administrator and an informal advisor to Wilson, did little to advance the Irish agenda. His encounter two days later with the president's military advisor, General Tasker Bliss, may have been actively counter productive. Wilson's first draft of the covenant established self-determination as the central instrument for adjudicating disputes. Bliss asked him if this would cover Ireland or India, prompting a re-think. The same passage did not appear in the version published later that month.[8]

The American delegation was under instructions not only to refrain from encouraging Irish aspirations but actively to discourage them. With this in mind, Wilson sent Creel to Ireland in February to meet with senior figures in Sinn Féin, including Michael Collins and Harry Boland, as well as with John Dillon, leader of a much-diminished Irish Parliamentary Party. The visit did little to clarify understanding on either side, Creel returning to Paris convinced Sinn Féin had understood there was no question of a hearing at the conference while the Irish side remained committed to seeking one despite the odds stacked against them.

---

[8] Manela, *The Wilsonian Moment*, p. 60.

With little to show for their efforts and no sign that their case would be taken up by the conference, it was decided to play the Irish-American card. In early April, reinforcements arrived in the form of a three-member American Commission for Irish Independence. Appointed by an Irish race convention held in Philadelphia in February, the commission's goal was to lobby Wilson to secure the necessary permits for the Irish delegates to travel to Paris. Its chairman was Frank P. Walsh, a labour lawyer who had served as chairman of the War Labor Board. He was joined by Edward F. Dunne, a former governor of Illinois, and Michael J. Ryan, a lawyer who had unsuccessfully run for the governorship of Pennsylvania. All three were Democrats and none had opposed Wilson's re-election in 1916 in contrast to some Irish-American leaders. The commission took rooms at the same hotel as the Sinn Féin delegation and took their cue from them. What the Irish failed to appreciate was that Wilson needed British support to overcome French opposition to his draft for the League of Nations. There would, therefore, be no question of intervening to secure a hearing for Sinn Féin at the conference table.

Wilson was prepared to persuade Lloyd George to allow the Americans to visit Ireland and this they did in early May. The visit was simultaneously a public relations coup for the republic and a setback for any hopes of getting the Irish delegates to Paris. The republican ministry feted the Americans, holding a special session of the Dáil in their honour. Rallies across the country were the scene of rousing speeches and an ill-judged police raid on a meeting of the Dáil during their stay generated blanket press coverage. The impact of the visit in Ireland was considerable. Even *The Irish Times* was moved to ponder whether there might be a head of steam building behind the idea of a republic, a proposition it had previously charged only 'fools and fanatics' would support.[9] The commission produced a hard-hitting account of British injustices that drew an immediate response from London. The British government accused the commission of stoking separatism in public while in private complained bitterly to the Americans for asking that permits be granted in the first place. The message was blunt: there would be no further talk of allowing an Irish presence at the peace conference.

The commission arrived back in Paris just as the text of the peace treaty with Germany was published on 17 May. A new dynamic now entered the peace negotiations. The terms to be imposed on Berlin, considered by many at the time as well as subsequently to be punitive and draconian, were drafted so largely at French insistence. Fearing the Germans would

---

[9] *The Irish Times*, May 1919.

baulk at signing and walk away from the table, the British sought to enlist American support in an eleventh hour attempt to water down some of the most egregious provisions. Once again, Anglo-American cooperation would stand in the way of Irish hopes for intervention in the negotiations. Although the treaty would not be signed until the end of June, the following day Eamon de Valera wrote to Clemenceau repudiating the British right to sign on behalf of Ireland.[10]

The debacle of the commission's visit to Ireland was a serious set back, leaving Ó Ceallaigh despondent. He had given up any hope of achieving anything at the peace conference and advised de Valera the time had come to 'take the fight to the United States'.[11] By late May, the commission had also accepted that there would be no Irish seat at the table and lobbied instead to represent the Sinn Féin case in Paris. This request was refused on the grounds that the commission members were not authorized to represent anyone but themselves. As British anger rumbled on, in early June the US Senate passed a resolution introduced by the Republican senator for Idaho, William Borah, expressing sympathy with the aspirations of the Irish people for 'a Government of its own choice' and requesting the American delegation in Paris to secure a hearing for de Valera, Griffith, and Plunkett.

Negotiations on the peace treaty with Germany continued through the summer, reaching their final stages as the Senate was passing its resolution. Clemenceau refused to act upon it and Wilson, whose over-riding aim was to see the League of Nations come to life, was not disposed to insist. Ó Ceallaigh had been quick to grasp that the primary French interest at the conference was to 'get the last ounce of flesh from Germany', yet there was limited understanding among nationalist leaders of the politics between the major powers as the negotiations progressed.[12] The embattled American president, increasingly out of his depth in negotiations with Lloyd George and Clemenceau and obsessed with his project to reform the world order, was unwilling to expend political capital on Ireland and made this clear when he met the commission on 11 June. The meeting with Walsh and Dunne was memorable for Wilson's description of the wide-scale misinterpretation of his policy of self-determination as the 'great metaphysical tragedy of today', but it did not advance the Irish cause. In the president's eyes, the Irish were but one of many national groups to

---

[10] Ó Ceallaigh and Gavan Duffy to Georges Clemenceau, 17 May 1919, NAI DFA ES Paris 1919.
[11] Ó Ceallaigh to de Valera, 17 May 1919, NAI DFA ES Paris 1919.
[12] Ó Ceallaigh to Cathal Brugha, 7 Mar. 1919, NAI, DFA ES, Paris 1919–21, original file 1919.

have misread his intentions and their pleadings were a distraction from his goal of securing the League. The *New York Times* published the correspondence between the commission and Wilson on 14 September 1919 as the Senate sat to debate ratification of the Treaty of Versailles.[13] Two months later the treaty was rejected by the Senate just weeks after Wilson had been awarded the Nobel Peace Prize.

Would there have been an Irish seat at the table if history had taken a different course and home rule had been enacted before the start of the war? The Home Rule Act had reserved foreign and defence affairs to London but this was broadly the case for the dominions, all of which sent representatives to Paris. Some, such as the South African General Jan Smuts and the Australian prime minister, William Hughes, played an influential role at the conference. The presence of the dominions at the peace conference was a sign not only of the shifting sands of power away from Europe but also of the shifting constitutional balance within the British Empire that was a direct result of the war. The infusion of dominion troops was a major fillip to the British war effort until the Americans entered the war. As the number of colonial troops grew, dominion premiers took their places in the Imperial war cabinet from 1917. The Ulster Unionist leader Sir Edward Carson held office from 1915; John Redmond was also asked but declined to take a seat at the cabinet table. Despite hostility to conscription, it is conceivable that the sacrifice of 50,000 Irish troops at the Somme, Gallipoli, and other battlefields might have earned for a home rule Ireland a seat at the table as well.

THE LEAGUE OF NATIONS

While the initial focus of the Sinn Féin delegation in Paris was to secure a hearing for the Irish case at the peace conference, there was also interest in the emerging details of Wilson's much anticipated Fourteenth Point: a new world League of Nations. The US president concentrated his energies in the opening months of the conference on drafting the new organization's charter himself, rightly calculating that it would have to be agreed first or not at all. The British and French were less enthusiastic, but conceded it as the price for securing American acquiescence in their plans to divide the spoils from the war between them.

[13] *The New York Times*, 14 Sept. 1919.

The draft text of the League covenant was published on 21 February and, the following day, Ó Ceallaigh presented a demand for Irish admission to the new organization. The issue of the League posed a dilemma for Irish nationalism. On the one hand, republicanism was in favour of moves towards creating a framework for international governance in which the rights of smaller states and subject peoples would be upheld. The Dáil voted in April to seek membership of 'a World League of Nations based on equality of rights' between large states and small and 'to accept all duties, responsibilities and burdens which inclusion in such a League implies'.[14] Membership of the new League would constitute the highest seal of legitimacy and international recognition for the newly-minted states of Europe, a fact not lost on the Irish. Admission had become an accepted aspiration across all but the Irish unionist spectrum by 1919. Canada, Australia, and the other dominions would be admitted as founding members of the League at its first sitting and even those segments of Irish political opinion which favoured a continuing link with Britain, such as the Irish Dominion League founded by the agriculture reformer and home rule advocate Horace Plunkett, wished to see Ireland join their number.

Irish republicans continued to place faith in Wilson's grand scheme, even though the British had been able to prevent a hearing at the peace conference, believing international opinion would ensure a different outcome with the League. But the new organization would be a club of established states and its rules were crafted with this in mind. Initial drafts of the covenant contained references to self-determination as a basis for the future adjustment of borders, but the term was absent from the published version, which offered little by way of encouragement for subject peoples hoping to find in the League a forum in which their grievances would receive a hearing. Article 10 enshrined the principle of territorial integrity, confirming the possessors in their possessions. Wilson had envisaged the League would determine claims to self-determination and arbitrate border disputes which the peace conference was unable or unwilling to take up but this was qualified by a stipulation that the consent of the occupying power was required. From an Irish perspective, this would rule out recourse to League arbitration without British consent.

By early March 1919, disillusionment had begun to set in, Ó Ceallaigh dismissing the League as 'a sham'.[15] While the hope of US intervention remained in republican minds, the movement refrained from publicly criticizing either Wilson or the League. The expectation was that Wilson

[14] *Dáil Éireann Official Record*, p. 76, 11 April 1919.
[15] Ó Ceallaigh to Brugha, 7 Mar. 1919, NAI DFA ES Paris 1919.

might be prevented from acting in support of Irish claims, not that he would refuse to do so. He quickly went from hero to villain when it became clear he would not intervene in support of the Irish case. By June, Ó Ceallaigh had correctly concluded that Wilson regarded the Irish question as a matter for the British to resolve and that the hoped for intervention would not be forthcoming. It had been decided not to break with Wilson publicly unless advised to do so by the Irish-American organizations. But as Wilson failed to deliver, attitudes cooled towards the US president and what Erskine Childers caustically dubbed his 'mystical mumblings'.[16]

The case for membership was again presented to Clemenceau in June, proposals to picket the signing ceremony on 28 June at which the League was born were dismissed and de Valera was conciliatory in his comments on the League upon arrival in New York at the start of his awareness raising campaign in the United States. Once the contours of the peace settlement became clear, however, the tone of comment became more critical as republican strategy in the United States switched to lobbying against the Treaty of Versailles, and with it American membership of the League, in the hope of pressuring the Wilson administration to intervene in support of Irish independence. They were not alone: Egyptian and other nationalists also campaigned for rejection of the Treaty in the hope this would bring about a change in the US position on their respective claims for recognition or support. They would equally be disappointed.

Ó Ceallaigh's prediction in March that the only way to force Wilson to intervene was 'by using the possibility of the non-ratification of his great scheme' by throwing Irish-American votes behind Wilson's Republican opponents would ultimately be proven correct but without the wished-for intervention from Washington in return.[17] As debate about US ratification of the Treaty of Versailles wore on, the Geary reservation passed by the Senate in March 1920 sought to link American support with Irish admission to the League once self-government had been secured. But this condition was ultimately moot as the United States would not ratify the Treaty of Versailles and the provisions on the League of Nations were omitted from the separate peace treaties the US negotiated with the belligerents.

The faith at first placed in Wilson and his ability to secure recognition for Ireland, and the assumption that he would actively seek to do so, was remarkable for a movement given to cynicism regarding the political process. This would turn out to be an unfortunate misreading of American

[16] Erskine Childers in *New Ireland Review*, 1919.
[17] Ó Ceallaigh to Brugha, 7 Mar. 1919, NAI DFA ES Paris 1919.

politics and of the extent to which the Irish question and Irish agitation could be bound up with American attitudes towards the League. How serious was Sinn Féin in its pursuit of a seat at the negotiating table in Paris? Opinions differed. Many in the movement were impatient of any diplomatic or political attempt to resolve the matter and would, according to Liam de Róiste, 'rejoice at failure to secure anything through the Peace Conference'.[18] Michael Collins reminded his colleagues the focus should be in Ireland and not Paris or New York, and P. S. O'Hegarty would later claim that the peace conference was 'a temporary weapon forged by circumstances'. For some there was undoubtedly an element deflecting criticism at home from the decision not to take up seats at Westminster.

The League met for the first time in Paris on 16 January 1920, six days after the Treaty of Versailles entered into force. The following day, Ó Ceallaigh wrote to its British secretary general, Sir Eric Drummond, dismissing it as an 'English simulacrum of an international League', but membership remained a republican aspiration.[19] Opposing American membership of the League in the hope of gaining leverage over the Wilson administration did not mean nationalism had turned its back on internationalism. Once it became clear the United States would not enter the League, Irish leaders reverted to a more positive stance envisaging an active role for Ireland in the organization. Michael Collins predicted the country would become a 'pivot' of the League.[20] Some even proposed Ireland as a seat for the League. Far-fetched though much of this comment may have been, Irish nationalists grasped the changing international landscape of the time. Despite the disillusionment of Versailles and realization that League membership could not be achieved until independence had been won, support remained for a broad internationalist vision as the best means of guaranteeing the rights of small states.

THE 'STAR-SPANGLED HARP'

The signing of the Treaty of Versailles on 28 June 1919 meant that Paris and the peace conference ceased to offer a forum for Irish hopes. Wilson and Lloyd George returned home leaving lower level officials to negotiate treaties with Austria, Bulgaria, Hungary, and Turkey. As hopes faded of securing a multilateral path to Irish independence, the focus shifted to seeking recognition from individual countries. Despite the

[18] Liam de Róiste diary, 16 Feb. 1919, CAI, U271/24.
[19] Ó Ceallaigh to Sir Eric Drummond, 17 Jan. 1920, NAI DFA ES.
[20] *The Manchester Guardian*, 7 Dec. 1921.

Figure 2. Éamon de Valera and supporters at San Francisco City Hall, 18 July 1919 (Image courtesy of UCD Archives P150/791(9))

disappointment in Paris, hopes remained high that Wilson's wartime pledge to support self-determination meant America would recognize the republic.

Ó Ceallaigh had predicted that the only means of bringing pressure to bear on Wilson would be to raise the prospect of the Senate blocking ratification of the League of Nations. He was half right. As hopes of achieving something in Paris faded and as the contours of the peace settlement became clear, the tone of nationalist comments changed and Irish strategy in the United States switched to lobbying against ratification of the Treaty of Versailles. Eamon de Valera arrived in America in June, establishing his base at the Waldorf Astoria in New York and embarked on a countrywide tour aimed at raising pressure on the government to recognize the republic or to pressure Britain into a settlement. His first official statement in New York was clear: 'from today I am in America as the official head of the Republic established by the will of the Irish people in accordance with the principles of self-determination'.[21] It was a challenge to Wilson and those who had denied him a hearing at the peace conference. A sizeable sum of money was raised through a bond drive that would keep the propaganda effort going around the world and a series of high profile speaker events held across the country aimed at keeping the issue of Irish independence at the forefront of US domestic politics.

News photographs depict crowded squares and meeting halls in every city he visited in an ambitious programme masterminded by his lieutenants Harry Boland and Patrick McCartan. Such was the throng of well-wishers and supporters to be greeted at every turn, de Valera quipped he would soon have the biceps of a blacksmith. But it was his skills as a wordsmith that were put to work, working crowds to indignation with his calls for justice for Ireland, spurring civic petitions, and generating acres of newsprint. The message was tailored to suit an American audience, with references to the Irish Congress rather than the Dáil, while de Valera conveniently elided the title of President of the Dáil with that of President of the Republic. An attempt was made to appeal beyond the Irish American constituency to reach a broader audience drawn from other emigrant backgrounds, for whom the cause of self-determination would also have resonance. All of this was conducted with a touch of the razzmatazz of US electoral politics—there was even a campaign song, 'There'll never be a League of Nations without Ireland'. De Valera was made an honorary chief of the Chippewa tribe while a meeting with the last survivor of the *Catalpa* escape confirmed his ties with the Fenian legacy. An impressive tally of meetings was arranged with governors, members of Congress, and a host of current and future political figures, including a young Franklin Delano Roosevelt.[22]

Despite initial success in securing sympathetic resolutions in both houses of Congress, further progress was blocked by damaging internal dissent. At issue was a power struggle between Irish-American leaders led by Judge Daniel Cohalan and John Devoy, who saw in an organized Irish-American movement a means to exert power within the United States, and de Valera, who wished to focus solely on the issue of independence. Political impetus was lost following a split into rival organizations, and

---

[21] 23 June 1919, Seán Cronin, *The McGarrity Papers* (Tralee, 1972), p. 77.

[22] Roosevelt recalled the experience when, as president, he received Minister of State Frank Aiken in Washington in April 1941.

Figure 3. Éamon de Valera dressed as a chief of the Chippewa Tribe, Wisconsin, 18 October 1919 (Image courtesy of UCD Archives P150/9)

de Valera failed to secure a pledge from either the Democratic or Republican parties to support Irish independence in the 1920 general election, despite a much-publicized presence at both party conventions. As the popular appetite for monster rallies faltered after a year on the road, it became clear that the republican road show suffered from a surfeit of access and a deficit of influence. Reluctant to abandon hope of securing recognition, de Valera remained in America until December 1920 but was forced to concede that Washington would not intervene with London. The Dáil cabinet instructed him to remain in the United States to lobby the new American government when it took office in March 1921, in the hope that recognition or at least intervention might be forthcoming, despite the fact that he had failed to persuade the Republicans to include either course in its election platform. De Valera ignored the request and returned to Dublin in late December, leaving Harry Boland and Mary MacSwiney to continue the propaganda effort. The republican regime mistook mass meetings for leverage. The British connection was of paramount importance, something the actual weight of the Irish-American lobby was never sufficient to force a change in policy.

EFFORTS TO COURT THE EUROPEAN POWERS

Efforts in the meantime were being pursued on the other side of the Atlantic. In continental Europe these efforts were concentrated towards France, Italy, and Germany. Despite historical links and religious affinity, there was no agent in Spain, 'a big field open and untilled', until late 1921.[23] Less surprisingly, links with the new states of Eastern Europe were almost nonexistent. The Allies did not recognize the Baltic States until 1920, when it had become clear that anti-Bolshevik resistance in Russia had failed, while in Finland a parallel civil war played out between Reds and Whites. The eastern boundaries of the new Polish state would not be fixed until after the Russo-Polish war in 1920; wedged uneasily between Bolshevik Russia and a humiliated Germany, the pressing priority for the resurrected Poland was survival. Likewise, the successor states of the collapsed Hapsburg Empire provided unpromising ground for Sinn Féin. Preoccupied with finalizing borders at each other's expense and imposing new state structures on restive minorities, they had neither the luxury nor the inclination to become involved with others' concerns. Thus, the new states of Europe, among whose number Irish nationalists sought to take their place and with whose cause Sinn Féin strove to associate Irish aspirations, offered little by way of example or encouragement. It was rather the old powers of Western Europe on which attention was focused.

The long-standing Francophile tradition in Irish nationalism meant that efforts to invoke the 'historical alliance' between the two countries were revived even though a cool-headed analysis would have revealed that a consistent unwillingness for official France to become involved had hardened into outright hostility to the republican cause during the war. Experience at the Paris peace conference bore this out. The republican mission was rebuffed at every attempt and while there were some successes

---

[23] Gavan Duffy to Brennan, 11 Mar. 1921, NAI DFA ES Box 33 File 232.

in influencing press coverage of events in Ireland, there was little sympathy in government circles for a separatist movement believed to have allied itself with Germany during the war.

The depth of French feeling on this score was under-estimated by the Sinn Féin envoys, who believed French political opinion could be won over in time. The extent of this antipathy is clear from the account left by Clemenceau's right hand man at the conference, the future prime minister, André Tardieu. It was a view shared by Clemenceau and by many others in post-war France. This did not prevent the Irish from making efforts to cultivate French opinion at both official and popular level. French newspapers were reluctant to take news from the republican mission, but as strains appeared in the Anglo-French relationship in 1920, coverage of events in Ireland gradually increased. This did not bring about a shift in French policy, however. Nationalists had traditionally over-estimated French interest in Ireland, whilst at the same time exhibiting little understanding of how the country might intervene in Irish affairs or whether it was in French interests to do so.

To strengthen links with France, some nationalists proposed that Ireland exploit differences between London and Washington, such as those over naval strength. Throughout 1920, George Gavan Duffy urged Irish-American organizations to adopt a pro-French line, writing to Patrick McCartan and Frank Walsh in Washington touting a 'big new orientation of international policy' without any real understanding of how feasible this proposal was while lacking any means of bringing it about.[24] It was scarcely realistic to assume that the reach of Irish-American opinion extended to the inner counsels of the American military or the State Department.

Rather than pursuing an alliance with the United States, French policy at the time aimed to anchor Britain in Europe as a safeguard against German revival and to counter the threat from Bolshevik Russia. Britain and France were at odds at the start of 1920 over the division of the Middle Eastern spoils of the Ottoman empire but, as the year wore on, unrest in the Arab territories, the risk of war with Turkish nationalists led by Kemal Ataturk and the failure of foreign intervention to topple the Bolsheviks from power combined to remind Paris and London that there was more to be gained by sticking together. French insistence upon maintaining a British alliance meant not just the frustration of Sinn Féin's 'big new orientation' but also a growing impatience with republican propaganda efforts. While the peace conference was sitting, the French

[24] Gavan Duffy to Frank P. Walsh, 7 April 1920, NLI mss 5582.

authorities had tolerated the presence of Sinn Féin envoys despite British protestations. But as the military campaign in Ireland intensified and nationalist unrest across the eastern flank of Europe for a time threatened to unravel the Versailles settlement, there was a limit to French willingness to tolerate separatists. Gavan Duffy was expelled from France in October 1920 for propaganda activities following the death on hunger strike of the imprisoned Lord Mayor of Cork, Terence MacSwiney.

Despite the setback of Gavan Duffy's expulsion and the lack of any sympathy for the republican cause in official circles, Sinn Féin did not give up on France—religious sympathies and republican myth ran too deep for that. He believed the Catholic interest to be worth cultivating on the grounds that it was sympathetic, on the ascendant in France and, he contended, saw Ireland as a 'bulwark of religion in a godless world'.[25] He believed a grouping of Catholic states with France, Italy, and Belgium at its core would emerge in the post-war landscape as a counter balance to Germany and in competition with the Anglo-Saxon powers of Britain and America. An independent Ireland would be a natural partner for such a grouping.

Gavan Duffy took advantage of his expulsion from Paris to tour Europe (he was also asked to leave Brussels by the Belgian authorities), assessing the potential for activity and propaganda, before settling in Rome in March 1921 to replace Seán T. Ó Ceallaigh who had been taken ill. The information he gathered resulted in a reassessment of short-term strategic thinking. Reporting on his findings, he placed less emphasis on Catholic countries: 'France is a decadent and decreasing country, Italy is in low waters and Spain belongs to other days' he reported, in part reflecting disillusionment at failure to record any real progress in Paris, Rome, or Madrid.[26] Instead he foresaw an alignment of America, Germany, and Russia based on American capital, German know-how, and Russian mineral resources that would emerge as an economic competitor to Britain.

The idea of such a grouping appealed to Sinn Féin leaders, combining the United States, where the regime perceived Irish influence to be strong, and Russia, the only state with which they had been able to establish contact. Neither were they alone in expecting that German economic power would soon rival that of Britain again. Discontent was growing with western military intervention in the Russian civil war, and American business concerns had expressed interest in exploiting Siberian mineral resources. The German government had established a *modus operandi* with

[25] Gavan Duffy memorandum on France, 10 Oct. 1920, NAI DFA ES Paris 1920.
[26] Gavan Duffy report, 11 Mar. 1921, NLI mss 5582.

the Bolshevik regime, and it was known that the British were seeking a similar trade agreement with Moscow. Gavan Duffy's analysis overlooked the political, economic, and social weakness of Germany, which was in no position to embark upon such a capital-intensive and ultimately risk-laden venture as exploiting Russian resources.

Little attention was paid at first to Germany, while the focus was on the peace conference in Paris. Germany had not been represented at the conference, its delegates arriving in May to be presented with a fait accompli, and there was therefore little potential for contact. Many in Sinn Féin viewed the terms imposed on Germany at Versailles as punitive and harsh, and concluded the country was a spent force which would have to throw in its lot with Britain in the face of French *revanchisme*. The political instability and economic, social, and psychological collapse in post-war Germany presented both obstacles and opportunities for the republicans. Turmoil at the political level was mirrored by conditions in the German capital that, in 1919, was a shady netherworld of arms dealers, revolutionaries, and hedonists.

The Irish scene in Berlin was a world of émigré intrigue and requiem masses for Roger Casement; its leading figures included sympathetic Ger-man professors, a former American consul at Munich, Thomas St John Gaffney, who had resigned in protest after the Easter Rising, the shady George Chatterton Hill, whom the British had linked to German and Russian communists, and an American lady, Agatha Grabasch Bullitt, who ran what remained of the wartime German-Irish Society. The calibre was varied to say the least and petty squabbles prevented this array of characters from working together. In the words of Nancy Wyse Power, who had been sent to Berlin in 1920, 'almost everybody in Germany who purports to be working for Ireland's interest is more concerned in blackening the character of everybody else than in doing useful work'.[27] Most were broke and suffered from an overly romantic view of diplomacy, the colourful Frau Grabasch writing to Dublin that she needed 'pure men who will do and dare and, if necessary, die'.[28]

Activities were only nominally under Dublin control and a source of considerable embarrassment. The Dáil ministry felt it owed them some thanks for their work during the war, but resolutely refused to sanction their present actions, and strove to distance itself from them. The diffi-culty was that post-war insurrection and British occupation made a Dáil representative impossible until late 1920. While a certain amount of sympathy existed in Germany for the Irish cause, given the precarious

[27] Nancy Wyse Power, 10 Dec. 1920, NAI DFA ES London File 1.
[28] Gavan Duffy to O'Hegarty, 17 Mar. 1920, NAI DFA ES Paris 1919–21.

political and economic situation no German government would risk entanglement with its powerful former foe over Ireland. The British had intervened at the last minute in negotiations in Paris to water down the punitive terms the French sought to impose on the Germans and exercised considerable influence in Germany through the presence of the Inter-Allied Commission of Control established at the end of the war. As crisis followed crisis, the prospects of German support for Ireland, never substantial, became increasingly remote. The vulnerability of the new German republic, its dependence on Britain in the face of French threats and the taint of Bolshevism meant that Berlin was not a promising centre for political activity.

But republican interest in Germany did not begin and end with the search for political allies. The country was awash with weapons left over from the war making it the arms bazaar of Europe. Political instability meant there was little control over how these weapons were used and there were numerous groups of various political hues with access to them willing to help the Irish, be it for adventure, money, or out of common cause against the British. A steady flow of emissaries, including the future Lord Mayor of Dublin, Robert Briscoe, arrived in Germany intent on securing arms and munitions for the fight in Ireland. Claims of Irish agitation and gun running were taken seriously by the British, who had some success in stopping the flow of arms. But despite the best efforts of British intelligence, shipments made it through naval blockade to reach Ireland. As late as October 1921, ten days after the start of negotiations in London that would result in the Anglo-Irish Treaty, the IRA was engaged in smuggling arms from a group of German communists. The incident provided further fuel to the British preoccupation with the growing red menace across the Irish Sea but in reality the relationship was a marriage of convenience. Sinn Féin was interested in importing guns not communism to Ireland.

If Sinn Féin was unable to elicit French or German support for Irish independence, the situation was little better in Italy. The Italian government had shown no interest in Ireland at the peace conference, busy persuing instead plans to add territory in the Adriatic. The creation of Yugoslavia had put an end to these deams, provoking public unrest back home. Combined with political instability and left–right tensions, the environment was hardly propitius to promote the Irish cause. The Catholic centre parties expressed some interest in Sinn Féin's campaign, largely on grounds of religious affinity, and there was sympathy from the left and from Benito Mussolini, whose fascist party had been founded in March 1919.

A 'thorough going friend and supporter of ours' in Diarmuid O'Hegarty's view, Mussolini agreed to publish fortnightly front-page stories on Ireland in his *Popolo d'Italia*.[29] He also facilitated contact between Ó Ceallaigh, now based in Rome, and the poet-radical Gabriele d'Annunzio, who made repeated overtures to Sinn Féin following his quixotic occupation of Fiume, the modern-day Croatian port city of Rijeka, in November 1919 in protest at the peace conference's failure to award the city to Italy. The Dáil ministry was quick to reject d'Annunzio's proposals for a league of oppressed peoples, rightly seeing it as bombast (despite claims by his 'foreign minister', the Belgian poet Léon Kochnitzky, that 'the indomitable Sinn Féin of Ireland' was a signed-up member), and poured cold water on plans for d'Annunzio to visit Dublin. There was interest, however, in exploiting both the popularity of his cause in Italy and the potential to acquire arms. Ó Ceallaigh made arrangements in the autumn of 1920 to ship arms and munitions from Fiume to Ireland in early December. However, a press statement at the last minute by the inveterate and theatrical self-publicist d'Annunzio resulted in a British naval blockade of Fiume, and the plan was aborted.[30] At an official level success was less forthcoming, though the establishment newspaper *Corriera della Serra* became increasingly sympathetic in its coverage.

THE REPUBLIC AND THE VATICAN

If the Italian state offered little prospect of political action, the reverse was the case in the Vatican. The large Irish presence at the Holy See offered opportunities and challenges for Sinn Féin diplomacy. The republican movement was quick to enlist the global network of Irish bishops and clergy who ministered to congregations wherever the Irish had emigrated in large numbers. Sympathetic bishops were provided with propaganda material and letters flowed from Sinn Féin representatives in Rome urging the Dáil ministry to fete senior clergy passing through Ireland while in Europe. A steady flow of English speaking bishops, many Irish or from Irish backgrounds, provided an opportunity to influence Vatican thinking on Ireland.

The ability to exploit networks of prelate patriots who were as comfortable on the hustings as in the pulpit provided a valuable additional platform to the international propaganda effort, even if the Irish bishops at home were cautious in their pronouncements regarding Sinn Féin. The support of senior clerics, such as the Cork-born archbishop of Melbourne, Daniel Mannix, an outspoken advocate of the Sinn Féin cause, was akin to

[29] O'Hegarty to Gavan Duffy, 18 Sept. 1920, NAI DFA ES 2/202/25.
[30] Ó Ceallaigh memoir, NLI mss 27,702(6).

celebrity endorsement given the prominence enjoyed by the clergy in Irish society at the time (Mannix's removal from an Ireland-bound liner by a British naval frigate in August 1920 became an international cause célèbre). The major Irish religious communities maintained houses in Rome, the most senior of which being the Irish College, which was sympathetic to the nationalist cause. The recently promoted superior-general of the Carmelites, Peter Maginnis, had sheltered many prominent nationalists, including de Valera, on arrival in America at the order's New York priory. The rector of the Irish College, Monsignor John Hagan, worked closely with both Ó Ceallaigh and Gavan Duffy during their time as envoys in Rome, guiding them through the Vatican bureaucracy and putting in a quiet word with curia officials. His insider knowledge was particularly influential in avoiding a Vatican condemnation of republican violence in 1920 and 1921.

Not all the Irish clergy in Rome were sympathetic to the Sinn Féin agenda (Mairéad Gavan Duffy described the Irish religious communities in Rome as broadly pro-English in sympathies, singling out the Christian Brothers in particular) and Hagan's efforts were seen as essential to counteracting both this and the perceived British influence in Rome.[31] Ironically, the British saw Rome as a hot bed of Sinn Féin sympathizers, a comment on both the Vatican's determination not to take sides in the struggle, its ability to play both parties and the extent to which Sinn Féin believed its own rhetoric of British omnipotence.

The Holy See was not a participant at the peace conference but had an observer at the talks in the form of its undersecretary of state, Monsignor Bonaventura Cerretti. Cerretti was kept up-to-date on developments in Ireland by Paschal Robinson, his Irish-American assistant, who would become the first papal nuncio to Ireland a decade later. Contact was established with Cerretti in Paris and, while he was unable to do anything to help the Irish cause, he offered Ó Ceallaigh a sympathetic ear. The value of the contact would prove more important in the course of efforts the following year to influence the Vatican to adopt a sympathetic, or at least neutral, approach to the military campaign in Ireland. Patrick McCartan had told Cerretti in New York that a formal request for recognition would not be submitted lest it embarrass the Holy See. The over-riding objective was to avoid the Vatican taking a hostile stance to Irish aspirations or the methods being used to achieve them. The threat of a condemnation of Sinn Féin was a very real danger. The Irish-born British envoy to the Vatican, Count de Salis, was repeatedly instructed

[31] Mairéad Gavan Duffy to Arthur Griffith, 11 Oct. 1921, NAI DFA ES Rome 1921–23.

by his superiors in London to secure a condemnation and sought to mobilize anglophile elements of the Curia in his support. Both Benedict XV and his secretary of state, Cardinal Pietro Gasparri, were reluctant to become embroiled on either side, seeking instead to maintain their freedom of manoeuvre.

Rumours began to circulate in May 1920 about a possible Vatican condemnation of republican violence in Ireland that would include censure of Sinn Féin. British efforts in Rome were focused on securing a condemnation on moral as well as political grounds, calculating that this would deal a blow to Sinn Féin's support at home and abroad. Ó Ceallaigh had remained in touch with Cerretti, now back in Rome, who advised him to prepare a counter argument to present to the pope. An audience with Benedict XV was secured on 12 May at which he set out the case for self-determination and firmly laid responsibility for the spiralling violence at Britain's door. A memorandum submitted stopped short of asking the Holy See to recognize the republic, although parallels were drawn with the new states of Eastern Europe and Poland in particular, whose cause the pope had championed during the war.[32] Benedict XV was not unsympathetic to the Irish cause but was careful not to be drawn into the dispute. His message to Ó Ceallaigh was nuanced: 'Ireland has every right to its independence. Ireland has every right to fight for its independence but remember my words, be careful of the methods you use.' For the time being no condemnation was issued although the Vatican reacted negatively when Ó Ceallaigh published the fact that the audience had taken place.

Ten days later, the republic secured a further advance, profiting from celebrations in Rome marking the beatification of Oliver Plunkett. This was Ó Ceallaigh's crowning moment, when he hosted a reception in the name of the Irish republic, pulling off the coup of getting Cardinal Logue and the entire Irish hierarchy, not to mention two Vatican officials, to attend. As his memoirs attest, Ó Ceallaigh was in his element cajoling Irish bishops of whom he was somewhat in awe, whilst enjoying the frisson of using them for his own political ends.[33] It was also about the extent of his diplomatic skills, and in his dealings with the Vatican he was dependent on Hagan, who advised on his every move.

As the war of independence dragged on, the British increased pressure on the Vatican, in particular following the death on hunger strike of the Lord Mayor of Cork in October. Despite the emotionally charged circumstances of the case, London failed to extract a condemnation and

---

[32] Ó Ceallaigh memorandum to Benedict XV, 18 May 1920, NAI DFA ES Paris 1920.
[33] Ó Ceallaigh memoir, NLI mss 27,702(3).

Foreign Office entreaties were rebuffed again in December. The issue of a condemnation arose again in early 1921, but visiting Irish-Australian bishops led by Daniel Mannix lobbied the pope and Secretary of State Cardinal Gasparri against such a move. The Holy See finally issued a statement on Ireland in May, which failed to denounce Sinn Féin whilst condemning violence on both sides. Crucially, it called for a negotiated settlement between the two sides. The statement was cautiously welcomed in Dublin while in London it was seen as 'just the kind of casuistic performance that might have been expected from the Vatican', in Lord Curzon's words.[34]

The Vatican never condemned the Sinn Féin government, despite considerable British pressure, both political and ecclesiastical, to do so and, in this sense, republican representation was a success. To a large extent, however, Irish republicans consistently exaggerated the extent of British influence in Rome whilst underestimating their own. Catholic and Irish may have been interchangeable identities for many, but this did not blind Sinn Féin to the temporal reality in which the Vatican operated. Ó Ceallaigh was convinced the Holy See was playing both sides, wryly observing there was 'no beating the Vatican State Department for diplomacy'.[35] Recognition, however, was never formally requested, as it was understood that it would not be forthcoming. The position of the Catholic Church in the British Empire was too valuable to be put in jeopardy.

THE REPUBLIC'S OSTPOLITIK

The October Revolution that swept the Bolsheviks to power in late 1917 permanently transformed the European political landscape. A fearful European body politic watched events unfold concerned that the contagion might spread beyond Russia's borders. Within weeks of the revolution the Soviet Commissariat of Foreign Affairs, Narkomindel, was given two million roubles to propagate revolution abroad. Irish republicans did not fail to notice that Lenin's peace plan, published on the eve of the Paris peace conference in December 1918, had called for self-determination for Ireland. The Third International, later renamed the Comintern, had also called for Irish freedom at its inaugural meeting the following March. The unfolding drama of the October revolution, civil war, and allied intervention in Russia was followed with as much interest in Ireland as anywhere

---

[34] Curzon minute, 31 May 1921, cited in Dermot Keogh, *The Vatican, the Bishops and Irish Politics, 1919–39* (Cambridge, 1986), p. 70. CO739/9/42855.

[35] Ó Ceallaigh to O'Hegarty, 19 Sept. 1920, NAI DFA ES Paris 1920.

and with as little understanding of the nature of the society that the Bolsheviks were building. The republican Countess, Constance Markie-wicz, confided to her diary in December 1918 that 'freedom has dawned in the East' and in April 1919 Eamon de Valera called on Ireland to prepare for the day 'when Europe may be run by councils of soldiers, workers and peasants'.[36] For McCartan, the two causes were based on a sense of brotherhood which 'a common experience endured for a common purpose alone can induce'.[37] Despite this, it was not until June 1920 that the Dáil contemplated an overture to Soviet Russia.

A British mission went to Moscow in late 1919 to open channels with the Bolshevik regime, but plans for a trade agreement were put on ice with the outbreak of the Russo-Polish war the following spring. As Marshall Pilsudski's armies swept east, for a time it seemed as though the Bolshevik regime was facing collapse and Lloyd George decided to wait to see if the Poles would finish it off. With the prospects of a deal with London receding, the Russians entertained overtures from Sinn Féin for a possible understanding between the Bolshevik and republican regimes. Desperate to put an end to allied military intervention, the Bolshevik regime hoped arming the Irish would divert the British and perhaps influence Irish-American opinion in favour of withdrawing US troops. The Russians were also mindful of the possible impact this might have on Indian and Egyptian nationalists.

Contact was first established in New York where, like Sinn Féin and other nationalists in search of a state, the Bolsheviks had opened a bureau to campaign and raise funds. Discussions over the summer of 1920 between Patrick McCartan and Santeri Nuorteva, the Finnish secretary of the Soviet Russian Information Bureau in New York, resulted in agreement in June on the text of a treaty of mutual recognition. The same month, the Dáil authorized a mission to travel to Moscow to finalize its terms with Patrick McCartan, selected for the journey to Russia he had been unable to make three years earlier. Despite sanction from Dublin, McCartan did not set out immediately (he would later blame de Valera for the delay) but sent instead an Irish-American labour figure, Patrick Quinlan, to sound out the Russians under cover of attending a meeting of the Comintern's second world congress in Moscow. By this stage the outlines of an eventual treaty were discernible, but Quinlan reported back that the mood in Moscow was not favourable to recognition. Instead he

[36] *Irish Independent*, 9 April 1919.
[37] McCartan to Ludwig Martens, 8 June 1919, in McCarten, *With de Valera in America* (Dublin, 1932), p. 109.

had broached the subject of training, arms, and trade, all of which were favourably received by the Russians.

Back in Dublin, the cabinet was considering a memorandum from de Valera favouring the proposed treaty. A few weeks later, they had before them McCartan's report from New York on the proposed treaty of friendship.[38] The text provided for both parties to use each other's diplomatic missions, and included commitments to promote the other's recognition and to prevent the shipment of arms for hostile purposes to each other's territory. Significantly, there was also provision for the right of political asylum in Russia for Irish revolutionaries, an important consideration given the plans to coordinate activities in India and the Far East from Moscow. A series of commercial clauses offered Irish firms significant concessions including in exploiting the lucrative flax trade, which were conceived in part as an inducement for unionist business interests to opt into an all-Ireland settlement at a time when the Government of Ireland Act was bringing partition to life. The most incendiary aspects of the agreement, however, were the proposed league of anti-imperial nations that the two undertook to establish, and Irish representation of the Catholic Church in Russia. The implications of this latter point for Sinn Féin strategy towards the Vatican seem to have gone largely unconsidered while the former proposal would clearly have undermined Sinn Féin efforts to win over reluctant governments and public opinion among the imperial powers of Europe.

On the basis of McCartan's findings, the go-ahead was given a second time for a mission to Russia, a decision subsequently affirmed by the Dáil on 29 June after little discussion. Contacts with the Bolsheviks continued into the autumn, and de Valera authorized a loan of $20,000 in October to the cash-starved Russians in New York. The following month the Dáil ministry rebuffed attempts by the Irish socialists Roderic Connolly, son of the Labour leader and 1916 rebel James Connolly, and Eamonn MacAlpine to insert themselves as the channel of communication between Dublin and Moscow and refused to deal with the Comintern. Yet despite all this, McCartan did not leave for Russia until almost six months later in December, by which time the tide had turned against the republican plan. The Soviets had sued for peace with Poland and seemed secure within their reduced borders, having defeated the main White Russian armies in the civil war. Western troops sent to Russia to support the Whites were being withdrawn. The military threat to the Bolsheviks had passed and, with it, hopes of the regime's collapse. As it appeared that the

[38] 'Draft of proposed Treaty between the Russian Socialist Federal Soviet Republic and the Republic of Ireland', May 1920, NAI DE 2/245.

Bolshevik state was becoming a permanent fixture, by late 1920 the British had revived the idea of a trade agreement with the Russians and a delegation from Moscow visited London to discuss terms towards the end of the year.

By the time McCartan finally arrived in Moscow on St Valentine's Day 1921, the Russians had gone cold on the idea of a treaty. At a meeting with Maxim Litvinov, commissar in charge of western affairs, McCartan was candidly told things were not as they had been six months ago, when the Russians had been prepared to sign a treaty. Negotiations were progressing for a trade agreement with Britain, a prize more valuable than anything the Irish could offer. The nationalist nature of the Irish revolution was also causing concerns for the Communists. In Moscow later that month, McCartan was told the same story by Commissar for Foreign Affairs, Georgy Chicherin. But further meetings with Nuorteva did not seem as unpromising. A British trade agreement would not necessarily preclude an understanding with the Irish, he claimed, and so McCartan remained in Moscow until June.

Back in Dublin, de Valera had regained his earlier enthusiasm for the proposals, seeing in Moscow a potential centre for propaganda in Europe and Asia. However, once the Anglo-Russian trade agreement was signed, ironically on 17 March, St Patrick's Day, the likelihood of a deal receded further. McCartan believed recognition was still possible on the grounds that the Soviets had not publicized his presence in Russia, despite the extra leverage this might have earned them in their dealings with the British. His cover was blown in April when a raid on a Dublin house secured for the British a store of Sinn Féin papers including the text of the draft treaty. Leaked the following month to the ultra-unionist *Morning Post* in London, the affair caused a sensation. The Russian government denied the story and the British published the texts in July.[39] Despite having stayed on in the hope of salvaging the treaty's commercial clauses, McCartan left empty handed in June.

Had the Bolsheviks signed a treaty of recognition with the republic in mid-1920 there is no guarantee they would not have disowned it six months later, when conditions favoured a deal with the British. It is also difficult to see how aligning the republic with the Bolsheviks would have advanced chances of securing recognition elsewhere. George Gavan Duffy, for one, was firmly opposed to the move, arguing 'we may as well at once give up all further political effort on the Continent'. Britain's wartime propaganda machine had moved almost seamlessly from linking Irish

[39] HMG Command Paper, 'Intercourse Between Bolshevism and Sinn Féin', Cmd. 1326, 10 June 1921.

nationalism with Germany to associating it with the new menace of Bolshevism. A war-weary public, alarmed by continuing social and political upheaval, was easy prey to scaremongering that depicted separatist nationalism of any hue as blocking a return to normality. On top of this was a Europe-wide paranoia about vernacular Bolshevisms. The breathless 1920 bestseller *Red Terror and the Green*, published by the Irish Unionist Alliance, played to a receptive audience too easily persuaded of the implausible menace of a communist rising across the Irish Sea.[40] With American and other troops on Russian soil, the Bolsheviks' commitment to exporting their revolution and a growing unease in Ireland and elsewhere about the anti-clerical nature of the Soviet regime, beyond possibly securing arms the gambit appears all the more strange.

One conclusion is that the mission to Moscow was pursued once hopes of securing American recognition had finally been abandoned. The Dáil ministry had urged Eamon de Valera in April 1920 not to take action unless the Americans had concluded a peace settlement with the Bolshevik regime. Two months later, the cabinet again asked him not to present a demand for recognition to Moscow until one had been placed in Washington. It is possible that de Valera calculated a move of this kind would put pressure on the British government. Whatever the reasoning, the thinking seems to have been confused: at one point he was convinced the draft treaty's commercial clauses would provide an incentive for unionists to opt into an all-Ireland settlement. Either way, it was a gamble. British propaganda sought to depict Sinn Féin as an offshoot of Bolshevism and publication of the full text of the treaty in June 1921 caused a sensation.

So why did Sinn Féin embrace the Bolshevik bear? The Russians were the only government prepared to deal with the Dáil, and whatever reports reached Dublin of the exact nature of the regime weighed less heavily than the perceived similarities between the two. Reliable information about Russia was in short supply and lurid accounts of Bolshevik terror vied with encomia of praise for the new society being born. Irish nationalists were not alone at the time in misunderstanding or misconstruing the nature of the Bolshevik revolution or from seeking to benefit from the convulsions it had unleashed. Bolshevik revolutions in Europe had failed and it was in terms of regimes rather than revolutionary movements that negotiations were couched. The short-lived Kiev Rada passed a resolution in favour of Irish independence, but there is no record of contact with Ukrainian nationalists. There also existed certain sympathy for socialism, or at least

---

[40] Richard Dawson, *Red Terror and the Green, the Sinn Fein-Bolshevist Movement* (London, 1920).

socialists. The revived Second International had recognized the republic at its conference in February 1919. There were also those, such as Darrell Figgis, who detected communistic elements in pre-conquest Gaelic society although few were as enthusiastic as the polemicist Aodh de Blácam, who considered the workers' republic 'an excellent translation of Gaelicism'.[41]

There was also the pragmatism of being allied with an enemy of Britain. A long-standing nationalist principle, this had been reaffirmed by de Valera at the Sinn Féin party conference in 1919, though with a significant qualification: 'the enemy of our enemy must, for the time being, naturally command our sympathy'.[42] Did this provide a rationale to pursue links with the Bolsheviks? British intelligence reports emanating from Helsinki in April 1919 alleged that the Russians were funding Sinn Féin. To a large extent this was political scaremongering—similar allegations also circulated in London.[43] But as concerns about the nature of the Bolshevik revolution emerged, fear of being tarred with the same brush fuelled uncertainty about the Russian treaty. The allies whom the regime sought were on the whole bourgeois-capitalist, as the essayist George Birmingham observed in 1919.[44] Seán T. Ó Ceallaigh reported concerned enquiries from French officialdom in November 1920 about links between Sinn Féin and Russia and recommended public assurances that the republic would not develop along Bolshevist lines. Art O'Brien in London was equally alarmed, believing an agreement would undermine the work achieved in London, Paris, and Rome.[45] The republic might regard no one as its enemy, but it was finding that it could not afford to be friendly with everyone.

Patrick McCartan similarly believed revolutionary Mexico offered potential and championed the Mexican cause in 1920 despite border skirmishes and rumours of war with the United States, again without considering the effect this would have on attempts to court American opinion. The following year this bore fruit. Responding to Independence Day greetings in September 1921, the Mexican president thanked the Sinn Féin envoy, Stephen O'Mara, for his good wishes expressed 'on behalf of the Irish people', using language normally accorded to the representative of a recognized state.[46] But McCartan's radical sympathies

---

[41] Aodh de Blácam, *Towards the Republic* (Dublin, 1919), p. 33. See also, Darrell Figgis, *The Gaelic State in the Past and in the Future* (Dublin, 1917).

[42] *Irish Independent*, 10 April 1919.

[43] Paul McMahon, *British Spies & Irish Rebels, British Intelligence in Ireland 1916–1945* (Woodbridge, 2008), pp. 121–3.

[44] George Birmingham, *An Irishman Looks at his World* (London, 1919).

[45] Ó Ceallaigh to O'Hegarty, 9 and 19 Nov. 1920, NAI, DFA ES Paris 1920.

[46] President Alvaro Obregon to Stephen O'Mara, 24 Sept. 1921, NAI DFA 50.

were not widely shared within the republican government, which preferred to court the United States and France. A bitter McCartan was convinced this lay behind reluctance to pursue matters with Mexico or Russia, and this may also have been the case in South America where sympathy for the republican cause was manifest in émigré circles.

The Dáil had two permanent representatives in the continent, Frank Egan in Chile and Eamonn Bulfin in Argentina, both of whom believed they could secure recognition for the Republic. The Buenos Aires-born Bulfin's activities on behalf of the republic were brought to an abrupt halt when he was conscripted for military service. He is a good example of the networks of Irish nationalists which made up the Sinn Féin movement. His father, William Bulfin, was owner of the *Southern Cross* newspaper in Argentina and famous for his *Rambles in Erin* and *Tales from the Pampas* which were serialized by his friend Arthur Griffith in the latter's *United Irishman*. Bulfin junior moved to Ireland upon his father's death in 1910, where he became a protégé of the 1916 leader Pádraig Pearse. Arrested after the Easter Rising, he escaped harsh punishment on account of his nationality and was deported to Argentina where he became a Sinn Féin activist. His sister would subsequently marry Seán MacBride, a future Irish foreign minister and Nobel Prize winner, whose own father was executed in 1916 and whose mother, Maud Gonne, was W. B. Yeats's muse.

There was a sizeable Irish emigrant population in Argentina, like the Bulfins largely drawn from the Irish midlands. With the young Eamonn Bulfin in military service, the Dáil decided to replace him with Lawrence Ginnell, who also hailed from this area of Ireland, and he arrived in mid-1921. He was feted by ecclesiastical and civic authorities and succeeded in obtaining an official interview with the Argentine foreign minister. At one point in 1920 Eamon de Valera had considered touring the South American republics himself in the hope of securing recognition, drawn by assurances that if one could be induced to recognize the republic the others would follow 'like dominoes'. But hopes that the Catholic states of South America would rally to the Irish cause were as wide of the mark as those pinned earlier on securing European recognition.

Who represented the republic abroad? Some were elected members of the Dáil, such as Seán T. Ó Ceallaigh, Harry Boland, and George Gavan Duffy. Others were IRB members, such as Patrick McCartan (although many of the Dáil members were also IRB members). A small number were defections from the Irish Parliamentary Party, such as the Westmeath MP Lawrence Ginnell or Osmond Grattan Esmonde, whose father had been a Wexford MP. Others again were from less obvious walks of life: Lindsay Crawford in New York was a former Grand Master of the Independent

Orange Order expelled for his conversion to nationalism; Gerald O'Kelly was a papal count and Marquis McSwiney a papal chamberlain. Count O'Kelly was a colourful character who would have a long career in the Irish diplomatic service. A papal count (the full title was Count Gerald O'Kelly de Gallagh et Tycooly), his wife was descended from an Austro-Hungarian diplomatic family and his uncle, Count P. J. O'Byrne, also a papal count, had served briefly as an Irish envoy in Rome in 1921 before siding against the Free State. Both Cáit Ní Cheallaigh and Máiread Gavan Duffy were active as envoys in their own right, while Nancy Wyse Power in Berlin was the daughter of Jennie Power, in whose Dublin restaurant the 1916 rebels had met. Colonel Maurice Moore had been an officer in the Connaught Rangers—his brother was one of the founders of the Abbey Theatre in Dublin and his father had been MP in Sligo for the Parliamentary Party. Many were appointed because of their connections to figures active in Sinn Féin or the IRB, because they held the right view of events in Ireland, or simply because they were in the right place at the right time.

The functioning of the Dáil network was limited by a communications system described as 'hopelessly inadequate' and a shortage of suitable individuals for posts.[47] The Dáil secretary, Diarmuid O'Hegarty, kept information flowing as best he could but was dependent on politically reliable couriers who travelled with documents sewn into their clothing. The Dáil's international activities were managed from a series of fake addresses in Dublin, one masquerading as a chemical import company complete with fake accounts and samples in case the special branch came calling. Another alias was an insurance agent with an address on Harcourt Street, a short walk from the oft-raided offices of Sinn Féin. It was an operation managed on the run from the police, whole departments disappearing, quite literally, down a drainpipe.[48]

The dominant position of British news agencies in the international news business and the wartime habits of pliant editors posed a challenge to Sinn Féin in getting its message across in the face of what the *Irish Independent* dubbed a 'campaign of calumny by inspired paragraphs'.[49] To counter this, a publicity machine was assembled to campaign via the newswires. The *Irish Bulletin*, a catalogue of British military injustices and arguments for independence, was published weekly and distributed throughout Europe and beyond. Publicity work in London was aided by Desmond FitzGerald's friendships with Ezra Pound and members of the

---

[47] de Valera to Boland, 29 April 1921, NAI DFA ES 54.
[48] Hugh Kennedy in *The Irish Independent*, 25 July 1924.
[49] *Irish Independent*, 19 April 1919.

Bloomsbury set and Erskine Childers' fame as author of the pre-war thriller, *The Riddle of the Sands.*

At home, Count Plunkett was minister in name only, with real decisions taken by Arthur Griffith until his imprisonment in December 1920. In response to growing suppression of Dáil activities in Ireland as the war of independence intensified, greater powers were devolved to Eamon de Valera in the States. He was particularly influential in those policy areas decided from America during his lengthy sojourn there, such as the mission to Russia where, as in other areas of policy, he set aside views of colleagues in Dublin. Distance meant he had less input to European affairs, where Gavan Duffy and Ó Ceallaigh were in charge. He sought to assert control in July 1920 by proposing to establish a foreign policy headquarters in Washington and vest responsibility for overseas appointments in him. His return to Dublin at the end of 1920 meant that this plan was never implemented. Circumstances were such that central control was frequently an aspiration with individuals largely left to their own devices. The Dáil's foreign affairs committee met when it could to hear reports from the field and retrospectively sanction decisions already taken, but the overseas network remained a decentralized operation staffed by a number of strong personalities. While this enabled it to function during the campaign for independence, it would pose problems once conditions permitted moves to centralize control in 1922.

Here the republic's diplomatic efforts largely drew to a close. No government would recognize the republic—to do so would have provoked a sharp response by Britain—but this did not make Sinn Féin's activities any easier to counter. As a British diplomat ruefully observed, anyone could set up as a diplomatic mission. They were, however, kept under close surveillance, and reports flowed back and forth between the Foreign Office and its offices abroad about the activities of 'our Sinn Féin friends'.[50] With the exception of the Bolsheviks, Sinn Féin stopped short of presenting requests for recognition to the United States or any other government. It was a step continuously under consideration but circumstances never seemed right; the risk of rejection was considered too high. Outliers such as the Bolsheviks or Mexicans flirted with Sinn Féin but ultimately did not bite.

The agreement of a truce in the War of Independence on 11 July 1921 signalled an end to British attempts to oppose Irish nationalism by force and a switch to a political track with the opening of negotiations in London between Irish and British representatives. A wait-and-see policy

[50] R. Sperling to Foreign Office, 22 April 1921, PRO FO 371/2886; Boston Consulate report, June 1919, PRO 371/102951.

was adopted. It was important to avoid any activity abroad that could jeopardize the talks or be used to derail them, whilst at the same time being in a position to resume efforts should they break up, as many believed likely.[51] There was, thus, no relaxation on the political front, and envoys abroad were warned to be ready to continue the campaign and push for bilateral recognition by European states should the negotiations break down.

---

[51] De Valera to Brennan, 27 July 1921, NAI DE 2/526.

3

'Director for International Bluff'

Imagining a Role for Ireland on the World Stage

Numerous delegations and groups were styling themselves as *de facto* governments, and claiming recognition as such from the Paris peace conference. On the same day that the Dáil held its first meeting, a constituent assembly of Ruthenians gathered to resist incorporation in the new Czechoslovakia. What distinguishes them now from the Irish is that they were ultimately unsuccessful. The eventual establishment of an Irish state, with government departments and internationally recognized diplomats, has lent the departments and envoys of the Dáil period a status that they did not enjoy at the time. Rather, the Dáil foreign ministry might more accurately be regarded as a propaganda bureau operating on an international scale. Taking a break from the pressure of interviews, meetings, and rallies during de Valera's sojourn in the United States in 1920, Harry Boland jokingly described himself as the 'Director of International Bluff'.

Much of Sinn Féin's international effort in the period 1919–21 can be characterized as propaganda, an effort that ultimately failed to result in recognition of an Irish Republic. While some of this may indeed have been 'bluff', the process of imagining a role for Ireland on the world stage that occurred as part of the campaign for independence would have lasting implications for the development of Irish foreign policy in the decades that followed. The Dáil government recognized the need to create an international rationale for independence. At times, this consisted in pinning hopes on a coalition of countries emerging capable of matching British influence and thereby bringing about independence. This had not worked in the past, yet hopes were, once again, invested in an external deliverance. Memoranda passed between Dublin and republican agents abroad, referring to Ireland 'backing' various 'alliances'. Headlines were scanned for signs of tension between Britain and its wartime allies that might signal the hoped-for intervention from abroad. In part, this was a reflection of the fluid nature of European politics at the time. There was also a lingering trace of Fenian legacies in Sinn Féin's worldview. It reveals a conception of Ireland's position in relation to other states out of all proportion to Sinn Féin's ability to influence their actions. Nationalist analysis of international events was not always wide of the mark: de Valera's warning in April 1919 that the peace terms France sought to impose on Germany would lead to another war proved to be remarkably prescient, even if the sentiment was unlikely to win friends in Paris at the time.[1] Ó Ceallaigh and Gavan Duffy's understanding of the dynamics at play in the peace conference was also realistic after the first blush of hope had given way to a more cold-headed analysis of the main actors' motives. The calculation that recognition should not formally be requested from any state testified to a realistic grasp of the fundamental situation. That talk of 'alliances' and international configurations was on such a grand and unrealistic scale is, perhaps, less remarkable than the fact that Sinn Féin was thinking in such terms in the first place.

The case for Irish independence was outlined in a number of documents drawn up by the IRB and the Dáil government. These texts contain a core set of ideas and images that were repackaged to suit different audiences. From them can be distilled a Sinn Féin view of Ireland's place in the world and the role the party envisaged an independent Ireland would play in international affairs. In essence, an embryonic diplomatic philosophy can be discerned. It is these ideas that the present chapter will examine.

One of the first texts adopted by the Dáil at its inaugural sitting on 21 January 1919 was a *Message to the Free Nations of the World*. It represents a first, officially endorsed view of Ireland as an international persona, and outlines an embryonic Sinn Féin diplomatic philosophy. The *Message* called upon the free nations to 'support the Irish Republic by recognizing Ireland's national status and her right to its vindication at the Peace Conference'. The document stressed the cultural distinctiveness of 'one of the most ancient nations in Europe'; enumerated the grounds for independence from Britain; committed the Irish to uphold 'freedom and justice as the fundamental principles of international law'; and a 'frank co-operation between peoples for equal rights'. The most interesting assertion is perhaps the following statement:

> Internationally, Ireland is the gateway of the Atlantic. Ireland is the last outpost of Europe towards the west; Ireland is the point upon which great trade routes between East and West converge; her independence is demanded by the Freedom of the Seas; her great harbours must be open to all.

[1] *Dáil Éireann Official Record*, 11 April 1919, p. 73.

This passage, or variants on it, appears in numerous publications and accounts of Ireland's claim to independence and represents an attempt to construct a geopolitical identity.

During the First World War and in the years leading up to it, propagandists had focused on military control of Irish harbours and the seas around the island. With peace restored, an attempt was made to demonstrate that the separation of Ireland from the United Kingdom was in the interest of free trade and commercial navigation. The Cork-based John J. Horgan provided an economic rationale for this concept in a prescient article published in March 1919. In it, he argued 'Ireland's geographical position makes her the natural European base for American commerce' and her harbours 'the front door to the European markets'.[2] He went on to propose an economic model for Ireland based on attracting US foreign direct investment, a strategy which would not become official policy in Ireland for decades to come: 'if we can enlist the support of American capital now seeking a foreign outlet, and adopt American business methods and machinery, the speedy development of Ireland is certain'.

The *Declaration of Independence* and the *Message* were drawn up by a committee appointed at a preliminary meeting of Sinn Féin on 7 January 1919, whose members included Seán T. Ó Ceallaigh, Eoin MacNeill, George Gavan Duffy, and Michael Collins.[3] In drafting these texts, they were able to draw on documents such as *The Historic Case for Irish Independence*. There were several workings of this text, with versions drawn up by Lawrence Ginnell and Darrell Figgis. The imagery and arguments were essentially the same in each, beginning with the premise that Ireland played an important role in the preservation of European culture after the Dark Ages and working its way through centuries of British injustice to argue for independence. The past was harnessed to suit the needs of the present and, for Sinn Féin, this meant proving Ireland had led a quasi-state like existence before British rule. The language of twentieth-century statehood was thus applied to describe conditions in medieval Ireland: 'from the sixth century to the eleventh the riches of Rome and Greece flowed over Europe through the Sovereign State of Ireland'. Similar imagery was used in the version of the *Case* sent as a memorandum by the IRB to President Wilson in 1917 and widely circulated abroad. Ginnell also sought to establish Ireland's credentials as

---

[2] John J. Horgan, 'Ireland and World Contact', *Studies*, Vol. 8, Mar. 1919, pp. 35–45.

[3] The full list of committee members was: Piaras Béaslaí, Harry Boland, Cathal Brugha, Conor Collins, Michael Collins, George Gavan Duffy, Thomas Kelly, Eoin MacNeill, Richard Mulcahy, James O'Mara, Count Plunkett, Liam de Róiste, Michael Staines, and J. J. Walsh.

a state, describing the 'ancient Sovereign State of Ireland' as one of 'the primary Sovereign States of Christendom'. The conclusion to be drawn is an obvious one: 'modern Europe therefore owes a vast unpaid debt to Ireland'.[4] By describing Ireland's prior existence in terms of modern statehood, however anachronistic, independence could be presented as a restoration rather than an innovation.

It was important to demonstrate a geopolitical rationale for an independent state. The countries of Eastern Europe had achieved independence largely because it suited allied interests. Nationalists therefore tried to conjure a similar rationale for Ireland. An important concept used was the idea of freedom of the seas. As an idea it was not new, but the recent war had given it new life, when British propaganda portrayed a German-controlled Ireland as a menace to international shipping and trade. With the defeat of Germany in November 1918, Irish nationalists tried to turn this idea on its head, arguing that British dominance of the Atlantic, a 'private avenue', was contrary to international interests, particularly those of the United States. The solution to this problem would be a neutral and independent Ireland, internationally guaranteed—a 'kind of Atlantic Belgium' in the words of a contemporary commentator.[5] This would transform the Atlantic into a 'free highway' open to international shipping between Europe and America. An emphasis on freedom of the seas chimed with the romantic image of Ireland as an island. As partition became a growing reality, it was important to establish the island as the unit in which self-determination was exercised.

With its emphasis on naval power, the First World War had brought about a change in the status of the United States and of European perceptions of that status. It also brought about a change in Irish perceptions of the country's geographical location. The growing importance of the Atlantic, both strategically and for global trade, meant that peripherality could now be considered a strategic advantage. These arguments were bolstered by the country's importance to transatlantic cable and wireless communications, its status as a ship-building centre and its location on the route plied by trans-Atlantic liners between the old world and the new. Griffith went so far as to claim that 80 per cent of trade routes passed through Irish coastal waters. A potential role in the fledgling aviation industry had been vividly demonstrated in June 1919 when Alcock and Brown's pioneering non-stop trans-Atlantic flight landed in County Galway. British negotiators would emphasize naval and aviation issues in the talks on Irish independence, reinforcing a sense of Ireland's strategic

---

[4] Darrell Figgis, *The Historic Case for Irish Independence* (Dublin, 1918), p. 6.
[5] John J. Horgan, *Parnell to Pearse* (Dublin, 1949), p. 233.

importance in global trade and communications. Enthusiasm for freedom of the seas also derived from a belief that removing British control from Irish ports would see them brimming with business. As we have seen, this belief was behind the proposals for an Irish trade and consular service as early as 1900. The problem with this was that, after the defeat of Germany, there was no one for whom freedom of the seas, or rather freedom of the Atlantic approaches to Europe, would strike a chord. The United States was broadly satisfied with its relationship with Britain despite occasional disagreements about naval strengths, while France and Belgium saw in a strong British navy protection from possible future German aggression.

The concept of freedom of the seas was closely linked to ideas of neutrality current at the time. Recognition of the need to make a concession to British security concerns lay behind proposals for Irish neutrality, as much as a desire to pursue a pacific policy. It received its most controversial treatment in 1920, when Eamon de Valera likened a possible arrangement with Britain to the relationship then existing between the United States and Cuba. In an interview with the *Westminster Gazette* in New York, he observed 'mutual self-interest would make the peoples of these two islands, if both independent, the closest of possible allies in a moment of real national danger to either' and asked 'why doesn't Britain make a stipulation like this to safeguard herself against foreign attack as the United States did with Cuba? Why doesn't Britain declare a Monroe Doctrine for the two neighbouring islands?'[6] His comments provoked a howl of opposition among Irish-American opinion and newspapers, alarmed at the notion that Britain would be granted a right of intervention in Irish affairs after independence along similar lines to that which the United States enjoyed in Cuba, which included (prophetically) the use of bases on the island. The proposal was all the more remarkable for being made without consulting colleagues in Dublin, who were caught off guard by his comments and the analogy was quietly dropped. The idea of making some form of accommodation with British security interests remained part of de Valera's calculation and he had made a similar statement to the Dáil in April 1919 before his departure for the United States. The idea arose again during the Treaty negotiations in the form of undertakings not to facilitate Britain's enemies.

Once negotiations with the British began, the idea of freedom of the seas became less important in the face of the need to satisfy British security concerns. It also posed a problem for the likes of Erskine Childers. An

---

[6] *The Westminster Gazette*, 6 Feb. 1920.

expert on British military organization, he effectively contradicted this line in a 1921 pamphlet, arguing that Ireland held no strategic value: British naval power would render an invasion from Ireland impractical and, should that naval power be defeated, there would be no need to use Ireland as a bridgehead from which to launch an invasion of Britain.[7] He had, effectively, turned the romantic nationalist concept on its head and his pragmatic analysis of Ireland's relative strategic importance was closer to reality. As an index of contemporary conceptions of Ireland's strategic and international importance, however, it is revealing.

Childers, with his military background (he had served with the British army in the Boer War and with the navy during the First World War), anticipated security arrangements featuring prominently in the negotiations with the British in London, but on the first day of discussions Arthur Griffith admitted he was disinclined to raise the matter beyond stating that 'in principle your [Britain's] security should be looked after'. Griffith and Collins considered a policy of neutrality to be incompatible with security undertakings necessary to secure agreement with Britain on the broader question of independence.

Childers seems to have been alone in believing that a commitment to neutrality would be compatible with Commonwealth membership, despite the prevailing convention that it was committed as a unit to war by a decision of the British government. In a memorandum prepared before the negotiations, he laid out the Irish position as he understood it: 'our preference is to stand alone, like the vast majority of small nations, with complete independent control of our territory, waters and forces, neutral in all ways and devoted to peaceful development'.[8] If this was to prove impossible, he contended that guaranteed integrity, that is a defence association without provision for a common defence, should be proposed. This was the line Childers pursued during discussions with the British on defence while Griffith conceded defence facilities in Ireland during the plenary sessions. This became evident when the word 'neutral' was deleted from the first draft proposals prepared in Dublin in October 1921, which referred instead to Ireland being recognized as a 'free state'. It is interesting to note that de Valera's subsequent alternative to the Treaty, Document No. 2, made no mention of neutrality, instead closely mirroring the defence arrangements agreed in the discussions leading to the Anglo-Irish Treaty.

The *Democratic Programme* also adopted by the Dáil at its first sitting contained a commitment to addressing labour issues through international

---

[7] Erskine Childers, *Is Ireland a Danger to England?* (Dublin, 1921).
[8] Erskine Childers memorandum, TCD, mss 7780/1415.

action, included with an eye to the Socialist International gathering at Berne and also the views of the Labour party, which had stood aside at the 1918 election giving Sinn Féin a free run in many constituencies. The Labour leaders, Thomas Johnson and Cathal O'Shannon, travelled to Berne where they succeeded in winning recognition of Ireland as a separate entity from Britain and support for a hearing at the peace conference. The two stopped off in Paris en route to exchange notes with Ó Ceallaigh. The idea was nonetheless forward looking, reflecting the growing importance of labour issues in the post-war period, a product of the war itself as well as the revolution in Russia. Concern to address labour issues lay behind proposals to establish the International Labour Organisation at the peace conference.

In an open letter to Woodrow Wilson in June 1917, the IRB had claimed that Irish nationalism was not based on grievances, but a quick perusal of nationalist tracts and speeches indicates this was far from being the case. The length and degree of Ireland's historical suffering was deemed to set it apart from other nations in moral terms.[9] Thus, Ireland's 'right' transcended that of other states which the allies had chosen to recognize and care was taken to demonstrate the superiority, in nationalist eyes, of Irish claims for consideration over these new states. An exception was made for Poland, the 'Ireland of the East', whose claim to statehood was regarded as being on a par with that of the Irish. Some even believed the Poles would support a hearing for the Irish case at the peace conference but hopes would be disappointed. In a similar vein, the tenacity with which the Irish maintained their Catholic faith was cited by some writers as an exemplar to other countries: 'it was to Ireland's honour that she has always suffered for her ideals', declared Count Plunkett at the opening session of the Dáil, and once again the country would become 'a torch-bearer when reactionary statesmen tried to befog and enslave the world'.[10]

Preoccupation with being the most sinned-against people in history entailed comparisons with others and thus also a horizon broader than the narrow world of Irish politics. Memoranda prepared in 1921 for the South African premier General Smuts on Sinn Féin's foreign policy highlighted past missionary activities and Christianity. Talk of the spiritual values of Gaelicism and Irish culture in general were translated onto an international plane, with the works of writers such as Darrell Figgis, Aodh de Blácam, and Eoin MacNeill providing an intellectual background for the projection of Ireland onto the world stage. Many of the sentiments expressed were made explicit in de Valera's American interviews in

---

[9] Eoin MacNeill, 'Representative Irishmen and International Resurrection', in *Ireland's Place Among the Nations* (Dublin, 1918).
[10] *Dáil Éireann Official Record*, 10 April 1919, p. 58.

mid-1918, and are best summed up in his remark that, as the most spiritual people on earth, the Irish would 'show [to the world] the might of moral beauty'.[11] The implication was that, because of its earthiness in spiritual and moral terms, Ireland would be a bulwark of the international community and a guardian of its values.

There was a millenarian strain to some thinking on the foreign role Ireland was to play. The Cork politician, Liam de Róiste, confided to his diary in September 1919 that God had decreed Ireland to be free so that she might 'show men the path of justice'.[12] Similar ideas can be found in the writing of others, such as de Blácam, who saw Ireland taking the lead in a world struggle for morality against the capitalist order. Ranged against her was the British Empire representing, in the Sinn Féin lexicon, commercialism and might over right. Whatever the premise, it was an assumption that Ireland's unique story and national purity equipped it to serve as a guardian to watch against the 'fatty degeneration of the morals', to use P. S. O'Hegarty's loaded phrase.[13]

Of course, however much some nationalists may have imagined an independent Ireland of antiquity, the lack of a separate state in modern times had afforded little opportunity to harbour enmity towards other states, with the perennial exception of Britain. In the international environment of 1919 this became an advantage. Having played no part (as nationalists saw it) in international affairs, the Irish were untainted by the war or the great power diplomacy that had led to it. As one writer put it, 'remote from the rivalries and political intrigues of the rest of the world' Ireland was equipped to play a constructive role internationally.[14] Arthur Griffith saw Ireland aspiring to the role of a second Switzerland, committed to peaceful co-existence with its neighbours. Who could imagine, he asked, that an independent Ireland would 'lose its head in a day of freedom by seeking to become an imperialist power?'[15] In an act of political alchemy, political peripherality and the country's perceived exclusion from international discourse were transformed into assets. Nationalists didn't pause to consider whether geopolitical irrelevance might also be an outcome for an independent Irish state.

Writers might dwell with some pride on the military exploits of the Wild Geese and the various Irish brigades that had fought in foreign

[11] *Eamon de Valera States his Case* (Boston, 1918).

[12] Liam de Róiste diary, 19 Sept. 1919, CAI, U271/28.

[13] Aodh de Blácam, *Towards the Republic* (Dublin, 1919); P. S. O'Hegarty, *The Victory of Sinn Féin* (Dublin, 1924), p. 180.

[14] Michael Cronin, 'The League of Nations Covenant', *Studies* Vol. 8, Mar. 1919, pp. 19–34.

[15] *Dáil Éireann Official Record*, 10 April 1919, p. 77.

armies (a consoling if contrasting record compared to more recent events at home), but militarism was not to be imputed to the Irish race as a whole. Rather, it was Ireland's 'most ancient native tradition' of pacifism and good will that was presented to the outside world.[16] Lawrence Ginnell, in an IRB memorandum to Woodrow Wilson, stressed that Ireland's intentions towards the world were essentially peaceful, a commitment reaffirmed in both the *Declaration of Independence* and in Sinn Féin's appeal for admission to the League of Nations in June 1919, which affirmed that 'Ireland's voice in the councils of the nations will be wholly in favour of peace and justice.'[17] Republican diplomatic philosophy was perhaps most simply captured in de Valera's pledge at a Sinn Féin meeting that the movement's aim was 'to get right predominant in this world.'[18] Ireland's 'international ambition' would be to contribute to international relations 'without thought of recompense or selfish advantage'. The experience of political horse-trading at the Paris peace conference was thus a bruising encounter with the hard-nosed reality of great power diplomacy, Ó Ceallaigh confiding his dismay that peacemakers had 'no time to listen to anyone like myself who wants justice and right to prevail'.[19] This was a theme upon which Louie Bennett likewise dwelt, urging her compatriots to make their rallying cry 'Ireland a nation amongst nations'.[20] It was not necessary to be a republican to share in this imagery. From Arthur Griffith to George Russell (AE), all sketched an ersatz missionary tradition with the latter as convinced as the former that Ireland had yet to give its best to the world.[21]

Entirely absent from this imagining was any attempt to accommodate the Irish unionist worldview, whose commitment to Britain and the empire stood juxtaposed to the emerging nationalist worldview under construction. It is difficult to imagine how Sinn Féin could have done so, as the foreign policy role it claimed stood at variance with the unionist belief in a United Kingdom in which Ireland, as a constituent part, should have no separate international voice or persona.

It was largely left to those who favoured a home rule solution and subsequently dominion status for Ireland (or 'dominion home rule' as it

---

[16] Erskine Childers article in *The New Europe*, reproduced in *New Ireland*, 21 June 1919.

[17] George Gavan Duffy papers, NLI, mss 15, 439(3).

[18] *Irish Independent*, 10 April 1919.

[19] Ó Ceallaigh to Cathal Brugha, 7 Mar. 1919, NA, DFA ES Paris 1919.

[20] Louie Bennett, *Ireland and the People's Peace* (Dublin, 1918).

[21] Arthur Griffith, *Dáil Éireann Official Record*, pp. 85–6; George Russell (AE), *The Inner and the Outer Ireland* (London, 1921), p. 12; Louie Bennett, *Ireland and a People's Peace* (Dublin & London, 1918), p. 2.

was briefly called), to articulate how a self-governing Ireland would relate to the dominions through Irish engagement in imperial and Commonwealth affairs. Beyond the aim of equal membership in the League with the dominions and other states, Sinn Féin writers left few clues. By the time detailed negotiations with the British had commenced in October, however, it had become clear that some form of association with the Commonwealth would be necessary in the field of external relations at the very least. The idea formed the basis for de Valera's proposal in August 1921 for external association between Ireland and the Commonwealth, a proposal rejected by the British. He would return to it in his short-lived alternative to the Treaty, 'Document No. 2' in December. As the negotiations progressed and the likely outcome of the talks became clear, the prospect of an Irish state capable of pursuing a distinctive foreign policy receded as the contours of a dominion solution emerged.

Would any nation rally to support the Irish cause? As we have seen, few if any voices were raised by delegates at the peace conference in support of a hearing for the Irish case, while the Bolshevik flirtation with Sinn Féin was short-lived. British power and influence made espousing the cause of Irish separatism an unattractive proposition for foreign governments. There was, therefore, little to show from Sinn Féin's propaganda efforts in the countries of Western Europe and the United States. There had been contact between Sinn Féin members and representatives of other European nationalists during the war. At the Congress of Subject Peoples held in New York in October 1917, disaffected subjects of the Hapsburgs had rubbed shoulders with Irish, Indian, and Egyptian nationalists. Campaigning for the Czecho-Slovak state the allies would recognize months later, Tomas Masaryk declared the Irish cause a 'beacon' for the Hapsburg lands.[22] With Austria-Hungary confined to history, the new states taking its place owed their existence to Britain and the Allies. Busy consolidating themselves within their newly drawn borders or attempting to redraw them at their neighbours' expense, they had little reason to think of Ireland.

Those who were thinking of Ireland found themselves in a similar position to Sinn Féin: separatist movements looking for support wherever they might find it. And like Sinn Féin, there were other European nationalist groups whom the peace conference had left disappointed. But Sinn Féin was not interested in proposals to collaborate with Catalans or other European nationalists, for fear of alienating Western countries whose sympathy they hoped to enlist. Thus the Dáil government regarded

---

[22] Hanna Sheehy Skeffington, *Impressions of Sinn Féin in America* (Dublin 1919).

as 'most unwise' any response to overtures from Flemish nationalists, rebuffed expressions of Catalan good will, and strongly denied any contact with the pro-German movement in Alsace-Lorraine.[23] When seeking admission to the club of nations, it was better not to associate with opponents of members who might blackball you.

THE ANTI-IMPERIAL REPUBLIC

Different considerations applied in the case of cooperation with national movements under the British flag. There, collaboration was to be encouraged, but on Sinn Féin's terms. Addressing the Friends of Freedom for India in New York in 1924, Seán T. Ó Ceallaigh recalled efforts to forge an association of oppressed peoples of the British Empire in Paris during the peace conference.[24] Throughout the period Dáil envoys maintained the 'closest possible contact' with nationalists from India, Egypt, and South Africa. Irish-American advocates of Irish independence were prominent among American supporters of Indian and Egyptian claims against Britain. The US-based National Congress leader, Lala Rajpat Rai, attended the Irish Race Convention in Philadelphia in February 1919 that appointed the American Commission to lobby for an Irish hearing at the peace conference in Paris. The Commission's chairman, Frank Walsh, became a vice-president of the Friends of Freedom for India, also established in 1919 and mirrored on the Friends of the Irish Republic that had organized the Philadelphia convention. Sinn Féin provided funds for its Indian counterpart and propaganda activities were coordinated in the United States. Its secretary, Sahindareth Ghose, maintained close contact with Sinn Féin, masterminding Indian participation in the St Patrick's Day parade in New York in 1920.

During his continental tour, de Valera met with Gopal Singh and Jagat Singh of the Hindustan Gadar party in San Francisco, receiving a ceremonial sword (years later as president he would impress a visiting Indian president by producing it). Harry Boland, Liam Mellowes, Patrick McCartan, and the writer Padraic Colum were active in Dudley Field Malone's League of Oppressed Peoples, founded in New York in September 1919, which also involved Indian and Egyptian nationalists. In the small and overlapping world of Irish organizations in New York, Field Malone would later advise the Irish mission on American politics. London and Paris also offered opportunities for contact with Indians and other

---

[23] Ó Ceallaigh memoir, NLI mss 72,702(6).
[24] Seán T. O'Kelly, *Ireland and India* (New York, 1925), p. 3.

subject peoples of the crown. There was close contact between Sinn Féin's London representative, Art O'Brien, and a number of Indian nationalists. O'Brien was sympathetic to Indian requests for political and financial aid and favoured sending an agent to India to cooperate in fomenting agitation. Rai had met de Valera in New York in the summer of 1918 and, although the encounter did not yield immediate results, it would leave a mark on the Irish leader.[25]

Some wished to go beyond political agitation and foment a general uprising in the British Empire. Harry Boland proposed the opening of a broad-based front against British imperialism in 1920 through combined agitation by Indian, Egyptian, and other militants, whom he considered natural allies, but little was done to implement this grandiose scheme.[26] The propaganda value would have been significant, as the Fenians had calculated fifty years earlier. Indeed, Boland's plans were a throwback to Fenianism, reflecting a growing IRB influence in the nationalist movement. They were also a reaction to the failure to secure recognition in the United States or elsewhere, to military stalemate in Ireland and an attempt to profit from nationalist unrest in Egypt and India. The suggestion that central control over such a network be exercised from Ireland betrayed a failure to learn the lessons of the bruising encounter with organized Irish-America. This unrealistic if seductive ambition assumed common cause could readily be forged but this would prove to be an elusive proposition.

As activity developed across the Atlantic, in Dublin a more cautious approach prevailed. Griffith had laid down a marker when the Dáil discussed foreign relations in June 1919, warning that the Irish case should not become linked with that of the Indians and Egyptians. Setting out the Dáil administration's approach towards collaboration with other nationalities within the British Empire in mid-1919, Count Plunkett warned:

> We have to keep our movement sharply distinct and this prevents our actual cooperation with others just at present. The claims made by Egypt, South Africa, etc. are not identical, and the way in which they are put differs from ours; and if they fail, or produce the enmity of some other nation, we must not be involved as a nation in their troubles.[27]

The risk of too close an association with other anti-British nationalist movements was illustrated later that month, when the *Freeman's Journal*

---

[25] See, for example, Kate O'Malley, *Ireland, India and Empire: Indo-Irish Radical Connections, 1919–1964* (Manchester, 2008); Tadhg Foley and Maureen O'Connor (eds), *Ireland and India, Colonies, Culture and Empire* (Dublin, 2007).
[26] Fitzpatrick, *Harry Boland's Irish Revolution*, (Cork, 2003), pp. 178–21.
[27] Plunkett to O'Brien, 24 June 1919, NA, DFA ES London 1919–21.

published reports that the Irish were to join the Egyptians, Boers, and Indians in a league of 'victims of empire'. This was quickly denied, despite contacts ongoing at the time in Paris. Griffith claimed the proposal had been intended to alarm the British. The British were indeed alarmed by intelligence reports—frequently exaggerated—of collaboration between Irish, Indian, and other nationalist movements within their empire. The prospect of a formal vehicle for such intrigues seemed to confirm these fears. George Gavan Duffy had proposed just such an initiative but it was one of many ideas born of frustration as the Paris peace conference drew to a close without yielding a hearing for the Irish case or admission to the League of Nations. Other ideas circulating at this time included a league of small nations and a gathering of fellow members of the *salon des refusés* in Paris, none of which would bear fruit. There were also feelers in January 1921 from the Turks proposing collaboration against Franco-British intervention in the Kemalist revolution, but these also came to nothing.

While Sinn Féin representatives in Paris and London were claiming to act 'in an advisory capacity' to the Boers and Indians, proposals advanced by Egyptian nationalists in July 1919 for an 'entente cordiale contre l'Angleterre' were dismissed as 'foolish and oriental' by Gavan Duffy.[28] There was more than a hint of exoticism to some nationalists' references to Indians and Egyptians at the time. Despite his sympathy for Indian nationalists, Ó Ceallaigh also recommended against linking the Irish cause too closely with any other, persuading Frank Walsh not to act as legal counsel for Egyptian nationalists in America. Later that year, Walsh also stepped down from his post with the Friends of Freedom for India and a gradual distancing became discernible in 1920 between Irish and Indian organizations in the United States and elsewhere.

There are a number of reasons for this. Neither Egypt nor India had been included as locations for activity in Griffith's original proposal for a consular scheme in 1905 and nor did they appear in a list of proposed locations for Dáil representatives published in October 1919. Some consideration was given to sending an agent to India in 1921 but ultimately not acted on. The idea of sending a representative to Cairo was not considered, despite the strength of the nationalist unrest led by Saad Zagloul's Wafd party in 1920–21, although contact was established with Zagloul until he was exiled by the British to Malta. In part this was not necessary because contact with these and other nationalist representatives was possible in London, New York, and Paris, while the peace conference was sitting. Lack of regular communications and the

[28] Gavan Duffy to O'Hegarty, 15 July 1919, NAI, DFA ES, Paris 1919–21.

decentralized decision-making that characterized much of the Dáil's overseas business effectively left decisions about cooperation with other nationalist groups in the hands of a small number of Sinn Féin agents abroad.

Strained relations within Irish-American politics, culminating in the acrimonious split between the Friends of the Irish Republic and the American Association for Recognition of the Irish Republic in 1920, put a brake on much activity. Despite the success of the bond drive, financial constraints also increasingly posed a challenge. There was an inter-play between nationalist agitation in Ireland and other parts of the British Empire that influenced both Sinn Féin and British government thinking in different ways. This became pronounced with the start of negotiations between the two sides in mid-1921, Lloyd George fearing the impact in Ireland of any concessions in response to the Wafd's demands in Egypt, while the Dáil refused to receive a delegation of Egyptians led by Zagloul's lieutenant, Makram Ebeid Pasha, once negotiations had begun.

It is interesting, in light of future Irish government support for decolonisation, that de Valera struck a clearer anti-imperial note than some of his contemporaries. He told a gala dinner for the Friends of Indian Freedom in February 1920 that Ireland and India had common cause against a common foe. Given the tight reins he maintained on Sinn Féin activity while in the United States, it is clear any cooperation would not have proceeded without his sanction and de Valera would remain an advocate of links between Ireland and India throughout his life.

But opinions differed within the Sinn Féin movement as to whether the Irish should stand for anti-imperialism per se, or merely an end to British rule in Ireland. For some, such as Patrick McCartan or the Sinn Féin representative in London, Art O'Brien, the two were identical. O'Brien was a consistent advocate of cooperation with nationalists within the empire and protested at the fall-off of contacts in 1921. The Indian-born British communist, Sharpurji Saklatvala, wrote to O'Brien days after the Anglo-Irish Treaty was signed asking if this meant Sinn Féin would abandon the cause of India and Egypt.[29] A Catholic middle class that supplied colonial administrators and had expected to assume power in a home rule Ireland may have seen things differently, lacking ideological or personal affinity with the cause of subject peoples elsewhere in the British Empire. In an age of imperialism, the British were not its only practitioners. The allies had decided at the armistice that the 'impartial adjustment of all colonial claims' promised in the Fourteen Points would only

---

[29] Sharpurji Saklatvala to O'Brien, 8 Dec. 1921, NLI mss 8421(27).

apply to the former realms of the vanquished and, at San Remo in April 1920, a system of League mandates was formalized, dividing the former colonial possessions of Germany and Turkey among the victors. While Britain and France were the principal beneficiaries, Australia, New Zealand, and South Africa also emerged as colonial masters. Critics of empire quickly found that it may not be wise to bite the hand they hoped would feed them.

There was also, in some Irish minds at least, an assumption that other nationalist movements within the British Empire should take their cue from Sinn Féin. In the words of Art O'Brien, 'our triumph will be the triumph of all and, consequently, it is really more in their interest in one way to work hard for our success'.[30] Viewing themselves as a white, European race with a large diaspora in the English-speaking dominions and the United States, many Irish considered themselves to be in a superior position to other subject peoples of the British crown and this is reflected in the way they referred to other nationalities. A memorandum addressed to Pope Benedict XV in May 1920 made the point that 'alone of all the white nations', Ireland had not been granted self-determination.[31] Gavan Duffy advised against cooperation with the Boers and Egyptians on account of the latter's being 'not quite white' and reported in July 1919 comments by an assistant to André Tardieu who warned against association with 'Fellaheens and Hindus' in view of their 'low state of culture and of the strong anti-colour prejudice'.[32]

Belief in a purer pedigree of national struggle convinced many that the Irish occupied a higher rung in the hierarchy of national claims. Alongside the Poles, they represented the epitome of suffering nationality and this was as much a part of nationalist identity for some as religious or cultural factors. Thus, the trade unionist Louie Bennett could call on 'lesser nations' to make common cause under the Irish. Within republicanism there was also a strong anti-colonial tradition and for those such as McCartan, the struggle against Britain was a struggle on behalf of all peoples 'suffering under the yoke of imperialism'. In his eyes, the treaty with Britain was a betrayal of them all.[33] This was not inconsistent with offering support to Indian and Egyptian nationalists or Japanese calls for a commitment to racial equality in the League covenant. Writing from Gloucester Prison in 1919, Arthur Griffith suggested appeal be made to Liberia and Haiti, highlighting the fact that Ireland had not been involved

---

[30] O'Brien to Count Plunkett, 24 June 1919, NA, DFA ES, London 1920.
[31] Ó Ceallaigh memorandum to Benedict XV, 18 May 1920, NAI DFA ES Paris 1920.
[32] Gavan Duffy to O'Hegarty, 6 July 1919, NAI DFA EAS Paris 1919–21.
[33] Patrick McCartan letter/article, 16 Dec. 1921, NLI mss 17,617(4).

in the slave trade.[34] This did not mean that claims for independence were not couched in racial terms. Subject people and European nation, anti-colonial and mother country; identities overlapped uneasily for many Irish nationalists.

'HOT AIR HARPS': THE DIASPORA

When the idea of a league of subject peoples of the British crown emerged again in early 1921, de Valera highlighted the opportunities for activity in the dominions: 'an entente between ourselves, the Scotch, Welsh and the Overseas dominions, as if they were nations independent of England, should be encouraged'.[35] For nationalists of all political hues, Ireland was a mother country and the global Irish diaspora a source of pride. For some, it was also a ticket to political influence and an important source of finance. The diaspora was both a potential well of support and a challenge for Sinn Féin. In April 1919, de Valera had declared that freedom would be won 'by getting the whole Irish race to enter the field as an army' and it followed that the millions of Irish abroad would allow Ireland to punch above its weight. The close cooperation during the peace conference between the republican office at Paris and the American Commission on Irish Independence was just one aspect of the complex and, at times, controversial interaction between Sinn Féin and Irish-America. In one of its final attempts to pressure Georges Clemenceau to grant a hearing at the peace conference, the commission warned of the negative impact on French interests that would be brought about by twenty million Irish-Americans but the French premier was unmoved. In a report to the Dáil in 1921, Count Plunkett saw no difference between the Irish at home and abroad, urging the shaping of the diaspora 'into a power at the disposal of Ireland'. Irish envoys believed they would command respect by claiming to represent the Irish abroad as well as in Ireland. George Gavan Duffy told the Vatican secretary of state, Cardinal Gasparri, that he was '*ipso facto* the spokesman of the Irish Race beyond the seas', while many believed the Irish vote alone had blocked American ratification of the Treaty of Versailles.[36]

The British were concerned with the influence of the Irish lobby abroad and in the United States in particular. The strength of the Irish-American

---

[34] Griffith to cabinet, 23 Jan. 1919, NLI, Plunkett papers mss 11,405.

[35] De Valera to Robert Brennan, 5 April 1921, NA, DFA ES London 1920.

[36] Gavan Duffy to Cardinal Gasparri, 30 June 1921, NLI, Gavan Duffy papers, mss 10,780.

constituency, and the success in getting the Senate Foreign Affairs Committee and Congress to pass resolutions in favour of Irish independence, encouraged an assumption that influence could be exerted through the United States. Even if domestic American political factors were primarily responsible for the Senate's rejection of the Treaty of Versailles, Irish republicans believed their actions had played a central role and it was believed that Irish objectives could be advanced in other areas by bringing influence to bear in Washington. Outlining the possibility of getting a trade representative accredited in Germany in late 1919, Diarmuid O'Hegarty suggested that this could best be achieved 'through our friends over across'. Not everyone in the nationalist movement was as sanguine about the value of courting Irish-America. In her engagingly direct manner, Hanna Sheehy Skeffington was dismissive of 'hot air harps' whom she accused of being motivated more by local concerns than a desire to advance the cause of independence, while Harry Boland prophetically warned they would be 'skinned alive' if the movement became too closely involved in domestic US politics.[37] But these views were in the minority nor were they consistently held; Boland was as convinced as de Valera that the Irish vote would lead the United States to recognize the republic and was the chief architect of the publicity tour that criss-crossed America in 1920.

Sinn Féin encouraged the establishment of Irish Self Determination Leagues in Britain and sought to use them to advance its agenda; in many cases IRB members secured leadership positions. Active Leagues existed in Scotland and England organizing protests and petitions in support of the effort at home. As the war of independence intensified, the Sinn Féin representative in London, Art O'Brien, found himself arranging prison visits for the families of republican prisoners transferred to British gaols, whilst contending with police raids, informants, and Fleet Street hacks. The Irish population in the dominions was also an attractive target. Émigré communities were active in Canada and Australia, lobbying provincial and local assemblies to pass resolutions in support of self-government for the motherland.[38] In doing so, many would have been unclear on what form self-determination should take and a wide spectrum of opinion existed within these communities.

While these efforts had a clear publicity value, translating them into politically useful action was much harder. Despite sizeable Irish populations

---

[37] Sheehy Skeffington, *Impressions of Sinn Féin*.

[38] For a comparison of Irish emigration to Australia and the United States, see Malcolm Campbell, *Ireland's New Worlds: Immigrants, Politics and Society in the United States and Australia, 1815–1922* (Madison, 2008).

electing politicians of Irish background, the English-speaking territories of the British Empire offered limited scope for nationalist agitation. The Great War provoked a revival of imperialist enthusiasm and patriotic sentiment in the dominions. The contribution of dominion troops to the fighting; the casualties suffered, which included soldiers of Irish background; and participation by dominion premiers in the British war cabinet contributed to this sentiment. A warm reception was by no means guaranteed for Sinn Féin envoys even where an Irish community was present. Dominion administrations kept close watch on Sinn Féin agents and the force of the law was used to hinder their activities. Fearing arrest, de Valera did not include Canada on his tour of North America despite its large Irish population. Hanna Sheehy Skeffington narrowly avoided such a fate when a bogus group of supporters tried to lure her across the border to Ontario from Buffalo, New York in 1918. Osmond Grattan Esmonde was not so lucky, spending two months in detention on a ship in Sydney Harbour in spring 1921 before being admitted to Australia, only to face arrest and trial on his subsequent arrival in Canada.[39]

Little thought was given to how Irish people living in Britain or the dominions would be affected by the creation of a republic: would they retain existing residence rights as British subjects or become alien nationals? The adopted identities and loyalties of Irish immigrants as well as the realities of emigrant life and the desire of many to build a new life in their chosen home combined to limit the scope for activity. John J. Kelly's ('Sceilg') suggestion that Irish living in the empire should renounce allegiance to the king in protest at the opening of the Northern Ireland parliament in June 1921 was dismissed as unrealistic. There was a limit to how far the diaspora in the dominions or the United States could be expected to go.

Once independence had been achieved, any government would be reluctant to let go of this 'army' if it could be used to advance its interests. The potential for political, economic, and cultural benefit from harnessing '*Magna Hibernia*' were apparent at the time, as was the appeal of an 'alternative Commonwealth' centred in Dublin. Nationalists saw in the overseas Irish a valuable ally and, potentially, an instrument with which to pursue their interests at home and abroad. Diverging views on the relationship between Ireland and its diaspora lay at the heart of the fracas that would surround a gathering of the global Irish held in Paris in January 1922. Even before it became mired in civil war controversy, the ministry

---

[39] 'Report on Mission to New Zealand and Australia by Osmond Grattan Esmonde,' n.d. but post-July 1921, NA, DFA ES Box 32 File 220.

was concerned to establish a directing role in an overseas race organization. In the Dáil debate on the establishment of a permanent secretariat to organize the Irish race abroad in March the same year, de Valera predicted the Free State would be glad to have a mechanism through which Irish interests could be safeguarded when it found itself stymied by Downing Street's 'grip'.[40] But plans to mobilize the overseas Irish foundered on the question of leadership: should the diaspora take the lead or take its cue from the Irish at home? There was no consensus on this question: exiles or sojourners, Irish or hyphenated-Irish; the problem of definition went to the very heart of efforts to engage the diaspora.

The Dáil's overseas operations were an important plank in the campaign for independence and the construction of a separate state apparatus. If the republic existed largely in a few back rooms in Dublin, freedom from police raids allowed a greater measure of activity abroad than was possible in Ireland while overseas offices and dispatch-carrying couriers lent an air of credibility to the Sinn Féin regime. In many respects, the regime was pulling off a confidence trick, by presenting to the outside world the edifice of a functioning government in the hope of enlisting international opinion to support independence. As the regime's overseas voice, its foreign operation played an important role in this effort alongside the Dáil's publicity machine. However, its value was not confined to influencing opinion abroad. As with other aspects of the parallel administration that Sinn Féin constructed within Ireland, activity abroad helped to build support at home. For Diarmuid O'Hegarty, secretary to the Dáil cabinet, 'actual constructive work will leave a bigger mark on the people than political work...it invests the Government with tangibility. It means that the Dáil has slipped out from the beaten path of political parties and their shibboleths, and that it is functioning as any progressive Government would be expected to function.'[41]

It is necessary to challenge the view that the foreign policy apparatus of the Dáil period was merely a symbol or a means to emphasize distance from a home rule solution. For some this was undoubtedly the case, de Blácam contrasting the disinterested internationalism the republic would espouse to a home rule Ireland, 'bourgeois and green-flag jingoistic'.[42] A vivid picture, it is fascinating to observe one imagined Ireland pitted against another, neither of which would, ultimately, be achieved. Equally, a focus on the peace conference and the quest for recognition undoubtedly helped divert eyes from Westminster while deflecting critics of Sinn Féin's policy of abstentionism. But there was more to the approach than just this.

[40] *Dáil Éireann Official Reports*, p. 214, 3 Mar. 1922.
[41] O'Hegarty to Gavan Duffy, 27 Aug. 1919, NA, DFA ES, U3 (a).
[42] Aodh de Blácam, *What Sinn Féin Stands For* (Dublin, 1921), p. 130.

Correspondence from 1919 onwards shows that, even after the disappointment of the peace conference, many involved in the international effort believed recognition could be achieved, however unrealistic this may have been. This belief was still held by some in the movement as late as mid-1921, by which time negotiations on the Treaty had begun with the British.

A MORAL FOREIGN POLICY?

Dáil-period thinking on the subject looked beyond an appreciation of the symbolic value of foreign affairs in the struggle for independence. Foreign policy was also to be an expression of the values that an Irish republic would stand for, as well as a means to promote the values of the Irish race around the world. It is implicit in earlier Sinn Féin tracts that, if independent, Ireland would be qualified to lead an international existence. This was seen as a right of nationhood, as the *Sinn Féin Catechism* stressed in its catchy way. The right to international action was the 'first principle' of nationhood according to *New Ireland* and Sinn Féin pamphlets averred that Ireland occupied 'the foremost place' among the small states of Europe. While journals and pamphlets of the day reveal a lively debate about Ireland's position in the world and her obligations and contributions to it, there was also a strong belief that independence should be achieved at home, either militarily or by constructing the institutions of a separate state, rather than through efforts abroad. The scientist and university lecturer Alfred O'Rahilly gave vent to this view in the Sinn Féin organ *New Ireland*, arguing that 'the strength of our international position is to be measured by our active and militant nationality here at home'.[43] Tension inevitably arose between those who held that Ireland's international persona would best be generated from within, by actions on the ground, and those who advocated international action. Even then, attitudes towards foreign policy were not unequivocal. Although Arthur Griffith urged the cabinet to concentrate first on the peace conference, he criticized those who espoused international causes without considering Ireland first. Ernest Boyd took an excoriating view of things international, denouncing the 'pathetic dreams of forward-lookers' as irrelevant unless they served the purposes of Irish independence. There was a visible tension between domestic and international concerns.

The workings of the diplomatic chessboard were regarded with mistrust in many quarters, Eoin MacNeill warning against solutions born of

[43] *New Ireland*, 15 Mar. 1919.

'wining, dining and undermining'. The fact that the conference doors remained firmly closed to the Irish served to reinforce the prejudices of many who had suspected that Britain and the other colonial powers would conspire to thwart Irish ambitions. It is in this vein that anti-Semitism and attacks on Freemasonry crept into some nationalist propaganda. The *Catholic Bulletin* was particularly virulent in its condemnation, believing European governments to be in the hands of Freemasons whose 'object is to prevent the establishment of Ireland as an independent and intensely Christian state'. Such sentiments were not the preserve of conservative Catholics. Griffith attributed the 'arrangement' of international alliances and even the prosecution of the war to Masonic influences while Ó Ceallaigh complained during the peace conference 'everywhere Jews and Masons are united against us in the foreign press'. Anti-Semitic comments can also be found in Count Plunkett's correspondence, in Gavan Duffy's dealings with the Vatican, and in the writings of Griffith himself.

Irish security was to be ensured by the maintenance of a law-abiding international environment, hence the enthusiasm for the League of Nations and the ambition to pursue a moral (or moralizing) approach to international issues. The Irish argued that they were essential to the functioning of the international order. One aspect of this was the focus on freedom of the seas, essentially an attempt to turn the country's geographical location to strategic advantage by arguing that an independent Ireland granting free access to its territorial waters would benefit international commerce and communications. Another is the idea that an Ireland free to speak out would contribute to the workings of international fora and arbitration. The belief developed that the Irish case would have to be addressed if the new rights-based world order was to be credible. Ireland was a supplicant before the 'court of international conscience', a turn of phrase coined by the writer and mystic George Russell. By the same formulation it was the 'test case' for the application of the right to self-determination and, as hopes in this direction faded, an 'acid test' by which the international community would be judged.

It was in this sense that the *Declaration of Independence* described Irish independence as a 'condition precedent to international peace', a theme developed in the memoranda submitted to the Paris peace conference, which claimed an independent Ireland would be 'a guarantee of the new international order and a reassurance to all the smaller nations'.[44] Just as an internationally recognized neutral Switzerland provided a home for the

---

[44] 'Memorandum in support of Ireland's Claim for Recognition as a Sovereign Independent State', n.d. (one of the papers prepared for presentation to the Paris peace conference), NA, DFA DE 4/8/8.

new League of Nations, an internationally recognized, pacific, and disinterested Ireland would provide the moral lubricant necessary for the system to work. The Irish would offer to the world a new kind of diplomacy based on honesty, an honesty Sinn Féin contended would be the hallmark of its dealings with the outside world. Free of ambitions, enmities, or agendas of its own, Ireland would be able to speak honestly on matters of international concern. As the Sinn Féin mouthpiece, *Nationality*, put it 'there are no skeletons in our cupboards, no bloodstains on our hands: no mark of hypocrisy on our face. We are Irish.'[45]

This belief sat comfortably with denunciations of great power diplomacy and reminders of Wilson's pledge for 'open covenants, openly arrived at'. Eoin MacNeill believed Ireland to be a teaching nation, setting an example with 'our ancient ideals, faith, learning, generous enthusiasm, self sacrifice—the things best calculated to purge out the meanness of the modern world.' For the UCD professor, Michael Cronin, it was only natural that they should 'consecrate the whole land permanently to peace' as a centre for the League of Nations.[46] As the League was being negotiated in Paris, he proposed Ireland as a location for its headquarters. The idea would resurface in 1922 when George Gavan Duffy, by then foreign minister, argued that the country's position between America and Europe would give it a claim to consideration against Geneva. Such a formulation would also provide the international order with a selfish reason for both calling for and maintaining Irish independence. The notion of Ireland as an honest broker, with no selfish agenda or international interests to pursue can be found in numerous writings at this time. The idea represents a coming-together of several identities advanced by nationalists— that of the moral people, whether its roots be Christian or Gaelic; that of the insulated island untouched by the failings of diplomacy or the modern world; that of the disinterested nation able to act as go-between; and that of the wronged people, whose redress would anoint the new era of self-determination and liberty.

The idea of appealing to the international community for support was not new; other national movements couched their claims for recognition in terms that advanced the strategic interests of the victorious powers or appealed to their sense of justice through claims of victim-hood requiring redress. Sinn Féin attempted to do this, too, as had the Fenians and others before them in seeking to involve European powers in Irish affairs. But the proposition that Irish independence would advance the interests of the

---

[45] *Nationality*, 8 Feb. 1919.
[46] Michael Cronin, 'The League of Nations Covenant', *Studies*, Vol. 8, Mar. 1919, pp. 19–34.

international community as a whole was new, as was the very concept of an international community with interests of its own, separate to those of its constituent states. Such an idea was in keeping with the liberal internationalism re-shaping the way international relations were conducted. In this sense, the Irish grasped the changing international landscape of the early twentieth century and, despite the disappointment of the peace conference, remained committed to internationalism as the best guarantee of the rights of the small countries. There is something modern in this understanding. It is tempting to dismiss these sentiments as naive, but these were optimistic times when many dreamt of a better world. 'In these days of rapid and extraordinary changes, what idea may be dismissed as merely Utopian?' asked Louie Bennett and the expectation that change was possible was not confined to the Irish.

Against this background, aspirations were nurtured for a prominent place in world affairs and an active role at the League of Nations once independence had been achieved. Before this could be embarked upon, an accommodation would first be needed with the British to secure an independent state. But the agreement reached in London on 6 December 1921 on the nature of that state would fall short of expectations in many respects, including the international sphere. In the weeks and months that followed, the focus moved from abroad to home, and from London where the deal had been struck to Dublin, where it would have to be sold.

4

A State-in-Waiting

Foreign Policy under the Provisional Government of 1922

The signing of the Anglo-Irish Treaty in December 1921 and its approval by Dáil Éireann a month later, on 7 January 1922, transformed the political situation in Ireland.[1] A transitional administration was created to take over from the out-going British government in the southern twenty-six counties (a separate parliament had been established in Northern Ireland under the terms of the Government of Ireland Act of 1920). Although the British had not recognized the republic during the Treaty negotiations, the Dáil administration would continue to exist until the electorate signalled its acceptance of the Treaty at an election in June, and the British acquiesced in this arrangement insofar as its members were no longer subject to arrest. A separate 'Provisional Government' was established in keeping with the terms of the Treaty to administer the transition from British rule.[2] Michael Collins was chairman of the provisional government, while Arthur Griffith became president and head of the Dáil cabinet, following Eamon de Valera's resignation when the Dáil voted in favour of the Treaty. There was much overlap between the two governments and joint meetings were held.

The provisional government was 'provisional' until the Irish Free State was legally established, which would occur when a constitution was adopted for the new state. Until then, its remit was limited to domestic affairs. In the field of foreign affairs, a separation was maintained. George Gavan Duffy, though a Treaty signatory, was appointed Minister for

---

[1] The term 'Treaty' is used throughout as shorthand for 'Articles of Agreement for a Treaty between Great Britain and Ireland'.

[2] The Provisional Government held its authority from the 'House of Commons of Southern Ireland', created under the Government of Ireland Act in 1920, which met for this purpose on 14 January 1922 and then adjourned.

Foreign Affairs in the Dáil cabinet alone and had no counterpart in the provisional government. Until the Free State was established, Ireland lacked a defined status and could not enter into relations with other states. The network of Sinn Féin envoys abroad, therefore, continued to represent the Dáil government alone, even if it increasingly functioned in conjunction with the provisional government. Thus, in addition to a British administration preparing to evacuate, as the year 1922 began there were two governments in what would become the Free State, each limited in remit and ability to act; neither recognized internationally.

This double system of government, or 'duality' as it became known, worked better on paper than in reality. It had been predicated on a politically harmonious passage of the Treaty, but it quickly became apparent that debate over the Anglo-Irish Treaty would be anything but that. Republicans refused to recognize provisional government ministers, addressing queries to them in their capacity as members of the Dáil government, even when, in many cases, the same individual held both posts. The irony was that, as Dublin Castle departments transferred to the provisional government, many Dáil ministers achieved real administrative power for the first time.[3] Against this backdrop, maintaining the distinctions in the republic's self-styled diplomatic service necessary to preserve the fragile political situation would prove a delicate task.

Confusion reigned from the beginning as to who was representing whom. Two days after the provisional government took office, Gavan Duffy told Monsignor Hagan in Rome that the government's new agent there, Count O'Byrne, was 'neither Black nor White, or rather he will in effect be both'.[4] Upon being asked in January to open a trade office in Rotterdam, Seán O'Duinn replied to Ernest Blythe, trade minister in the Dáil cabinet, accepting his 'Provisional Government posting'. It was not clear to foreign observers, either, who was in charge or what the Treaty meant in early 1922, an understandable confusion, perhaps. The American consul called on Collins, as chairman of the Provisional Government, on 19 January to offer congratulations on the new government, while his Italian counterpart addressed his congratulations the following day to Griffith as president of Dáil Éireann.

Despite this, at the start of the year there was considerable optimism that the country would soon be able to take its first steps on the world

---

[3] For an account of the creation of the Irish administration, see Martin Maguire, *The civil Service and the Revolution in Ireland, 1912–1938, 'shaking the blood-stained hand of Michael Collins'* (Manchester, 2008).

[4] Gavan Duffy to Monsignor Hagan, 16 Jan. 1922, NAI DFA ES Rome 1921–23,1922 subject file, Vatican sub-file.

stage. For the previous three years, activity had been largely confined to publicity and propaganda. The initial reason for keeping the network of Dáil envoys in place was to be ready to resume this work should the British fail to implement their side of the Treaty. But it was assumed that consolidation followed by expansion would occur once the political situation was normalized. Gavan Duffy told staff abroad on 25 January that passage of the Treaty had opened 'many portals formerly closed to us through fear of England. It should, therefore, be possible immediately to widen the circles of Irish influence on the continent and to develop "relations" political, diplomatic, intellectual, economic and social, to a very much greater extent than anything that has hitherto been attempted.'[5] A reorganization of the Dáil's overseas representatives in early spring was based on this expectation.

Improving communications and an end to police harassment of Dáil activities meant that, for the first time in three years, it was possible to direct affairs from Dublin. It was no longer necessary for departments to disappear down drainpipes. Gavan Duffy set about reorganizing the apparatus that had grown up under the Dáil along lines more suited to peacetime conditions. An audit of offices abroad was carried out in February and a raft of administrative instructions issued. Gavan Duffy was anxious that a ministry and a corps of diplomats be ready to represent the Free State once it was recognized. Detailed plans regarding recruitment and training were drawn up and contact was made with the National University of Ireland to identify suitable candidates. Offices were sought for the foreign ministry in the form of the eighteenth-century Ely House, and a cabinet committee was set up in May to consider appointments to the foreign service. Abroad, enquiries were made about buying premises in Berlin, Paris, and in the United States to house the future state's diplomatic missions while enquiries were made to the Canadian and Italian foreign ministries seeking information on their structures and organization.

The end of hostilities also transformed the external environment. In the months following signature of the Treaty, Sinn Féin envoys reported a gradual opening up of official contact from foreign governments that had previously turned a cold shoulder. Michael MacWhite reported from Geneva in March that diplomats were now willing to talk to him and a department of trade report the following month also noted a less cautious approach from foreign governments and business. These overtures stopped short of official recognition, but they nonetheless encouraged a

---

[5] 'Foreign Office Memorandum No.1', 25 Jan. 1922, NAI, DFA ES 74.

belief that some measure of interaction would be possible during 1922. Ironically, it was frequently assumed that Sinn Féin envoys were now representing the Free State and this lay behind moves to establish contact. In foreign eyes, the Treaty was central; MacWhite had warned the previous December 'we might as well close all European offices as everything will be undone' should the Dáil fail to ratify it.[6]

This situation created its own pressure on the structures of duality. As opportunities for activity opened up, envoys were confronted with the ill-defined nature of their status: they could not claim to represent the Free State, which did not yet exist, while they remained representatives of a republic that did not exist either. A Foreign Office memorandum in May summed up the situation succinctly: 'no official recognition can be accorded to any person purporting to represent the Government of Southern Ireland in foreign countries' until the Free State was legally established and British diplomats were accordingly instructed to block Irish approaches to foreign governments.[7] Count O'Byrne experienced this problem at the Vatican, when his Dáil credentials were used as an excuse to refuse a papal audience in February, while others found there was a limit to how far they would be received in foreign capitals. There was no easy solution to this problem. In an attempt to avoid questions about status, envoys were told to stick to economic or international issues and avoid anything political.[8] As divisions over the Treaty began to emerge at home, this would quickly prove impractical.

The first signs of trouble emerged at the Irish race conference that opened in Paris on 24 January.[9] The conference had been designed to showcase the unity and purpose of the nationalist movement and to establish a transnational structure to link the diaspora to Ireland. Instead, it laid bare the divisions at the heart of Sinn Féin over the Treaty. While an attempt was made to paper over the cracks, things got off to a bad start when separate pro- and anti-Treaty delegations travelled from Ireland while no one turned up from the United States or Canada. The idea of holding a race conference was first proposed in 1921 by the Irish Self Determination League in South Africa, but organization was taken over by the Dáil administration. The task had fallen to Robert Brennan, as

[6] MacWhite to Gavan Duffy, 10 Dec. 1921, NAI DFA ES Geneva 1921–23, confidential file 1922–23.

[7] Foreign Office memorandum, 26 May 1922, PRO, FO371/726/A3447.

[8] Joseph Walshe to MacWhite, 13 Jan. 1922, NAI DFA ES Geneva 1921–23, subject file 1922, constitution sub-file.

[9] For a fuller account of the Race Conference see Gerard Keown, 'The Irish Race Conference, 1922, reconsidered', *Irish Historical Studies*, xxxii, no. 127 (May, 2001), pp. 365–76.

undersecretary for foreign affairs. Brennan had been recruited into the IRB in 1913 by Ó Ceallaigh and owed his post to his close friend, de Valera. He shared both men's opposition to the terms of the Treaty. Fearing Brennan would exploit his role as conference organizer to lobby against the Treaty, Gavan Duffy refused to send him to Paris, and asked Desmond FitzGerald to go in his place. Although director of publicity in the Dáil cabinet and therefore responsible for promoting the republic, he was in favour of the Treaty. Brennan promptly resigned in protest, becoming the first casualty of the split in the Dáil's foreign service, and travelled to Paris where he played a key role in turning the proceedings to republican advantage.

A series of sleights, both real and imagined, exacerbated by strained communication between the two sides soured the atmosphere and plans for a world organization of the Irish disapora were stillborn. Even had things been different, the experience in the United States should have suggested it would not be easy to organize a global structure controlled from Dublin. But the charged atmosphere among the Irish delegates and attempts to derive political gain meant that it had little chance of success. The anti-Treaty group, led by de Valera, out-manoeuvred the pro-Treaty side dominating the speaker list and packing the board of the new 'Fine Gaedheal' organization ('family of the Gael') with republican sympathizers hostile to the provisional government. De Valera himself was elected president of the body, a useful title having resigned as president of the Dáil two weeks earlier; Brennan was appointed its organizing secretary.

Despite instructions that the Dáil's foreign network was to stand above politics, it mirrored the broader split in the nationalist movement over the Treaty. Seán T. Ó Ceallaigh assisted the anti-Treaty group during the conference despite his responsibility, as Dáil representative in Paris, to look after the interests of all the Irish delegates. De Valera was accordingly installed in a grand suite while the pro-Treaty grouping lacked a room in which to meet. Michael MacWhite was brought back to Paris from Geneva to look after Eoin MacNeill and the other members of the pro-Treaty group. MacWhite's sympathies lay with the Free State, which he saw himself as representing from the moment the Treaty was ratified by the Dáil. The issue was brought to a head when members of the pro-Treaty group met the French premier, Raymond Poincaré, after the conference had closed on 30 January. The meeting was facilitated by Albert Thomas, Director-General of the recently founded International Labour Organisation, whose letter of introduction simply referred to representatives of the 'new Irish government', even though the group included Michael Hayes, education minister in the Dáil cabinet and Eoin MacNeill, minister without portfolio in the provisional government.

MacWhite had been Ó Ceallaigh's secretary in Paris in 1919 but, cutting his former boss out of the picture, accompanied the group meeting Poincaré, claiming the meeting meant France had officially recognized the new Irish government.[10]

The Poincaré meeting and the political intrigues that marred the conference provoked uproar on both sides of the divide in the Dáil. A committee of enquiry was set up to examine charges of political point scoring levelled by both sides but its report in March was inconclusive. Both episodes weakened Gavan Duffy's position as foreign minister: having occurred without his knowledge, it raised doubts not only about his control over his own staff but also the good faith of provisional government ministers in implementing the understanding between the two sides regarding the Treaty. It would become harder to maintain a firm line after this incident, and revelations of further partisan actions by both sides would follow. The shaky edifice of duality was at risk of collapsing under the weight of the contradictions it supported.

The problem was that, in Gavan Duffy's estimation, most of the Dáil envoys were 'die-hard' republicans. As debate over the Treaty descended into mutual recrimination at home, it became clear that steps were needed to assert some measure of control over representatives abroad. Responding to the problems at the race conference, he instructed overseas envoys at the end of January to refrain from propaganda for or against the Treaty.[11] In keeping with the non-partisan line, they were also told it was 'no part of your business to do anything towards popularising the proposed Irish Free State'.[12] The ink had barely dried on these instructions when a new row erupted over a letter published by Ó Ceallaigh and Boland urging party members to reject the Treaty at an extraordinary party meeting called to discuss the matter on 21–22 February. Both men had been allowed to return to Dublin to take part in the Treaty debates in the Dáil. As a member of the Dáil, Ó Ceallaigh contended his role as an envoy abroad did not preclude him from political action at home.

The situation was made worse by Gavan Duffy's decision to recall Ó Ceallaigh's assistant, Joseph Walshe, to Dublin at the end of January to fill the undersecretary position vacated by Robert Brennan. Ó Ceallaigh had recruited Walshe, a former Jesuit seminarian who had studied French at UCD under his wife, Cáit, to run the Paris office in 1919. He reacted angrily to the move, seeing it as a shot across his bows. He was right, although Gavan Duffy had also worked with Walshe during his time as

[10] MacWhite to Gavan Duffy, 2 Feb. 1922, NAI DFA ES Box 27.
[11] 'Foreign Office Memorandum No. 1', 25 Jan. 1922, NAI DFA ES 74.
[12] Gavan Duffy to Bewley, 16 Jan. 1922, NAI DFA ES 239(6).

Paris envoy and wanted to find a competent administrator to implement his organizational reforms. The decision to move Walshe would have long-term implications for the direction of Irish foreign policy, as he would hold onto the post of secretary of the department until 1946. Relations between Gavan Duffy and Ó Ceallaigh were already strained from their days together as envoys in Paris, and the latter resented moves to assert control from Dublin. An increasingly acrimonious correspondence between the two resulted in Ó Ceallaigh's resignation in mid-February. He was not the only envoy to go. After the acrimonious party meeting, the split in the republican ranks widened and the foreign service began to fracture along pro- and anti-Treaty lines. Boland resigned as US envoy on 16 February. O'Brien was sacked in May and legal proceedings begun to recover funds from the London office. Lawrence Ginnell stood down as South American envoy and Donal Hayes quit as agent in Italy. A dejected Ginnell wrote to Eamonn Bulfin in March, 'the unfortunate crash at home blasted our main purpose here and reduced us to the task of salvage'.[13]

As the split spread, republicans in the embryonic diplomatic service began to openly preach against the Treaty. Ó Ceallaigh nominally handed over the Paris office but in reality began to campaign against the Treaty, claiming to be the legitimate Irish representative in France. Elsewhere, others followed suit, using confusion over their status to undermine the provisional government. MacWhite complained in June that the guidelines restrained pro-Treaty envoys while anti-Treaty opponents had a free hand. Identifying Ó Ceallaigh as a particular problem, he urged Griffith to make him a roving envoy to counter anti-Treaty propaganda ahead of the 16 June election.

The mental gymnastics required of those who, however reluctantly, accepted the Treaty placed a strain on efforts to portray a coherent image of Irish politics abroad. As Gavan Duffy told his friend and colleague, Colonel Maurice Moore, in June before sending him to Paris, when 'dealing with foreigners make it clear that little as most of us like the Treaty, we are determined to put it through, because there is no rational alternative'.[14] Moore was one of a handful of IPP supporters who had sided with Sinn Féin. A career in the Connaught Rangers left him with a clipped military manner and a tendency not to suffer fools lightly. Going further, Gavan Duffy told Moore 'there is no reason why you should conceal the fact that the ultimate end of the great majority of the Irish people goes far beyond the concessions contained in the Treaty'.[15]

---

[13] Ginnell to Eamonn Bulfin, Mar. 1922, Bulfin papers.
[14] Gavan Duffy to Moore, 14 June 1922, NLI mss 10,583.
[15] Ibid.

While this probably reflected the views of many on the pro-Treaty side, the message was not without risk. The chancelleries and editorial offices of the continent viewed with suspicion anything that might cause difficulties for them in their relations with Britain and this included anti-Treaty propaganda by members of Sinn Féin or attempts to stir up hostility to the old foe. French intelligence reports following the race conference in January reveal a concern that Irish nationalists would push for complete separation from Britain and seek to involve France in the process, concerns shared by the French consulate in Dublin.

The attitude was the same in Paris and Berlin, where neither government welcomed continuing Irish agitation. The Quai d'Orsay in particular was wary of becoming involved in Irish affairs, fearing that to do so would complicate relations with London, and the official French line on Ireland remained one of disinterest even after electoral endorsement of the Treaty in June.[16] In Berlin, the German foreign ministry refused to recognize any Irish representative until a green light had been received from the British. A similar policy was pursued in other capitals.

As independence approached, old-style anti-British propaganda was increasingly out of step with political reality for the pro-Treaty side. The legal advisor to the provisional government, Hugh Kennedy, urged a change of approach in August, warning that 'the campaign of slanging England is not our only asset'.[17] Long-standing shibboleths of the nationalist canon would have to be dropped, in itself no small task, but a change in personnel would also be necessary to ensure reliable mouthpieces. The continuing involvement of politicians, many of whom were now anti-Treaty, could only hamper moves in this direction. But there was a shortage of reliable replacements. The departure of anti-Treaty figures at first eased the situation, only to free them from the non-partisan restrictions imposed on those who remained.

As the year progressed, Gavan Duffy was reduced to juggling an ever-decreasing number of people in attempts at damage limitation. John Chartres, who had served as advisor to the Treaty delegation, was briefly sent from Berlin to Paris following Ó Ceallaigh and Kerney's defection to the anti-Treaty side.[18] Colonel Maurice Moore replaced him in June, with instructions to open a line of communication with the government (even if it rankled that the French had blocked an Irish appeal to the peace

---

[16] Minister of Defence to Raymond Poincaré, 8 Feb. 1922, QO, CPC, Europe 1918–40, Irlande, vol. 1, pp. 195–9.
[17] Kennedy to Ernest Blythe 29 Aug. 1922, UCDA P4/860.
[18] For an account of John Chartres, see Brian P. Murphy, *John Chartres, Mystery Man of the Treaty* (Dublin, 1995).

conference, and expelled Gavan Duffy in 1920). Relations between Chartres and Charles Bewley in Berlin deteriorated over Bewley's anti-Semitic views (concerns that would resurface in the 1930s, when Bewley was Free State representative in Berlin). Chartres himself lacked German. Ill-suited to the task as continental representatives, expediency dictated their assignment.

An even bigger challenge was posed by the strength of anti-Treaty sentiment in the United States. Membership of Irish-American organizations had fallen off as many considered independence achieved, while others were turned-off by the split within nationalist ranks. Despite this, the potential for party political agitation was clear to both sides. Timothy Smiddy was sent in early March to assume control or salvage as much as he could of the quickly splintering Irish organization in the United States. Michael Collins mandated him to secure control of the funds raised by the bond drive. A smart man from Cork sporting a clipped moustache and bowtie, Smiddy had been professor of economics at University College Cork. In the small social world of post-civil war Ireland, his daughter would marry the head of the North East Boundary Bureau, Kevin O'Shiel. The IRB leader, Denis McCullough was also sent out, ostensibly on an anti-partition ticket, but in reality on a mission to re-unite or neutralize Irish-American organizations as a factor in the Treaty debates at home.

To counter this, the republicans sent Lawrence Ginnell to New York shortly after his resignation from the Dáil, where he was joined by Robert Briscoe. From a Dublin Jewish family, Briscoe had worked for Collins buying arms in Germany where he had witnessed at first hand Bewley's anti-Semitism. Established in New York as the republican representative, Ginnell instructed Briscoe to seize the republican 'consulate' in the city which the provisional government had taken control of. Briscoe provides a colourful if one-sided account in his memoirs of the seige at the office on Nassau Street, a short distance from City Hall, in which rival sets of Irish representatives and the New York Police Department played a starring role.[19] The affair generated publicity, none of it flattering for either side. Ginnell's real target was the list of subscribers to the bond drive believed to rest in the office safe and, through it, access to an estimated $2.5 million in funds collected in the name of the republic. Briscoe was assisted by John B. O'Brien, who took annual leave from his job at Fordham University to join in the escapade. In the small world of Irish political agitation in New York, O'Brien was related by marriage to the brothers James and Stephen O'Mara, whom de Valera had appointed to manage the republican bond

---

[19] Robert Briscoe, *For the Life of Me* (London, 1958).

drive and who had opted for different sides in the Treaty split. The register was not found and lengthy legal proceedings would see the Free State fail to secure access to the funds that would eventually be used to finance the establishment of the *Irish Press* newspaper. Ginnell's sudden death in April 1923 was a setback for the anti-Treaty cause in the United States. The small world of Irish and Irish-American activism in the United States helps explain the vitriol of the split that was second only in intensity to the conflict in Ireland.

THE CONSTITUTION AND FOREIGN POLICY

While Gavan Duffy was drawing up plans for an expansion in foreign affairs, the provisional government was preoccupied with the urgent business of drafting a constitution for the Free State. A drafting committee nominally headed by Collins had the difficult task of reconciling republican aspirations with the terms of the Treaty. The constitution offered an opportunity to establish a position favourable to the pursuit of an independent foreign policy, Gavan Duffy believing it was on this question that 'the real fight with England will come'.[20] At the height of deliberations over the constitution in mid-May, he asked Collins to use growing concern in London over prospects for implementation of the Treaty to extract from the British a commitment that the Free State would be entitled to diplomatic and consular representation overseas.[21] A final draft completed in May provided for a constitution essentially republican in form and substance. Rejecting the notion of the diplomatic unity of the Empire, it provided instead for complete Irish autonomy in the field of foreign policy.[22] Michael Collins had been hesitant to include much detail on foreign policy in the draft constitution, fearing the British would reject anything that could be construed as affecting the status of the Anglo-Irish Treaty.[23] This was precisely the objection that London made, arguing that the clause on international treaties left open the possibility that the Irish parliament could unilaterally alter or repeal the Anglo-Irish Treaty.

A matter of days before the draft was forwarded to London, the Foreign Office had written to Lionel Curtis, secretary to the British cabinet's Provisional Government of Ireland Committee (he had previously served as secretary to the British delegation during the negotiations for the Anglo

---

[20] Gavan Duffy to Collins, 9 May 1922, NAI DFA ES 112.
[21] Gavan Duffy to Collins, 18 May 1922, NAI DFA ES 112.
[22] Provisional Government Cabinet minutes, 25 May 1922, NAI G1/2.
[23] See, for example, Collins to Gavan Duffy, 25 May 1922, NA, DFA ES box 17.

Irish Treaty), warning against any impression that Irish representatives would hold the same status as diplomats from other countries.[24] Hopes of securing some comfort in the field of foreign policy were dashed in a British re-draft sent back to Dublin in early June. The entire section on foreign affairs was deleted. The revised draft constitution was reluctantly approved by the cabinet on 12 June and published the morning of the general election on 16 June. Gavan Duffy was appalled at the retreat, and threatened to resign three days later.

FIRST OF THE SMALL NATIONS?

The debacle of the constitution dealt a blow to hopes for an early expansion in foreign affairs activity. It also hastened Gavan Duffy's departure from government. He had painted himself into a political corner: having signed the Treaty he felt compelled to support it while voicing increasing disquiet at both its terms and the actions considered necessary by his colleagues to ensure its survival. He told Arthur Griffith on 19 June he did not support the constitution, believing it conceded more than was necessary under the Treaty, but agreed to remain on as minister if given a free hand to take a dissenting line. A month later the number of issues on which he disagreed with the provisional government had widened and he resigned at the end of July.

Perhaps sensing the way the wind was blowing, partly also in a desire to ensure the emerging Irish state would have a distinctive foreign policy along the lines imagined during the Dáil period, Gavan Duffy had set about drafting a detailed report on how the country's foreign relations could be developed. The nationalist movement had thrown up many ideas and, in the three years since 1919, many had been taken up and laid aside as expediency dictated. War conditions had not allowed the development of a coherent or consistent image of Ireland as an international actor. The question now was how to formulate a set of specifically Irish interests? It was necessary to construct for the first time a national policy.

Gavan Duffy had prepared an interim report in April. It was a short manifesto for a principled and active foreign policy, taking advantage of the protections available to small states under the umbrella of the League of Nations and drawing on the image of a principled and pacific country propagated by nationalist propaganda. In it, he made the celebrated claim

---

[24] Foreign office minute, 26 May 1922, PRO, FO 371/7266/3447. The committee, chaired by Colonial Secretary Winston Churchill, was established on 21 December 1921 to advise the cabinet on Irish affairs.

that 'no country ever started its international career with better prospects than were ours after the war. . . . Ireland had every reason to expect rapidly to become recognised as the First of the Small Nations.'[25]

In a fuller report presented to the Dáil two months later, on 21 June, he set out the basis for a comprehensive Irish foreign policy. There were, he argued, four reasons why Ireland could aspire to a prominent role in international affairs:

> First, that Ireland is a world-race with great possibilities; secondly, that we are supposed to have great influence upon American politics and policy; thirdly, that we know England better than the continental peoples and that the friendship of an Ireland lying on England's flank may at any moment be very useful; moreover, we have a reputation for frankness and fearlessness which stands us in good stead.[26]

The report was as ambitious as it was comprehensive in scope, covering issues such as passports, information services, publicity, and people-to-people exchange. It contained many forward-looking elements, for example recognizing the value of academic exchange in promoting the image of Ireland. The United States and the diaspora featured prominently and, despite the failure of the race conference in January, a new global body was envisaged to organize the overseas Irish in support of government objectives. He also foresaw the new state playing a prominent role in the constitutional evolution of the dominions, and recommended the creation of a legal section to deal with Commonwealth affairs. This policy would be supported by a network of twenty missions abroad, with priority accorded to opening offices in London, Washington, Berlin, and Geneva, followed by a second tier of offices in Paris, Rome, the Holy See, and Ottawa.

The cornerstone for this vision was membership of the League, which Gavan Duffy saw as offering the greatest opportunities. He believed other countries would welcome Irish membership on the grounds that Irish representatives would be free to 'say plainly the things that everyone is thinking and that the other Powers are too cowardly to be the first to say'.[27] Ireland would be able to say these things because, unlike other states, it would have no selfish national interests to prevent it adopting a principled stance in international affairs. Much of this thinking was encouraged by Michael MacWhite's reports from Geneva. 'By maintaining

[25] Ministry of Foreign Affairs Dáil report, April 1922.
[26] 'Confidential Memorandum by the Outgoing Minister of Foreign Affairs on the Position of Ireland's "Foreign Affairs" at date of General Election', June 1922, DFA, p. 3.
[27] Ibid.

a diplomatic reserve,' he told his boss in May, an Irish representative at the League 'could ingratiate himself with all those who had axes to grind and make his country an important factor in international diplomacy.'[28] It had been the goal of three years of Sinn Féin propaganda to establish this image of Ireland and it was now advanced as a basis for foreign policy. Having propagated the image of an internationally-minded Ireland making a positive contribution to the conduct of international affairs, when this was repeated back by foreign diplomats, it was cited as reasons why an Irish state could aim to play a positive role in international affairs. Nationalists had become consumers of their own propaganda.

Gavan Duffy was not the only voice in favour of an active foreign policy. In August, Hugh Kennedy saw the possibility for 'a big view of world affairs [which] would introduce us into the world in a new capacity and with new possibilities'.[29] A joint memorandum submitted to the cabinet on 15 September by the secretary of the Post Office and Sinn Féin historian, P. S. O'Hegarty, with the support of the Postmaster General, J. J. Walsh floated similar ideas. Their vision was every bit as ambitious:

> Ireland's position is unique. By virtue of our special history, our special position, we can not only lead the British Dominions in an anti-Imperial policy against the British Empire, but we can, through the League, organise the small nations in a Small Nations League against the Empires. We can make of the League a reality by going into it and supplying honesty and passion and decency in its councils. We can become a pivot for Europe and for America as well.[30]

Despite having claimed a role in blocking American entry to the League, it was now argued that Ireland would be the 'bridge over which America will pass on the road to Geneva'. This belief was based on the misplaced assumption that the Harding administration would find a way of bringing the United States into the League. Failing that, Irish representatives at Geneva would be in demand, as they would know the mind of America thanks to the influence of the diaspora. This would place the Free State in the 'vanguard of European states', enabling it to propose the unproposable, such as German membership of the League.[31]

---

[28] MacWhite Geneva report, May 1922, NAI DFA ES.
[29] Kennedy to Blythe, 29 Aug. 1922, UCDA P4/860.
[30] P. S. O'Hegarty memorandum, 15 Sept. 1922, UCDA P4/860.
[31] Michael MacWhite memorandum on League of Nations membership, 21 Aug. 1922, UCDA mss 859 (1).

While some of this is undeniably far-fetched, what is interesting for the development of Irish foreign policy is the synthesis of disinterest and self-interest it proposed. For all the principled reasons for joining the League, Gavan Duffy justified it on the grounds of self-interest: 'there is no other sphere in which we have equal opportunities for making ourselves seriously felt by England'.[32] The need to guarantee the Irish position in the international arena against possible British encroachment and the espousal of a disinterested foreign policy were seen as being complimentary: one would support the other. An important premise of early Irish foreign policy was thereby established.

The June report should be seen against the circumstances in which it was issued. It was published five days after the new constitution had been adopted and in the knowledge that it lacked the clear assertion of autonomy in the field of foreign policy for which Gavan Duffy had argued so strongly. The day before he delivered it in the Dáil, he warned cabinet colleagues of the 'very great possibilities which are apt to be lost sight of in the rush of more insistent matters'.[33] If the War of Independence had made reluctant internationalists of some in Sinn Féin, those most associated with ideas for an Irish foreign policy were now in the anti-Treaty camp. Those who remained, including W. T. Cosgrave, who had taken over as acting chair of joint cabinet meetings in Michael Collins's absence, took a more pragmatic view of world affairs. In a separate letter, Gavan Duffy challenged Cosgrave's assertion at a recent cabinet meeting that foreign affairs would be 'a matter of no importance' in the new state. His proposal for a cross-party parliamentary committee to oversee foreign policy may have been motivated by a desire to prevent the sidelining of international affairs.

The report was ahead of its time and hopelessly unsuited to the political situation in mid-1922. Begun in the more optimistic days of April, by the time it was completed two months later the chances of it being implemented had shrunk. A first attempt to set out a comprehensive agenda for the country's foreign relations, it was as much a lament for what might have been, as a blueprint for action. It captured a moment in time in which the imagined world of a nationalist foreign policy parted company with the messy reality of compromise and accommodation that characterized the real world of international relations. Gavan Duffy himself retreated to the certainty of the law. Against a backdrop of looming civil war, his foreign schemes must have appeared a distraction at best. Yet, they contained many forward-looking elements that would come to

[32] Michael MacWhite Geneva report, May 1922, NAI DFA ES, p. 4.
[33] Gavan Duffy circular letter to ministers, 20 June 1922, NAI DFA. ES 37(2).

characterize Irish foreign policy in the succeeding decade and a half. The Free State would become an active member of the League and play a significant role in Commonwealth evolution and, by 1938 diplomatic offices had been opened in each of the locations proposed in 1922.

THE LEAGUE OF NATIONS

Not all of Gavan Duffy's proposals were dismissed. Membership of the League had become a nationalist goal almost as soon as Wilson had propounded the idea of a League, albeit with a brief flirtation with hostility to the project in the belief it would bring about US recognition of the republic. By late 1921, opinion was back on track and a seat at Geneva was seen as a means to assert the new Irish state's international status once it was established: 'what was right in 1919 is not necessarily right now'.[34] Michael MacWhite was sent to Geneva in September to open an office and prepare the path for membership. Fluent in French, having served in the Foreign Legion and decorated with the Croix de Guerre, MacWhite would become one of the leading diplomats in the early decades of the Irish state, eventually retiring as ambassador to Rome in 1950. He quickly became convinced of the opportunities presented by participation in the work of the League and would become a consistent advocate for Irish involvement in all areas of League activity in the eight years he would spend as representative in Geneva.

MacWhite had the ear of both Griffith and Gavan Duffy, and encouraged the idea that League membership could be achieved in 1922, before the Free State had been legally established. A letter from MacWhite to Griffith in late December advocating membership of the League was read out in the Dáil during the debate on the Treaty as evidence of the international status provided under the agreement with London. The two were politically close and MacWhite would later claim in a letter to the writer Padraic Colum that Griffith had intended him to become foreign minister in August 1922, but had died before making the appointment.[35]

The issue of League membership became associated early on with efforts to secure support for the Anglo-Irish Treaty. The attraction of the League was as a forum in which to assert and affirm the new international status Ireland would enjoy once the Free State was established. This was equally true of a number of international organizations linked to the League responsible for regulating different aspects of

---

[34] Gavan Duffy to Smiddy, 10 Mar. 1922, NAI DFA ES Box 30 file 199.
[35] MacWhite to Padraic Colum, 27 Jan.1953, UCDA P194/664.

relations between states. As early as March, Gavan Duffy instructed MacWhite to seek membership of the International Telegraphic Union and Universal Postal Union using credentials drawn up by the 'Department of Foreign Affairs Dáil Éireann, at the request of the Provisional Government' in an attempt to get around any reservations about the legal status of the country.[36] The following month, he urged his cabinet colleague, Patrick Hogan, to send a representative to meetings of the International Institute of Agriculture as a means to advertise the country's independence.[37] Gavan Duffy sought to enlist Collins' support for these efforts, but he was not convinced the time was right and told Gavan Duffy in early April to wait until they were 'in a stable position'.[38] The plans were dropped, but Gavan Duffy did not abandon hope and set his sights on a far bigger prize: membership of the League of Nations.

The criteria for League membership were set out in article 1.2 of its covenant, which provided that 'any fully self governing State, Dominion or Colony not named in the Annex may become a member of the League'. League membership gave the dominions their new international status—they were founder members, with separate seats to the British at Geneva. It was hoped admission would compensate for the restrictions which Commonwealth membership would impose: 'the very fact of admission is considered in international law to be the permanent test of sovereignty', as Desmond FitzGerald would tell the Dáil later that year.[39]

The fly in the ointment was the inconvenient fact that the provisional government could not bind the as yet un-constituted Free State. Gavan Duffy argued that the criteria for membership had been fulfilled, as the Treaty had been ratified and contained within it the essence of the new constitution. MacWhite reported from Geneva that the League's secretary general, Sir Eric Drummond, had given the impression that moves towards membership would be possible if the British agreed. The Finns had been allowed to take part in League meetings in 1920, as the League took up the question of the Åland Islands, without being full members and MacWhite pressed Drummond to accede to a similar status for Ireland. Enquiries were made whether a form of 'associate' membership would be possible, to allow Irish representatives to attend at League meetings before becoming a full member. The secretary general would not be drawn, however, making clear that little could be done without a letter of support from London. The British had already told Dublin in

[36] Gavan Duffy to Collins, 31 Mar. 1922, NAI DFA ES 148.
[37] Gavan Duffy to Hogan, 21 April 1922, NAI DFA ES 114.
[38] Collins to Gavan Duffy.
[39] *Dáil Éireann deb.*, vol. l, col. 398, 18 Sept. 1922.

December that they envisaged the Free State becoming a member of the League, but a letter from Lloyd George to Griffith during the Treaty debates made clear that this could only happen when the Free State constitution had been adopted, pouring cold water on hopes for an early seat at Geneva.[40] The constitution would not be adopted until 6 December 1922, at which point the Free State became a fully self-governing entity in law. In the rush to secure the country's international position, this important stipulation was overlooked.

There were a number of calculations behind the enthusiasm for early League membership. It was hoped becoming a member would strengthen the pro-Treaty side in the civil war by illustrating the international status gained under the Treaty. Partition was another factor. Under the Treaty, Northern Ireland had the right to opt out of the Free State within a month of its establishment. Along with many of his colleagues, Gavan Duffy was anxious to join the League, fearing that the Belfast government might attempt to do so (something which both the League covenant and unionist inclinations would make unlikely).[41] There were other considerations. Gavan Duffy and others, such as O'Hegarty, saw in the League a potential arbitrator or guarantee should the British fail to implement the Treaty. Opinion at Geneva was believed to be favourable to Irish membership, and MacWhite reported an air of expectation about Irish intentions, outlining the possibilities for Ireland at the League: 'as Ireland has no international embarrassments and excites no international jealousies the sincerity of our motives would not be questioned,' he wrote. This would enable it to play a role in international affairs to which 'no other country could aspire'.[42]

The idea remained on the table even after the British redraft of the constitution in June had removed references to a separate foreign policy and reaffirmed the Commonwealth link. The Dáil had voted funds for famine relief in Russia in April, Arthur Griffith recognizing that 'the claims of suffering humanity do not stop at National Frontiers', but the unfolding civil war diverted attention from international initiatives.[43] Cabinet minutes reveal an administration overwhelmed by the challenge to public order. A crowded domestic agenda—the Belfast boycott, negotiations with the Northern Ireland government, and efforts to retain some nationalist unity in the run up to the June elections—left little time for

[40] Lloyd George to Griffith, 13 Dec. 1921, UCDA P4/863.
[41] Gavan Duffy to Hugh Kennedy, 14 July 1922, NAI DFA ES 31 (193).
[42] MacWhite Geneva report, May 1922, NAI DFA ES Geneva 1921–23, 1922 subject file, reports sub-file.
[43] Griffith to Saor an Leanbh Committee,10 April 1922, NAI DE 2/269.

matters further afield. These were hardly propitious circumstances in which to lay the foundations for a foreign policy. Collins told Gavan Duffy on 22 July that the moment was not right to push for League membership, correctly believing efforts to assert an international existence should wait until the Free State was fully established.[44] Overseas representatives could be no more than 'inquiry agents', paving the way for the establishment of proper relations when the time came, and days before his death in August he tried to put a stop to efforts in Rome to seek a formal audience with the pope.[45] His death was a further blow to prospects for an activist foreign service.

Gavan Duffy's resignation removed the main proponent of early membership. Griffith succeeded him as foreign minister but, with the unfolding political and constitutional crisis, had little time to devote to the brief. Following his sudden death on 12 August, Michael Hayes took over as a temporary measure. Two weeks later, Desmond FitzGerald was appointed minister for external affairs on 25 August and took office on 4 September, having confirmed in writing his acceptance of the Treaty. With the survival of the provisional government under threat, there was little time to consider the merits of taking a seat at Geneva. The problem was that new members could only be admitted at the annual meeting of the League's general assembly in September. The day after the assembly opened on 3 September, MacWhite raised the issue again, in the hope of securing a last-minute application while it was sitting. He believed the British would yield on the issue of status, as they would be obliged to support the pro-Treaty side, and his arguments were persuasive.

A head of steam built up behind the idea, and the new cabinet agreed to seek immediate admission on 1 September. Faced with a bleak political landscape at home, the appeal of some good news abroad is not hard to imagine. But MacWhite's assessment was incorrect. In response to a request from the cabinet for assistance in submitting an application at Geneva, the British reaffirmed their position that only after the Free State was legally established could such a step be taken. The firmness of the British note poured cold water on the prospects for membership. A memorandum circulated to the cabinet the previous day by P. S. O'Hegarty had concluded that immediate membership was not an option, a view shared by Hugh Kennedy, who advised the provisional government could not bind the Free State. Two days after receipt of the British note, a government motion to defer indefinitely the question of League membership was passed in the Dáil by forty-four votes to nineteen.

---

[44] Collins to Gavan Duffy, 22 July 1922, NAI DFA ES 193.
[45] Collins to Gavan Duffy, 25 May 1922, NAI DFA ES Box 3 file 17.

Figure 4. Desmond FitzGerald, Minister for External Affairs 1922–27 (Image courtesy of FitzGerald family)

Why did the idea of membership persist so long? The proposal had been based on the mistaken assumption that, following electoral endorsement of the Treaty in the 16 June election, the reconvened provisional government would be able to act as though the Free State had come into being. That Gavan Duffy should so completely misunderstand both the rules for league membership and the status of the provisional government is unlikely given his legal background and experience as a Treaty negotiator. More likely is a calculation that these could be set aside if the British became convinced the threat to the Treaty meant it might not be implemented. He mistakenly believed London would give ground on the constitution and was equally convinced that British reticence over early League membership could be overcome. But this was a misreading of the signals coming from London. British opposition to Irish aspirations in this field remained firm and hopes to leverage anti-Treaty agitation and uncertainty over its adoption to secure concessions proved wide of the mark. In the aftermath of the death of Griffith and Collins in August, Foreign Secretary Lord Curzon informed his officials 'now would not be a good time to point out to the Provisional Government that they are not entitled to separate representation'.[46]

---

[46] Foreign Office minute, 15 Sept. 1922, PRO, CO739/9/42855.

RETRENCHMENT

Against this background, retrenchment became the order of the day. Horizons were lowered and the ambitious plans of earlier in the year were shelved. The deaths of Griffiths and Collins removed two key figures who had taken an interest in international issues. W. T. Cosgrave's statement in the Dáil that the war of independence had not been won by foreign affairs seemed to set a new tone.[47] Plans to acquire a headquarters for the foreign ministry were abandoned in July and the envoys abroad told to dispose of assets. Instructions from a renamed department of external affairs in October set the parameters for the following years: envoys abroad would no longer be considered 'representative of the Irish government as such and therefore can claim no recognition'. Count O'Kelly in Brussels was ordered to sell all ostentatious assets: 'efficiency alone must be the foundation of our right to the esteem of foreign peoples'.[48] The same day a note was sent to the Colonial Office in London clarifying his status as trade agent rather than the consul of a recognized state.

The degree of retrenchment came as a surprise to many supporters of the new government. Upon his return from Paris in September, Maurice Moore denounced the new spirit, warning: 'the hand of Ministerial France is held out to Ireland but there is no Envoy to take it'.[49] Seán Murphy recommended that the Paris office be replaced by an information bureau and a trade office; Osmond Grattan Esmonde described his role in Madrid as 'ornamental and unnecessary'.[50] The same was true for other 'consuls' who, henceforth, would represent the trade department alone and should 'avoid anything which might give rise to the belief that you are acting as consul of a recognised state'.[51] In early November, 'Republic of Ireland' was dropped from notepaper. The last act of the Dáil foreign ministry was to notify the world of the establishment of the Free State on 6 December. By then all that was left to distinguish the old from the new was a change of letterhead. Observing the conventions of duality to the end, this was done on Dáil ministry notepaper.

What of the future? The civil war changed international perceptions of Ireland: the conflict was difficult to understand for foreign audiences and

---

[47] *Dáil Éireann deb.*, col. 554, 21 Sept. 1922.
[48] FitzGerald to Count O'Kelly, 2 Oct. 1922, NAI DFA ES 243(1).
[49] Colonel Moore memorandum, Sept. 1922, NLI mss 10,583; Moore to Ministry of Foreign Affairs, 25 Aug. 1922, NAI DFA ES Box 28.
[50] Grattan Esmonde to FitzGerald, 30 Oct. 1922, NAI DFA ES 42.
[51] FitzGerald to O'Duinn, 5 Oct. 1922, NAI DFA ES 197.

contrasted sharply with the moral tone of the preceding three years' propaganda. A tragedy at home, it was a disaster abroad. Reports from agents loyal to the Free State catalogued the growing damage to the country's image as the civil war took its toll. The French consul in Dublin described a situation 'worthy of Soviet Russia'.[52] Representatives abroad had the unenviable task of explaining the civil war to a foreign opinion unable to comprehend the issues that had split the nationalist movement. Arguments over the Treaty fell on largely deaf ears abroad, where foreign public opinion understood simply that Irish demands for self-rule had been met. Not only did the outbreak of civil war risk alienating international sympathy built up during the previous three years, it seemed to confirm British characterizations of the Irish as unready for self-government. It was against this backdrop that the Irish Free State began its international existence. The civil war would cast Irish aspirations in a very different light, and leave the Irish Free State harbouring more modest ambitions. Until this happened, Ireland was a state-in-waiting.

[52] Etat-Major de l'Armée to Raymond Poincaré, 4 April 1922, QO, CPC, Europe 1918–40, Irlande, vol. 2, p. 2.

5

'The Irish Harp in the Orchestra of Nations'

First Steps on the International Stage, 1923–1924

Surveying the changes in Ireland in its last edition of 1922, the *New York Times* predicted the Free State would soon have ambassadors in the principal capitals of the world. But as 1923 began, the over-riding priority was to create the institutions at home necessary to breathe life into the new state, while seeing off a challenge that threatened to choke it at birth. Events beyond the country's shores would have to wait. The country had become independent not as a republic, but as a dominion in the British Commonwealth, and not as Ireland, but the Irish Free State. The Canadian Prime Minister cabled congratulations, perhaps because the country's status had been pegged to that of his own. Otherwise, the appearance of the Irish Free State passed largely unmarked by the chancelleries and foreign ministries of the world. There was no exchange of diplomatic relations or messages of congratulation; no gathering of ambassadors or any of the diplomatic niceties that usually mark the birth of a new state.

Internal autonomy was secure, but in the field of foreign affairs, Commonwealth members were not yet free to pursue an independent line. Like the other dominions, the Free State was entitled to appoint a high commissioner in London and trade commissioners elsewhere, but neither would have diplomatic status. The British Empire acted as a diplomatic unit: treaties negotiated by the British applied also to the dominions and London shaped foreign policy after consultation with dominion premiers when it saw fit. Because of the diplomatic unity of the Empire, internal Commonwealth agreements were not regarded as international treaties and international treaties were not deemed binding on relations between Commonwealth members.[1] The new Irish state

---

[1] See D. W. Harkness, *The Restless Dominion* (London, 1969) for an account of this development.

would have to communicate this anomalous status to the outside world and find for itself a place on the international stage. These objectives would occupy Irish diplomacy in the first years of the Irish Free State. In seeking to achieve them, policy-makers would find their task was made all the harder by the ill-defined nature of the country's independence and its continuing links with Britain.

The challenge of building a new state meant attention was focused at home. The French occupation of the Ruhr in January and the Lithuanian seizure of Memel (Klaipeda) the same month accordingly passed without much comment or reaction in Ireland, where the focus was on bringing the civil war to an end. If the overarching focus was domestic, three decisions were taken in the early months of 1923 that would have a direct bearing on the Free State's international status and signal the direction that the government would take in its foreign policy: to seek membership of the League of Nations, to appoint a fully-accredited diplomat in Washington and to register the Anglo-Irish Treaty at Geneva.

Before these could be pursued, however, the government was faced with a more immediate external challenge in the form of Vatican efforts at mediation in the civil war. The Holy See had not become actively involved in efforts to bring the civil war in Ireland to an end beyond issuing calls for both sides to show restraint. This changed in March 1923, when an ill-judged attempt by the Holy See to become involved in mediating between the two sides prompted the Free State government to seek the withdrawal of a Vatican envoy sent to gather views on the situation in Ireland. The status and purpose of the mission by Salvatore Luzio was cloaked in confusion from the moment of the Monsignor's arrival in Ireland on St Patrick's Day. Instead of making contact with the government, he met first with the Irish bishops and then with Eamon de Valera and other anti-Treaty leaders before seeking a meeting with W. T. Cosgrave on 11 April, three weeks after his arrival.

Luzio's progress through the country was marked by petitions from town councils for the Vatican to condemn the policy of executions that the government had adopted in its prosecution of the civil war. Prompted by anti-Treaty agitators, they were embarrassing for the government, which was determined to resist any outside attempt to interfere. By early March, the civil war was drawing to a close with the government having the upper hand. Efforts to engage with the anti-Treaty side were far from welcome and the government dispatched an envoy to Rome to demand Luzio be recalled, a request the Vatican agreed to immediately without admitting that its diplomat had visited Ireland in an official capacity. The government had successfully resisted an attempt at outside intervention but did not wish to damage relations with the Vatican. The issue was

considered sensitive enough to dispatch foreign minister FitzGerald to
Rome at the end of April in a bid to smooth over any ruffled feathers at the
Holy See. He was assured there were none.[2]

THE CIVIL WAR LEGACY

The activities of anti-Treaty representatives after the civil war had ended in
Ireland were a thorn in the government's side. Intelligence reports supplied by the British charted anti-Treaty activity in Europe and North
America while Sinn Féin-appointed envoys loyal to the Free State strove to
generate support for its government. Reports provided to Dublin in late
1923 by the British suggested contact between republicans and communists in mainland Europe.[3] Earlier that year, Michael MacWhite had
reported a series of visits by anti-Treaty activists to the Soviet mission at
Geneva, although he did not believe they were taken seriously by the
Russians.[4] Having courted the Bolsheviks two years earlier, the official
attitude was now one of suspicion. The secretary to the government,
Michael MacDunphy, was sent to investigate the situation in Geneva
and, on return, recommended close cooperation with British and French
authorities to counter the continental network he believed was assisting
'Irregular and allied Bolshevist activity'.

The situation was particularly acute in Paris. Concerned the French
would expel all Irish representatives because of anti-Treaty activity, he
proposed the immediate opening of diplomatic relations. No action was
taken and the Free State office in Paris remained stymied by French
confusion between it and the rival republican 'consulate' operated by
Leopold Kerney who had been Dáil agent in France.[5] By January 1925,
the entire Irish community in Paris was under police surveillance. It
proved almost impossible for foreigners to differentiate between the two
and even the British embassy mistakenly directed callers in 1924 to the
republic's 'consul' rather than the Free State's office. This confusion
reached farcical proportions the following year when both held rival

---

[2] Dermot Keogh, *Ireland and the Vatican, the Politics and Diplomacy of Church-State
Relations 1922–1960* (Cork, 1995), pp. 10–30.
[3] Eunan O'Halpin, *Defending Ireland, The Irish State and its Enemies Since 1922*
(Oxford, 1999), pp. 22–4.
[4] E. O'Connor, *Reds and the Green, Ireland, Russia and the Communist International*
(Dublin, 2004), pp. 248–55.
[5] Michael MacDunphy reports to the cabinet, Berne and Paris, 19 and 23 Jan. 1923,
NAI, DT53147. Kerney was also in touch with the communists as evidenced by a letter
from him published in the Moscow press in December 1923.

St Patrick's Day banquets in adjoining rooms of the same hotel. However, it was to prove difficult to take action and Joseph Walshe eventually decided to drop the matter rather than ask the British embassy to become involved.

In the United States, Professor Smiddy's efforts to counter anti-Free State activity and propaganda were met with concerted opposition. Cables from Smiddy to Dublin reported on the movements of known anti-Treaty activists and socialists who had moved to the United States.[6] In New York, where a large and vocal opposition to the Free State was active, the Free State's agent, Lindsay Crawford, was told to avoid all mention of politics, so that 'every category of Irish man' might be persuaded to use the trade office in the city. The government was anxious to avoid undermining its credibility by admitting that it was threatened by republican activities at home or abroad. During the civil war, assistance from the British had been a necessity, but the government wanted to avoid calling on British support, even if it were to be at the expense of clarity in its relations with the French. Legitimacy was all in post-civil war Ireland, and nothing could be ventured that would risk tarnishing the authority of the new state.

The difficulties experienced in the United States accelerated moves to seek a permanent solution to the question of legitimacy by appointing a diplomat in Washington. Dwindling cash flows, and the creation of Fianna Fáil in 1926, diminished republican activity abroad. Even after the civil war had ended, concerns remained about its impact on how the country was seen abroad. James McNeill hoped for the day when the Free State would be seen 'as a highly organised community and not merely as a hive of poets, revolutionaries, and decadent farmers, redeemed by a few capable individuals whose control might be upset any day'.[7] No longer viewed as an oppressed people, the Irish would be judged by the same criteria as other states: on how they managed their own affairs.

SHOULD THERE BE AN IRISH FOREIGN POLICY?

The Luzio mission occurred as the final stages of the civil war were drawing to a close and the government began turning its thoughts to creating the institutions of the new state. With moves towards political stability, it was possible to question assumptions that had shaped policy during the campaign for independence. One of these was the importance

---

[6] Paul McMahon, *British Spies & Irish Rebels, British Intelligence and Ireland 1916–1945* (Woodbridge, 2008); Gavin Foster, 'No "Wild Geese" this time?: IRA emigration after the Irish Civil War' *Éire-Ireland*, vol. 47, issue 1 & 2 spring/summer, 2012, pp. 94–122.
[7] McNeill to Ernest Blythe, 12 Aug. 1925, NAI DFA G10/1923.

that had been accorded to international affairs. The cost of the civil war and construction of the new state made financial savings an imperative and the foreign ministry, having no counterpart in the old administration and viewed as dangerously political in some quarters, came under scrutiny.[8] During the campaign for independence, it had been necessary to open as many offices as possible without regard to the cost or desirability of keeping them. Even had a republic been achieved, this would have been unsustainable. In the straitened circumstances in which the Free State found itself, many questioned whether they were a luxury that could be afforded at all.

Loose cannons at best and politically partisan at worst, Cosgrave considered most of the Sinn Féin era envoys 'generally poor stuff' and warned Desmond FitzGerald 'we cannot have them making a mess of things'.[9] FitzGerald agreed, and the government set about getting rid of what he dubbed a '*damnosa hereditas*' of unrecognized envoys left over from the campaign for independence who 'handicapped themselves' with the title of ambassador while lacking any real status.[10] Such pretensions were now a liability; what was needed was full diplomatic status. There was a need to draw a line under this political past and establish the non-partisan principle as the basis for the foreign ministry. Moves to bring overseas representatives under Dublin control had contributed to the fragmentation of the foreign network in 1922. Conditions of administrative normality under the Free State would see this process pushed forward, but not without provoking its own share of tensions. It was not just the difficult financial situation in which the new state found itself that dictated a scaling back.

It was by no means certain at the start of 1923 that there would even be a foreign ministry. The initial report in March by a cabinet committee appointed to draw up plans for the new administration found no need for a department of external affairs, suggesting its functions could be subsumed into the prime minister's office. The same proposal was made by those such as Darrell Figgis who believed foreign policy should be handled by Cosgrave's office as a sign of their importance. Either way, the prospects were bleak for the fledgling external affairs department, its dejected head warning that abolishing it would set the country on a path to 'national obliteration'.[11] The change of name from foreign to external affairs was criticized in the Dáil, where it was seen as a mark of the

[8] Walter Doolin to Walshe, 27 Jan. 1923, NAI, DF F596/25.
[9] Cosgrave to FitzGerald, n.d. (1923), UCDA, P80/415.
[10] *Dáil Éireann deb.*, vol. 3(ii), col. 2393, 25 June 1923.
[11] Walshe to Joseph Brennan, 27 Mar. 1923, NAI, DF F851.

country's inferior status, but it had more to do with partition than with Commonwealth usage: as FitzGerald explained, his department had responsibility for 'everything external to our territory'.[12] It survived, in part because Cosgrave considered himself to have no aptitude for foreign policy and the department's place in government was confirmed by the Ministers and Secretaries Act in April 1924. But the debate was damaging for those who advocated a foreign policy, revealing a degree of ambiguity about the value of international activity within the pro-Treaty consensus.

SCALING BACK

If the civil war challenge might have been used as an argument to increase the number of offices abroad as part of the Free State's quest for legitimacy, it resulted instead in a scaling back of foreign activity as the political and financial costs took their toll. Requests for funding in April 1923 for high commissioners in Paris, Ottawa, and Rome, and trade agents in Denmark and Argentina, met with a cool response in the finance department, where British-trained civil servants on loan from London brought with them the methods and assumptions of Whitehall. The newly-created department of finance was heavily influenced by its secretary, Joseph Brennan, an Oxford-educated former Dublin Castle officer who had served as finance advisor to Michael Collins during the Treaty negotiations. Brennan's realist view of state finances made him unsympathetic to claims for expenditure on offices abroad.[13] Reacting to the proposals for offices abroad, a memorandum from his department outlined a foreign service far smaller than that sought by the department of external affairs. Its conclusions were blunt: all offices abroad were to close within six months, with the exception of London, Washington, or New York, and either Paris or Berlin.[14]

Attempts to sway opinions by citing the practice of other countries including the dominions were unsuccessful. The irony of finance officials, many from home rule backgrounds, justifying the cuts with arguments of Sinn Féin-style self-reliance cannot have been lost at the time. In private, the views of British counterparts were sought on requests for expenditure on anything foreign, a back channel that would persist for over a decade.[15]

---

[12] *Dáil Éireann deb.*, vol.3(ii), col. 2395, 25 June 1923.
[13] See, also, Ronan Fanning, *The Irish Department of Finance, 1922–58* (Dublin, 1978).
[14] C. A. Ryan memorandum, 14 Mar. 1923, NAI, DF F596/25.
[15] See Department of Finance file NAI, DF E105/39/29 for a series of enquiries regarding Foreign Office practices spanning the period 1922–36, including M. J. Beary memorandum, 15 Sept. 1927.

An exception was the secretary of the department of industry and commerce, Gordon Campbell whose father, the southern unionist Lord Glenavy, was chairman of the Senate. An advocate of state intervention to stimulate economic growth, Campbell would play a key role in developing the Shannon hydroelectric scheme in the 1920s, but his arguments for the appointment of trade commissioners in key foreign markets fell on deaf ears at the department of finance.[16] Closures were the order of the day and future appointments would have to wait 'until happier times'.[17]

The shutters came down in Berlin, Rome, and Buenos Aires and other closures would follow. Until something could be done to change the dominions' incomplete international status, the Foreign Office was the channel for communication with other governments; in the absence of diplomatic status, business would have to be conducted unofficially or not at all. Following enquiries from London in February 1923, the British were asked to notify the American and French of the appointment of Professor Smiddy and Seán Murphy as Free State 'general agents' in Washington and Paris; neither had diplomatic status. Guidance from Dublin on where their roles began and ended boiled down to avoiding any definition of the word 'general'. Murphy's successor in Paris, a young Irish-Australian, Vaughan Dempsey, complained that the only people who would meet him were shopkeepers and tradesmen. It was the same elsewhere. In New York, Lindsay Crawford remained on as trade commissioner, a role performed in Brussels by Count O'Kelly. With James McNeill as high commissioner in London and Michael MacWhite as delegate to the League in Geneva, the Free State's reduced overseas network was in place. Less than six months after coming into existence, Arthur Griffith's grand scheme of consuls and envoys had been dismantled.

Living up to earlier aspirations would prove a challenge as the constraints of statehood imposed themselves. A more questioning attitude to the value of international action was a measure of how closely it had been associated with the pursuit of independence. It was perhaps inevitable, therefore, that there would be a reassessment following the Treaty split and failure to secure a republic. Confusion surrounding the constitutional basis for pursuing a foreign policy and more pressing demands of state building at home were further reasons. Many of those most closely associated with the external projection of the republic took the opposing side in the civil war; in effect the idealists left and the pragmatists remained while, for some, an external dimension had never been an important part

---

[16] Gordon Campbell to W. B. Gilbert, 20 June 1923, NAI, DF F818/3.
[17] Joseph Brennan to W. B. Gilbert, 28 July 1923, NAI, DF 851.

of the nationalist project. From ex-unionists and former home rule supporters on the one hand, to those who viewed with suspicion the corrupting influence of ideas from abroad or took a literal interpretation of Sinn Féin to mean efforts at home, voices were raised questioning the need for a foreign policy. Loudest among them were the Farmers Party which, together with Labour and a scattering of independents of various hues, comprised the opposition in a chamber boycotted by anti-Treaty republicans. A party of large farmers, its leader Denis Gorey questioned the need for a foreign policy in a country that had 'no colonies and . . . no interests to clash with any other nation'.[18] In Gorey's view, the country's limited resources would be better used for economic development than wasted on international issues in which it had no direct interest. His plainer-speaking colleague, Michael Heffernan, dismissed the international ambitions of some in the Dáil as being out of proportion to the reality facing the country, warning the chamber was in 'danger of bursting just with the sense of our own importance'.[19]

The views of unionists and home rulers are easily accounted for; as an editorial in the *Church of Ireland Gazette* explained, membership in the Empire was a larger prize than participation in the League of Nations. Complaints by the Farmers' Party about wasting money on the 'theatricals' of a foreign policy encapsulated the latter viewpoint. W. T. Cosgrave shared some of these concerns, conceding that pronouncements on international affairs had 'expanded a little more than the merits of the case warranted'.[20] The decision to fold the publicity office into external affairs prompted accusations that administrative resources were being used for party gain. The civil war had made the question of propaganda sensitive and the publicity bureau's new home encouraged many to conclude the foreign ministry was an organ of the government party and not the state.

The Labour party was more supportive. Internationalist by inclination, its leader, Thomas Johnson, encouraged the government throughout the 1920s to adopt a principled line on questions of foreign policy. The historian Denis Gwynn later attributed to his influence a more active Irish policy on international issues.[21] Until he lost his seat in the August 1923 election, George Gavan Duffy was a lonely backbench voice calling for an ambitious foreign policy, listing off the points from his report of the previous June and asking what was being done to implement them. The former Sinn Féin envoy Osmond Grattan Esmonde was another advocate

[18] *Dáil Éireann deb.*, vol. 4, col. 940, 16 Nov. 1923.
[19] Ibid., vol. 4, col. 1412, 5 Dec. 1923.
[20] Ibid., vol.4, col. 1410–12, 5 Dec. 1923.
[21] Denis Gwynn, *The Irish Free State 1922–27* (London, 1928), p. 92.

for a more active policy on international issues, but otherwise there was little time for events beyond the country's shores as reconstruction, the economy, and continuing debate on the Treaty settlement dominated the political agenda. Questions about the value of pursuing an Irish foreign policy were also raised in the Senate, reflecting its largely ex-unionist and vocational composition. Interest in the upper house was confined to a small number of senators, including the former Sinn Féin envoy Colonel Maurice Moore and James Douglas, a Quaker humanitarian from a family of Dublin drapers. For the rest, the former unionist Colonel Hutchinson-Poe summed up the Senate's feelings when he told the upper house it should not be wasting time on 'unimportant bills'.[22]

The burden of articulating the case for a foreign policy at the cabinet table and in the Dáil fell on Desmond FitzGerald's shoulders. This entailed walking a fine line, balancing calls for more action with those wanting none at all, while educating some in the responsibilities and obligations of statehood. His frequent assertions that the government might change its mind, when pressed on a constitutional point or particular course of action, exasperated some parliamentarians, who found his replies to their questions evasive and vague. But there was a limit to the information he could share when discussing foreign policy or the clarity he could bring to the status of the dominions. It was a difficult task, particularly when funding was the issue. FitzGerald assured a sceptical Dáil in June 1923 'we are not anxious to have elaborate Embassies in other countries where the representative will spend money in entertaining people' and, with a nod to the finance mandarins, took pains to stress that value for money would be the guiding principle.[23] But he enjoyed an uneasy relationship with the Dáil, where his polemical debating style did not always go down well. Nor did he always enjoy the confidence of his staff, the head of his department, Joseph Walshe, complaining that he allowed himself to be put off when pressing cabinet colleagues for funding. He was described as a 'link of inefficiency' by the writer and wit, Oliver St John Gogarty.[24] Putting the department of external affairs on a professional basis was a significant achievement, given the circumstances of the time, and FitzGerald faced an uphill task countering the apathy that greeted foreign affairs in many quarters. Defending his department against calls for its abolition during debates on the Ministers and Secretaries Bill in December 1923, he warned against 'a home rule mentality,' a loaded

22 *Seanad Éireann deb.*, vol.1, col. 1546, 30 July 1923.
23 *Dáil Éireann deb.*, vol.3(ii), col. 2394, 25 June 1923.
24 Oliver St John Gogarty to MacWhite, 26 Dec. 1922, UCDA P194/1876.

charge.[25] Freedom entailed its own responsibilities, and there could be no avoiding the question of foreign affairs.

It was with some justification that external affairs was called the 'Cinderella department', cohabiting uneasily with a finance department unconvinced of its need to exist.[26] Joseph Walshe presided over a handful of staff at headquarters, chief among whom were Seán Murphy, from a prominent Waterford home rule family—his father had been John Redmond's election agent; and Seán Lester, a Carrickfergus-born journalist with the *Freeman's Journal* who joined the department in 1923 as director of publicity, a post FitzGerald had held before becoming minister. Murphy's steady hand would see him rise in the department, eventually succeeding Walshe as secretary in 1946. His calm head and measured tone, in contrast to that of Walshe, saw him entrusted with key tasks including the sensitive matter of securing the recall of Monsignor Luzio. He would spend the war years in France.

Lester was one of a number of northern Protestants for whom the Irish language movement provided a path to nationalism. His appointment first as head of the League section at headquarters in 1925 and then as permanent delegate at Geneva in 1929 set him on an international career path, serving first as League high commissioner in Danzig and, eventually, keeping a lonely vigil in wartime Geneva as the last secretary general of the League. Walshe and Murphy were contemporaries at Dublin's UCD. Both had been recruited to the Dáil's Paris office by Seán T. O Ceallaigh, as had Michael MacWhite in Geneva and Count O'Kelly in Brussels. In the small social world of post-civil war Dublin, relationships established during the campaign for independence transcended the divide between politician and official that would later develop. Making arrangements for ministers when not travelling on official business might seem relatively benign, but Vaughan Dempsey prepared FitzGerald's election mail from Paris in 1923, something Seán Lester did for his former colleague and future boss, Patrick McGilligan, and FitzGerald sought assistance 'as a friend' from Michael MacWhite in Washington for a fund-raising visit for Cumann na nGaedheal in 1929. There was a feeling of fellowship between those who had weathered the civil war together and the boundaries of appropriate interaction were slow to emerge. Personal ties between government and civil service were close and would be tested with the arrival of Fianna Fáil in power in 1932.

---

[25] *Dáil Éireann deb.*, vol. 4, col. 1397, 5 Dec. 1923.

[26] The Department of Foreign Affairs did not move to its present accommodation in Iveagh House until May 1941.

The dominions each maintained a high commission to represent them in London; a move the British were slow to reciprocate. The cabinet decided on 2 January 1923 to appoint James McNeill, brother of Eoin MacNeill, as high commissioner in London. McNeill was reluctant to take the post, but his nationalist pedigree and background in the colonial service in India made him an ideal choice for the job. The role was a difficult one, lacking diplomatic status. Navigating the corridors of Whitehall, McNeill encountered widespread reluctance among senior British officials to countenance an active dominion role, with a particular *froideur* from the Foreign Office, which viewed with suspicion and distaste any attempt to encroach on its turf. He complained of being bypassed by his colleagues in Dublin, in particular finance officials who preferred to deal directly with counterparts in the British Treasury. He had allies in his Canadian and South African colleagues, whose countries shared the Irish desire to push the boundaries of dominion status. For a brief period in 1923, he was assisted by Patrick McGilligan, whose decision to enter politics at the end of the year would see him become McNeill's boss as foreign minister five years later. Two years into the job, he was looking to return home, frustrated by the obstacles in his way: if a high commissioner was not an ambassador, 'he need not be an office boy' either.[27] McNeill was granted his wish to come home in 1928, succeeding Tim Healy as governor general, a role in which he would come up against Fianna Fáil's efforts in government to remove the crown from Irish constitutional life.

JOINING THE LEAGUE OF NATIONS

There was a need to re-establish a link between the external dimension and the nationalist project by demonstrating that consolidating the country's constitutional status and other government priorities could be advanced through international action. One of the first priorities was to complete the unfinished business of joining the League of Nations. The cabinet decided on 20 March 1923 to revive the issue, based on the Dáil vote from the previous September. The official application, submitted the following month, contained a clear commitment to accept all obligations of membership. It was couched in similar terms to the commitment made in the headier days of April 1919. In contrast to the previous year, the British were fully supportive and the application proceeded smoothly over the summer in Geneva.

---

[27] McNeill to FitzGerald, 2 Mar. 1923, NAI DFA Letterbooks (Department of the President 1923–28).

The Free State was admitted as a member of the League at the annual sitting of the assembly in September. Cosgrave's decision to travel to Geneva was a testament to the importance he attached to League membership and a sign of his growing political confidence at home, setting out before learning the results of the August general election. The first Free State passports were issued especially for the journey. Stopping off first in Paris, he travelled on to northern Italy for a commemoration of St Columbanus in Bobbio, his first official engagement abroad having the air of a pilgrimage before his appearance at the secular League assembly. The historical scene setting suggested what was happening was a return to Europe. The Irish newspapers followed his journey to Geneva, where he was accompanied by Desmond FitzGerald, education minister Eoin MacNeill, and attorney general Hugh Kennedy. Following completion of the necessary preliminaries, the Free State was unanimously voted a member of the League on 10 September, its delegates taking their seats in the assembly hall to a standing ovation. The rules of procedure were set aside to allow Cosgrave to address the chamber. Taking to his feet in a hushed hall, he pledged the support of Ireland, 'one of the oldest and yet one of the youngest nations', in promoting 'the peace, security and happiness, the economic, cultural and oral well-being of the human race'. He did not mention the Free State once, referring to Ireland throughout.

The Free State was admitted at the same session as Ethiopia. It would be the League's failure to act in the face of Italian aggression against Ethiopia twelve years later that would prompt a reassessment of Irish policy towards Geneva and its collective security architecture. But in 1923, the League was in its springtime and hopes were high that it would succeed in its mission of banishing war as an instrument in the relations between states.

The League assembly was the first major diplomatic outing for the Free State. A basic primer prepared for delegates by Joseph Walshe covered everything, from how to behave (adopt continental manner including doffing of hats; avoid idiosyncrasies) to whom to be seen with (avoid Commonwealth gatherings; seek out small state representatives, especially Europeans).[28] The delegates were feted on arrival; in demand on the dinner circuit; their views sought out in committees. With perhaps a little exaggeration, Desmond FitzGerald told his wife, Mabel, it was enough for a proposal to have Irish support for it to succeed. There was an undeniable interest in these revolutionaries-turned-statesmen who had brought the

---

[28] Joseph Walshe, Memorandum for members of the Irish delegation to the League of Nations Assembly, 28 Aug. 1923, NAI DFA ES Box 37.

Figure 5. Irish delegation to League of Nations Assembly, Geneva, September 1923: Hugh Kennedy, W. T. Cosgrave, Eoin MacNeill, Michael MacWhite, Marquis McSwiney (Image courtesy of UCD Archives P194/779)

world's leading power to terms, just as there would be a decade later when Eamon de Valera made his diplomatic debut at Geneva.

It was a demanding schedule, with complaints about the round of social engagements, at which the Marquis McSwiney was 'in heaven' but Mac-Neill in 'mild purgatory'. The 'strain of politeness, good behaviour and overeating' told on all. After the initial excitement had died down, FitzGerald found the assembly sessions 'dull enough' as delegates set to work on the various committees and commissions that were the bread and butter of the League's work. The star performer was Michael MacWhite, who revelled in talking to 'people of all tribes and tongues' and whose two years at Geneva enabled him to ease the way for the Free State's diplomatic debutantes.[29] A natural diplomat, he was immediately at home in the world of corridor conversations, gossip, and horse-trading that was the

[29] FitzGerald to Mabel FitzGerald, undated Sept. 1923, UCDA P80/1404; MacNeill to Agnes MacNeill, 6 Sept. 1923, UCDA LAI/G/215; MacNeill to Agnes MacNeill, 14 Sept. 1923, UCDA LAI/G/217.

M. Kennedy.   M. Cosgrave.   M. Mac Neil.

.a délégation irlandaise à la Société des Nations. — *Phot. H. Jullien.*

Figure 6. Clipping from French newspaper, Irish delegates arriving at League of Nations Assembly, 10 September 1923 (Image courtesy of UCD Archives LA30/PH/418)

League. MacWhite's verdict on their first outing was that it had passed off without hitch or faux pas. The attitude of the British delegation was judged to be correct, although it was noticed that a junior diplomat had been sent to sit on the Irish bench each morning, presumably to listen in and remind others of the new arrivals' continuing links with the Commonwealth.

The assembly session was over-shadowed by a dispute between Greece and Italy that had broken out over the summer. In August, the Italian head of a boundary commission delimiting the Greek–Albanian frontier had been killed on Greek soil, probably by Albanian bandits. Mussolini blamed Greece and demanded compensation. When this was not paid, the

Italian navy bombarded and temporarily occupied the island of Corfu. Preoccupied with absorbing a flood of refugees from Turkey, Athens appealed to the League for redress. At Italian instigation and in the face of protests from the small states, the dispute was referred instead to the Conference of Ambassadors, a body left over from the peace conference where the British, French, and Italians were able to conduct business behind closed doors. The outcome was largely a foregone conclusion: the Greeks were found guilty and fined. In return, the Italians withdrew from Corfu at the end of September, but not before finalizing their annexation of Fiume. The deal was given a veneer of respectability when the League assembly was asked to endorse the package.

The Corfu dispute was the first international issue on which the Free State was called to comment and the first failure of the League. Cosgrave had alluded to it in his opening address. Eoin MacNeill's comments when it came up for debate in the assembly were more direct. He lamented the resort to arms, before reminding members of their commitment to submit disputes to the League (a veiled swipe at the Italians who had opted for the Conference of Ambassadors route). He was careful not to lay the blame solely on either party, however, preferring to strike a balanced tone, drawing general conclusions about the League's work. It was the first example of what Michael Kennedy has dubbed the Free State's policy of 'critical support' for the League.[30] MacNeill's verdict on his return from Geneva was pessimistic: the League was 'too immature to make full use of its formal powers' against a large member state. His prescription was to strengthen the role of the small states (those 'not looking for bits of Africa or Asia') with the aim of strengthening the League as a whole, believing it could not function properly until the smaller states acted in unison rather than spread themselves between different geographical groups.[31] This was an issue that would emerge as a major feature of Irish League policy three years later.

Membership of the League was greeted in Ireland by many as a sign that the country was beginning to find its place in the world after the upheaval of the previous four years. The unionist turned dominion home ruler, Horace Plunkett, expressed this desire most clearly when he wrote 'we want the Irish harp to sound in the orchestra of nations'.[32] For the government it was vindication of the Free State's status under the Treaty.

[30] Michael Kennedy, *Ireland and the League of Nations, 1919–1946: international relations, diplomacy and politics* (Dublin, 1996), p. 41.

[31] Eoin MacNeill, 'Report on the Fourth Assembly of the League of Nations (September 1923)', 4 Oct. 1923, NAI DT S3332.

[32] *Irish Statesman*, 15 Sept. 1923.

Admission was also an important step in a process of normalization after the civil war and a source of legitimacy for Cosgrave personally, although he would not attend another League meeting. On his return from Geneva, he was met by a civic reception, complete with army and police bands, flags, and a fly-past by the fledgling Free State air force. For republicans, League membership was a bitter pill to swallow or an irrelevance by what they considered an illegitimate entity and Hanna Sheehy Skeffington and Mary MacSwiney mounted a lonely protest outside the League chambers while the Free State delegates took their seats inside.

The Irish question had been the subject of newspaper headlines and diplomatic chatter for a generation and there was considerable interest in what the newly independent Irish would do and how their former masters would behave towards them. In some quarters it was feared Free State membership would mean another vote for Britain, to be added to those of Australia, Canada, New Zealand, South Africa, and that great anomaly of League membership, British-ruled India (Indian nationalists pointed out that the only claim for self-determination Indian representatives at Geneva could not vote for was their own). Opinion was won over to the idea that the Free State would adopt an independent and principled stance in its dealings at the League. Having spent years trying to persuade foreign opinion of the positive contribution an independent Ireland could make, the Irish were taken by surprise with their success. 'Somehow or other,' MacWhite mused, 'Ireland occupies a much larger place in the eyes of the foreigner than any other country of twice our size or population. It corresponds more to what we presumed ourselves to be before our recent disillusionment, than to any claims which we would be likely to advance today.' In order to capitalize on this, a well-defined and clearly identifiable League policy was needed. MacWhite was ambitious: a good first impression at Geneva and the country could soon hope to be regarded as one of the 'directing states', with a seat on the council a possibility for the future.[33] Translating interest into influence would not be straight forward, however, and six months after joining, his reports from Geneva revealed a sense of anti-climax. State building at home, the issue of partition and the business of day-to-day government were more immediate priorities. The first vote in the Dáil on the cost of League membership passed without comment in March 1924.

Geneva became the country's window on the world, and its representative there 'ambassador to the rest of the world'.[34] The Free State was

---

[33] Michael MacWhite report on the League of Nations, June 1923, NAI DFA Berne embassy box 6.
[34] *The Connacht Tribune*, 19 Jan. 1929.

keen to sign up to all the rights and responsibilities of League membership, including the collective security provisions enshrined in its covenant. While these 'guarantees of peace' as the League's instruments of arbitration and arms control were known at the time would ultimately remain untested, there was remarkably little debate in the Dáil on their import. The League of Nations (Guarantee) Act, adopted in 1923 to authorize membership of the League, comprised just two short articles committing the Free State to fulfilling the obligations of membership, including the imposition of economic or military sanctions if voted for by the League. How binding were these commitments on the Free State? The council of the League had ruled at its second meeting in March 1920 that neutrality was incompatible with the obligation on members to apply sanctions. Only Switzerland sought and received a derogation from imposing military sanctions, its neutral status formally recognized by the League. Other neutrals joined the League without making reservations. The covenant was amended in October the following year to allow each member to determine the extent to which a call for sanctions would be binding on it, a move that essentially made possible a position of military neutrality. The Free State would thus be able to reserve decisions on whether to commit troops in the event that military sanctions were voted for at Geneva.

Despite the constraints on its ability to act on the international level, the Free State wished to be seen as a model member of the League, meeting its commitments, paying its assessed contribution to the budget in full and transposing conventions from the International Labour Organisation (ILO) into law. This was done even when a similar provision was already on the statute book, prompting criticism from one member of the Dáil that funds were being wasted on 'a blessing from internationalists in Geneva'. The International Labour Organisation and the other technical bodies of the League were an important source of information which departments were able to draw on when preparing legislation. Enthusiasm for the work of the ILO was in keeping with the commitments contained in the *Democratic Programme* of January 1919 and reflected the influence of the Labour party.

The Free State aspired to a responsible and disinterested foreign policy and to act as a model international citizen. Aspiration alone would not enable Irish delegates to adopt a disinterested line on international issues. Like other small states at the time, the Irish were helped in their efforts to map out a foreign policy by the League. Possessing few resources and less clout, a small state is only able to pursue an active foreign policy when the international system provides an opportunity to do so. The League not only strengthened the sovereignty of small states, it also provided an arena in which they could pursue a multilateral foreign policy. Keeping an office at Geneva in a context of a small staff, and even smaller budget, was itself a statement of support for the League, one only some of its members would make. Geneva provided the Free State with a flow of information on world affairs and enabled it to engage directly with the League's fifty-four member states.

Despite the commitment of the League and its members to engage in a new form of diplomacy, the reality fell short of aspirations. The war had broken the mould of diplomacy and chancelleries across Europe struggled to adapt. As wartime alliances faded, America retreated into isolationism, Britain looked to its imperial possessions, and France faced the familiar problem of a European landmass dominated by Germany. New actors joined the stage: Czechoslovakia, Romania, and Yugoslavia formed the Little Entente to guard against Hapsburg revivalism; France looked to Poland and Romania as a buffer zone to constrain Germany and contain Russia. The search for security preoccupied the continental states but the resulting web of alliances and cooperation agreements would ultimately prove to be worthless.

With Germany and the Soviet Union outsiders, the decision by the United States not to join the League left the way clear for the European powers (they occasionally included Japan) to resurrect the concert of Europe through a series of conferences and meetings in the tradition of the nineteenth century. For all the talk of open diplomacy, meetings of the League were often a sideshow, the real decisions taken behind closed doors in Geneva hotels or at gatherings in continental spas and seaside resorts dubbed the '*politique des casinos*' by French president Raymond Poincaré. The scope for any small state to engage on matters beyond its concern was limited and the major international issues of the 1920s would be determined largely without reference to the Irish. This was equally true for other small states, which were neither consulted nor included in the schemes of the British, French, and Italians, while the challenge for medium sized states was to remain relevant.

A POLICY OF PRECEDENTS

It had been decided at the imperial conference in 1921 that the periodic gatherings of dominion premiers would be the foreign policy organ for the Empire, with Britain responsible for implementing policy in consultation with the dominions. The nature of this consultation was a topic for consideration at the Imperial Conference in October 1923 (another fall-out from the Chanak affair), the first attended by the Free State. The outcome was a commitment to periodic Foreign Office consultation with dominion high commissioners in London at which Irish participants would mostly listen, maintaining a reserved position on active engagement in the formulation of British foreign policy. Fresh from attending the assembly in Geneva, Eoin MacNeill's main contribution to the conference was to stress the need for Commonwealth policy to be based on the principles of the League.

It was a routine fisheries agreement rather than a full-blown international crisis that would present the Free State with its first opportunity to assert a right to a separate foreign policy. The Canadians had been negotiating agreements with the Americans since the 1870s, which were signed for them by British ambassadors in Washington, and there was nothing special about a treaty regulating halibut fishing agreed in March 1923. What mattered was not the subject but the signature affixed to it—that of a Canadian minister rather than a British ambassador. It was a breakthrough that Dublin would use to catch a far larger fish. If a dominion could sign a treaty without the need for a British intermediary, then in Dublin's view there was nothing stopping the dominions from appointing their own diplomats. Constitutionally speaking, both would be acting on behalf of the king. A first crack had appeared in the diplomatic unity of the empire.

Getting this view accepted and then copper-fastened became the Irish objective at the imperial conference. The issue was, in Walshe's assessment, the only point 'which really matters' on the agenda. The Irish delegation supported Canadian efforts to secure formal recognition of the dominions' right to negotiate and sign treaties that affected their interests through the work of a sub-committee conveniently chaired by Ernest Lapointe, the Canadian minister who had signed the halibut treaty. The resultant recognition of the precedent in the conference outcome cleared the way for the Free State to appoint its first properly accredited diplomat in the United States the following year.

The imperial conference did not alter the British insistence that agreements between Commonwealth members were not the same as other international agreements or that the provisions of international treaties, including those agreed at the League of Nations, did not apply between Commonwealth members. The British had secured the inclusion of a clause to this effect in an otherwise innocuous agreement on communications and transit negotiated in Barcelona in 1921. It quickly became known as the *inter se* clause as it excluded the terms of the agreement from applying between, or '*inter se*', Commonwealth members. The move was designed to clip dominion wings (they were not present in Barcelona) before they strayed too far from the concept of the diplomatic unity of the empire. It was also part of London's efforts to recover some of the constitutional ground lost to the dominions through their participation in the peace conference and admission to the League as individual members. It was one thing to recognize that a dominion government could use the agency of the king to sign a treaty with another country, as in the case of the halibut treaty. What the British were unwilling to accept was that the king could act severally in the same treaty on behalf of each of the dominions individually as to do so would undermine the idea of the diplomatic unity of the empire. In this sense, the halibut treaty represented a 'change of machinery' that did not affect the concept that the king represented the Commonwealth collectively. The *inter se* clause would prove to be a major obstacle for Irish foreign policy, as it effectively relegated the dominions to a secondary status in multilateral agreements. More importantly, it undermined the position of the Free State and other dominions as full and equal League members. It was thus essential to challenge its provisions from an early date.

The Commonwealth was an inescapable aspect of the Free State's external relations and the government sought to put a positive spin on membership in what justice minister, Kevin O'Higgins, called a 'miniature League of Nations', stressing the opportunities it presented to further establish the country's constitutional status.[35] As Joseph Walshe explained to his staff in March 1923, 'it is essential that you should realise how vague the position of the nations forming the British Commonwealth still remains with regard to foreign affairs'. To benefit from this, 'new customs and new precedents would have to be created'.[36] This would have to be done carefully, given the political, economic, and administrative weakness of the Free State, with much depending on the discretion of individuals. Walshe summarized the government's position as follows: 'our status will only be recognised by the world in proportion as we exercise the powers of a sovereign state through concrete acts'.[37] A policy of establishing precedents was adopted to exploit the ambiguity surrounding dominion status in the field of foreign policy.

USING THE LEAGUE: REGISTERING THE ANGLO-IRISH TREATY AT GENEVA

If the halibut treaty opened the door for changes in the way the Commonwealth states were represented abroad, it was a treaty nearer home that

---

[35] *Dáil Éireann deb.*, vol. 6, col. 3045, 9 April 1924.
[36] Walshe to Murphy, 1 Mar. 1923, NAI DFA letterbooks Paris, 1923–34.
[37] Walshe to MacWhite, 11 Mar. 1924, UCDA [MacWhite papers].

offered the first opportunity for the Free State to flex its constitutional muscles. Article 18 of the League covenant invited member states to register with the secretariat treaties concluded with another member state. The idea of registering the Anglo-Irish Treaty with the League had first been put forward in December 1921 and George Gavan Duffy had urged or this to be done on several occasions in 1922, but action could only be taken once the country was a member of the League. The cabinet decided in October 1923 that the Treaty should be registered in principle, but wanted to establish the likely reaction in Geneva and London before taking any action. There was no precedent for registering an agreement between two Commonwealth members with the League as none of the dominions had taken the step (the United States was not a League member so the issue of registering the halibut treaty did not arise). The attitude of the secretariat in Geneva would be crucial. Rejection of a bid to register the Treaty would damage the Free State's standing at Geneva and undermine its sovereignty, as the League would effectively be upholding the British view that dominions were not equal members of the organization.

Feelers were made during the winter of 1923 and into the following spring. A valuable source of information was the Waterford-born Edward Phelan, who was working as chief of the diplomatic division at the International Labour Organisation. Phelan's path to Geneva was via the British civil service where he had been employed on labour issues (he had been part of the first British mission to revolutionary Russia in 1919). He became one of the first employees at the ILO after its establishment by the Paris peace conference and would rise to become head of the Organisation during the Second World War, taking it into temporary exile in Montreal (with Seán Lester guarding the League in Geneva, two of the world's three international bodies had Irishmen at the helm for the duration of the war). The consummate Geneva insider, Phelan was a committed international-ist who believed in the League's mission to better mankind while remain-ing intensely patriotic and proud of the Free State's achievements since independence.[38] His political sympathies lay with Cumann na nGaedheal, dispensing advice to the Irish government on all aspects of League affairs, tipping Dublin off to British attempts to use the League secretariat to undermine the dominions' status and advising on ways to use the Geneva machinery to advance the Free State's goals. From his Geneva vantage point, Phelan was a convinced advocate of Treaty registration, grasping

---

[38] Fragments of an unpublished memoir by Phelan were published by the ILO— *Edward Phelan and the ILO, The Life and Views of an International Social Actor* (Geneva, 2009).

the implications for the Free State's status, and urged an initially cautious W. T. Cosgrave to take the step. After considerable deliberation, the cabinet finally decided on 1 July 1924 to lodge the Treaty with the secretariat directly, and this was done three days later on 4 July. The British were not informed until the following day.

It was hoped that registering the Treaty would accomplish a number of aims. League acceptance of the Treaty would establish its status as a full international agreement. It would provide a legal basis should the Free State wish to take action against Britain over non-implementation of the Treaty's provisions. Registration would also establish the formal equality of dominion membership with that of other states and punch a hole in British arguments that intra-Commonwealth agreements did not have the same legal status as treaties between other countries. Following internal consideration, the secretariat registered the Treaty on 11 July, confirming its status as an agreement between two equal members of the League. The decision grabbed the headlines, one Geneva correspondent calling it a 'diplomatic revolt'.[39] Everyone held their breath and waited to see how the British would react.

The news was greeted with surprise and anger in London. The British contended that the Treaty was not a treaty at all but a political document or an agreement between two Commonwealth members. Either way, it should not be registered with the League. This was not just an Irish issue for London—the British did not want agreements between any Commonwealth members to acquire the status of an international agreement and the Irish move, if not challenged, would achieve just that. The Colonial Office wrote to Cosgrave in August expressing concern at the Irish move but London did not formally react until early November, when the newly appointed Colonial Secretary in the conservative government, Leopold Amery, lodged a formal complaint with the Secretary General of the League. In it, the British government rejected the Irish position that the Treaty qualified for registration on the grounds that it was an agreement between two Commonwealth members. Crucially, however, it did not call for the registration to be undone.

In Dublin, the government was alarmed by the British move. In a lengthy memorandum in early December, Joseph Walshe summarized for FitzGerald the implications should the secretariat accept the British protest. At issue was whether or not the Free State was an equal member of the League. The other dominions had joined with Britain as a bloc and the British sat on the League council not as the United Kingdom or the

---

[39] *New York Times*, 24 Dec. 1924.

Commonwealth but as the British Empire. The Free State had not joined in this way, having been voted in by the League membership in its own right, but was nonetheless bound by Commonwealth practice. If the British position went unchallenged, Irish freedom of action at the League and elsewhere would be circumscribed. So far, no issue had arisen at the League on which the outcome depended on the number of Commonwealth votes, but this could not be ruled out. In the circumstances, it was essential that the Free State be free to determine its position independently and not be bound by or associated with a British vote. To accept the British view of the Treaty would be to acquiesce in 'the most barefaced explicit denial of equality'. Walshe's conclusion was stark: if the secretariat yielded to Britain and cancelled the registration, the Free State should give notice of its intention to quit the League.[40]

In the end, it did not come to this. Michael MacWhite reported widespread sympathy for the Irish position at Geneva, where the British note was the subject of considerable controversy among delegates gathered for a conference on opium production. A detailed legal analysis of the British case prepared by Edward Phelan upheld the Irish position and helped soothe nerves in Dublin. The government replied to the secretariat on 18 December, rejecting the British claims out of hand. On receipt of the note, League secretary general Drummond told MacWhite the British had 'no grounds to stand on'.[41] In public, the Irish response was presented as a defence of the equal rights of all League members, large and small. Privately, the government wondered what would have happened had the British note arrived before the secretariat had registered the Treaty. A major crisis in Irish League and Commonwealth policy had been averted. British objections continued into 1925, when the matter was quietly dropped, only to arise again in December that year when the Irish registered the Treaty amendment incorporating the outcome of the Boundary Commission (the British protested again, but this time half-heartedly).

Registration of the Treaty dominated discussions in the Dáil, the first time since membership that the chamber had held a proper debate on the benefits of League membership. In light of the outcome achieved in 1924, it is questionable whether the degree of caution pursued was justified. It would take time for the Irish to develop a sense of confidence vis-à-vis the British and when using international machinery to advance their interests. An important precedent had nonetheless been established, and a practice that would continue after its constitutional value became obsolete with the

---

[40] Walshe to FitzGerald, 1 Dec. 1924, NAI DFA 417/105.
[41] MacWhite to Walshe, 23 Dec. 1924, NAI DFA 417/105.

registration at the UN of subsequent agreements between Ireland and the United Kingdom relating to Northern Ireland.

PARTITION AND NORTHERN IRELAND

One of the main reasons for registering the Treaty was the looming problem of the Boundary Commission it established to finalize the border between the Free State and Northern Ireland. The North Eastern Boundary Bureau, established in 1923 to manage the Free State's engagement with the commission, took a keen interest in the machinery of the League, hoping to find a lever or a useful precedent to support Dublin's case for boundary change in Ireland. The peacemakers had failed or found it impossible to craft ethnically homogenous states in 1919 and had compensated by creating a number of commissions charged with overseeing boundary polls in Upper Silesia, East Prussia, and Carinthia. They had also imposed a raft of treaties and conventions intended to protect the many minorities included within the new states in Eastern Europe, minorities whose own right to self-determination the conference had overlooked or ignored.

The Bureau closely studied these cases as well as the League arbitration between Sweden and Finland over the status of the Åland Islands. As we have seen, the Bureau's Tyrone-born director, Kevin O'Shiel, advocated joining the League before the Boundary Commission began its work as a way to highlight the different status of the two jurisdictions on the island of Ireland.[42] He pressed for registration of the Anglo-Irish Treaty on similar grounds. On their first appearance at Geneva, Irish delegates supported Finland in its dispute with the Soviet Union over autonomy for the Finnish-speaking province of Karelia ('a kind of Finnish Six Counties') and took particular interest in the workings of the League's machinery for dealing with minorities, including its commissioner for refugees, the Norwegian polar explorer Fridtjof Nansen. The terms of the Treaty of Lausanne were also seen through the prism of partition (sympathy for Turkey).

Official preoccupation with international parallels to partition was mirrored in the public sphere by the interest journals such as *Studies* took in minority issues in Czechoslovakia, Alsace-Lorraine, and elsewhere. These were also viewed through the lens of Northern Ireland, as testified

---

[42] For an account of O'Shiel's life and career, see Eda Sagarra, *Kevin O'Shiel, Tyrone Nationalist and Irish State-Builder* (Dublin, 2013).

by a 1923 description of Catalonia as 'a tiny six county state'.[43] The League was viewed with suspicion by the unionist establishment in Belfast not because of any potential to interfere in the way Northern Ireland was run but because of the challenge it was seen as posing to Britain and the Commonwealth, a challenge in which an up-start Free State was playing a prominent role. Commenting on the decision to register the Treaty in Geneva, the Belfast-based *Morning Post* ruefully observed 'it is curious how at every turn this League of Nations comes up to hit us in the eye'.[44]

From their Geneva perspective, both MacWhite and Phelan repeatedly urged the government to use the League machinery to highlight the issue of partition. But, in contrast to the sore thumb policy pursued at the Council of Europe in the late 1940s, partition was not raised at Geneva.[45] The widely held assumption in Dublin was that the boundary commission would resolve the issue by awarding sufficient territory to the Free State to render Northern Ireland unviable. When this turned out not to be the case, and the commission's report of 1925 resulted in no change to the border, the government effectively shelved the problem of partition. It was unwilling to adopt a confrontational policy abroad on the North fearing international opinion would side with Britain. Cosgrave explained his reasoning to Edward Phelan the month after publication of the boundary commission report:

> What I feared more than anything was an appeal to the League. Putting myself in the position of, say, France or Spain, or even one of the South American members, my inclination would be to say go home and solve your domestic difficulties—that the League had more than enough to do to solve international problems. [There was an attempt to place the problem on an international basis.] (sic) It was originally an international question. But I am afraid the five years that elapsed made it no longer a question to be solved between the British and ourselves: it developed into a difficulty for solution between Irishmen.[46]

For *The Irish Times*, it was not the government's policy at Geneva but its ambitions in the Commonwealth sphere that provoked the greatest concern, which the newspaper would frequently link to the issue of partition. Opposed to any loosening of the bonds with London and the dominions

---

[43] J. Ryan, 'A new era in Spain', *Studies*, no. 13, Sept. 1924, p. 467.

[44] *The Morning Post*, 17 Dec. 1924.

[45] The issue of discrimination against nationalist workers in Northern Ireland was raised by the Free State at the ILO in the context of rules governing the issue of work permits.

[46] Cosgrave to Phelan, 16 Jan. 1926, NAI DT S5985. Brackets inserted by hand in original.

on principle, the need to placate imperially-minded Ulster was cited in defence of the status quo, as on the eve of a Commonwealth gathering in 1929, when the newspaper would warn ministers that reunification would not be brought any nearer by the Free State becoming 'a simulacrum of a dominion'.[47]

The problem of partition led external affairs in different directions at different times, sometimes seeking to accentuate the difference between the Free State and Northern Ireland while on other occasions pursuing a less confrontational approach towards its existence and that of the British tradition on the island. At all times, however, the goal was the same—the ending of partition. Efforts were made to refer to Ireland instead of the Free State where to do so would not create legal or constitutional difficulties. Responding to League circulars, officials were told to include general details for the whole island while providing statistics for the Free State alone. The use of a map of the island unblemished by the border on postage stamps and elsewhere in the public sphere were psychologically satisfying gestures.

At a practical level, the free travel area between the Free State and the United Kingdom constrained policy freedom in areas such as visa requirements, where British practice would be followed.[48] Official support was provided to the Dublin-based Football Association of the Irish Free State in its bid to secure international recognition alongside the Belfast-based Irish Football Association from which it had split. Concern was also voiced at the 'lamentable effect' of the exclusion rules regarding soccer and rugby adopted by the Gaelic Athletic Association which, in Joseph Walshe's words, left these games 'in the hands of the shoneens (sic)'.[49] James McNeill was instructed to lay a wreath at the cenotaph in London on armistice day in 1924, it having been agreed that the tricolour would be carried by the Irish veterans parading: the display of the Irish flag by unionist elements at such 'British' events was to be encouraged until they were 'completely absorbed in the Saorstát and weaned altogether from their attachment to British institutions'.[50] The official line was to stress the service of Irishmen in the war as Ireland's most recent contribution to

[47] *The Irish Times*, 29 Oct. 1929.

[48] For a detailed examination of this issue, see Elizabeth Meehan, *Free Movement between Ireland and the United Kingdom: From the 'Common Travel Area' to the Common Travel Area* (Dublin, 2000).

[49] Walshe to Vaughan Dempsey, 20 April 1923, NAI DFA box 28. 'shoneen' an anglicization of 'seánín', or 'little John' as in John Bull, was a term of abuse used to describe the pro-British element in Irish life.

[50] Walshe to James McNeill, 2 July 1924, NAI DFA letterbooks, High Commission London, 1924.

international peace. The position was different where remembrance ceremonies would have a purely British character, such as the inauguration of
the Munster memorial at the Somme in 1924. On that, as on other such
occasions, the Free State representative was advised not to attend.[51]

TROUBLE WITH TREATIES

The Free State had succeeded in using the League machinery to register the
Anglo-Irish Treaty, but the country's role in relation to broader international agreements was less easy to resolve. Having no hand in their
conclusion did not mean the Free State could disassociate itself from the
outcome of big power deals. As a Commonwealth member, it was required
to ratify a range of international agreements so that they could take effect;
some of them had been negotiated before it had even existed. This raised
awkward questions for the Free State about its status, its responsibility for
deals agreed by London, and its ability to conclude its own treaties.

These questions crystalized in the spring of 1924, when the Free State
was asked to ratify the Anglo-American Liquor Treaty, a prohibition-era
arrangement allowing the United States to search foreign vessels within an
hour's sailing of the American coast. The British negotiated the treaty with
the Americans, having told the dominions that they would do so in a way
that would not require any action by them. What emerged, however, was a
treaty that would have to be approved by each Commonwealth parliament. Uncomfortably for the Irish government, it was signed by a British
ambassador in the name of the 'United Kingdom of Great Britain and
Ireland' on behalf of the British Empire. Desmond FitzGerald found
himself in hot water when he tabled the treaty for approval in the Dáil
without the preamble containing the offending references. Forced to
confess it had been left out to avoid focusing debate on the royal title (a
move which failed), he admitted to the house that the government had not
yet asked for a change to the Royal Titles Act while discussions were
ongoing on the issue of the Northern Ireland boundary (which, the
government hoped, would change the nature and extent of the United
Kingdom by rendering partition unviable).[52] An angry Seán Milroy
expressed the views of many when, with more than an echo of Woodrow
Wilson, he warned the government 'let us not start with that old game of

---

[51] See file at NAI DFA GR225.
[52] This was a source of dispute between the two countries, as it required British
legislation to change the royal title. This was achieved in 1926.

secret diplomacy in this new-born state'.[53] FitzGerald was forced to concede that the government had been consulted in advance and that the British had acted for the Free State in signing the treaty. This prompted angry calls that the Free State should not be associated with international agreements in which it had little or no interest. The government was in a weak position arguing for treaties it had neither initiated nor had a role in negotiating but it had sufficient votes to pass the treaty. The Dáil had put down a marker that it would not unquestioningly rubber stamp treaties concluded by the British.

The problem arose again a few months later, when Dublin was invited to ratify the Treaty of Lausanne with Turkey. The last piece of the post-war peace settlement, it was necessary because the Turkish Republic had repudiated the Treaty of Sèvres which the allies had imposed on the Ottoman Empire in 1920. The Free State had not existed when negotiations for a new treaty began in November 1922. Once agreed, it could only enter into force if ratified by each of the dominions, which now included the Free State. The government thus found itself under pressure from London to signal its assent.

The eastern Mediterranean might have seemed far away (and many questioned whether it was really necessary for the Free State to make peace with Turkey), but the treaty's military clauses raised very real questions. It was unclear whether the British could commit the dominions to war as a group or whether one of them could remain at peace if the others took military action. The dominions had flexed their constitutional muscles in 1922 by refusing to commit troops at Chanak, and they did so again now, declining to ratify the Treaty of Lausanne. The Canadians objected first and were followed by the Irish: both wished to make sure they would not be committed to military action if the treaty were broken.

In the Dáil, debate focused on this key question and the wider authority of the British to negotiate and conclude treaties on the Free State's behalf. The motion to ratify made clear the government's view that only Britain would be committed to hostilities if the treaty's terms were broken, a position in keeping with article forty-nine of the Free State constitution which required parliamentary approval on matters of war. Privately, the government told London it would ratify the treaty in return for movement on Dublin's agenda of issuing its own passports and appointing a minister in Washington (negotiations were dragging on both fronts). The need for dominion ratification afforded some leverage but an important political point was also being asserted. In Irish eyes, parliamentary ratification was necessary because the Treaty of Lausanne was about questions of war and

[53] *Dáil Éireann deb.*, vol. 6, col. 2931, 4 April 1924.

peace. As Darrell Figgis astutely observed, if a Dáil vote was needed to end a state of war, it followed that one was also needed to declare one, a further chink in the diplomatic unity of the empire.[54]

RAISING THE FLAG IN WASHINGTON

The Boundary Commission consumed resources, time, and political capital, dominating exchanges between Dublin and London in 1924 and 1925. The issue may have been a political priority, but it was not pursued at the expense of other objectives in the external sphere. Desmond FitzGerald and his officials became regular visitors to London for a series of ad hoc conferences with the British on issues such as passports, visas, and the role of British diplomats in handling Irish affairs. Discussions were often difficult, the Foreign Office seeking to resist Irish moves, the Colonial Office seeking to smooth the way, occasionally acting as umpire. The main prize that Dublin set its sights on was appointing its own diplomats abroad and the first location selected was Washington. As FitzGerald told the Dáil, it was more important to have one properly accredited minister than a long list of unrecognized ones.[55] In linking the Free State's status to that of Canada, the Treaty had created an opening as Ottawa had secured the right in 1920 to appoint a minister plenipotentiary in Washington. Opinion in the Canadian capital was divided on how to manage relations with the great neighbour to the south, however, and the option had not been taken up. Despite the changes since the war, British embassies still represented the interests of dominions, colonies, and the motherland.

The cabinet decided in early 1923 that it would begin moves to open a legation[56] in the American capital and a reference to this goal was included in the first draft of the Ministers and Secretaries Bill. The reference was removed following a British reminder that consultation was needed before external appointments could be made, but the government remained keen to secure diplomatic status for Smiddy in Washington. Eoin MacNeill sounded out the British on opening a legation while attending the imperial conference in October. The proposal met with a cool response. Negotiations on issuing Irish passports were stalled at the time and,

---

[54] Ibid., vol. 8, col. 173–5, 9 July 1925.

[55] Ibid., vol. 8, col. 835, 9 July 1924.

[56] At the time it was the practice for major powers to exchange embassies headed by ambassadors. Other states maintained legations in foreign capitals headed by diplomats with the rank of minister, as did the major powers in smaller countries. This practice would change with the formal recognition of the equality of all states in the UN Charter.

preoccupied with the Ruhr crisis and economic collapse in Germany, the Foreign Office played for time.

It would be anachronistic to attribute a nascent special relationship between the Free State and the United States based on ties of kin, or suggest a desire to forge relations with the new state lay behind early moves. As we have seen, successive US administrations wished to remove the Irish question as an irritant in relations between Washington and London and a factor in domestic politics. The reasons for seeking to establish diplomatic relations with the United States were more prosaic: a pressing need to counter anti-Treaty activity; a desire to raise much-needed funds for the new state and an underlying nationalist dream of wielding influence through the diaspora. Intelligence sharing and cooperation between security services were a further impetus. Throughout 1923, anti-Treaty activity based across the Atlantic posed a very real threat to the interest of the Free State government and its efforts to bring the civil war to a close. The political machine built up during the campaign for independence was a valuable prize and if the Free State could not capture it, it aimed to shut it down.

The issue that spurred the government to act was the need to secure a separate Free State quota in US immigration legislation. Smiddy had reported growing difficulties engaging with the administration on this and other issues. His efforts to influence opinion on Capitol Hill were hampered by a lack of diplomatic status meaning he had to resort to 'back door methods' that did not always yield the desired result.[57] This highlighted the limits of the semi-official nature of dominion representatives abroad—were they trade representatives alone or should there be a political aspect to their work? The cabinet decided on 1 March to press ahead with the appointment. The Colonial Office was officially notified two days later and, citing the Canadian precedent, asked to approach the Americans for their agreement. The request met with a mixed response in London. The Foreign Office was determined to ensure that the Irish would not take up the Canadian precedent. The Colonial Office was more sympathetic, raising the prospect of disagreement between two branches of the British government over how to respond to Irish demands.

When the Irish had first raised the idea of appointing a diplomatic representative in the summer of 1923, Lionel Curtis had warned Dublin would press ahead with more far-reaching demands if its requests were denied. Curtis, who was now working as the Colonial Office's advisor on Irish affairs, predicted the Free State would succeed in opening diplomatic

---

[57] Smiddy to Walshe, 25 Jan. 1924, NAI DFA D2055A.

relations with the United States one way or another and urged his counterparts at the Foreign Office to work with the Colonial Office to bring this about in a way that did least damage to British interests. Failure to do so, he cautioned, would risk the Irish developing 'a whole paraphernalia of diplomatic relations' with unwelcome knock-on effects on the dominions.[58] Opposed to the idea of dominion foreign policy in general and to Irish ambitions in particular, this was advice many in the Foreign Office were unwilling to heed. Senior officials resented the speed at which concessions were being granted in the diplomatic field. They were also put out at the Colonial Office's involvement in their affairs as well as the disregard, as they saw it, for the diplomatic unity of the empire, complaining that 'the Colonial Office go too fast as usual'.

The advent of the Labour government of Ramsay MacDonald in March was a fillip to Irish aspirations. Although short-lived, it provided a window in which progress could be achieved on Dublin's agenda that might not so easily have been achieved had the Conservatives remained in power. A combination of personality and politics meant the new Colonial Secretary, J. H. Thomas, was an easier proposition for the Irish to deal with on this issue. A breakthrough seemed close when Thomas responded to the Irish note on 24 April, conceding that the Canadian precedent entitled the Free State to appoint a minister in Washington. However, weeks of wrangling and inaction followed, with the Foreign Office frustrating progress, prompting Joseph Walshe to conclude 'we have no friends there'.[59]

The Americans were at first reluctant to see an Irish legation open its doors, fearing this would result in the other dominions following suit, thereby complicating their relations with the British. Concern at the potential influence on the Irish community in America was also a factor. The experience of Irish agitation over the previous four years provided ample evidence to sustain such fears and doubtless this was a concern encouraged by the British. Ironically, it was this argument, or rather its reverse, which the Free State used to press its case, asserting that the presence of an Irish legation operating through recognized diplomatic channels was the best way to prevent unwelcome political activism on US soil. That year, 1924, was also an election year in the United States and the administration calculated that agreeing to the Irish request would help with the Irish vote. The State Department nonetheless checked at every step with the British before acceding to the Irish request.

[58] Lionel Curtis memorandum, 14 June 1923, PRO, CO 739/21/28787.
[59] Walshe to James McNeill, 21 May 1924, NAI, DFA letterbooks, High Commission London 1924.

The wheels of diplomacy move slowly at the best of times, but in Dublin the delay in progressing the appointment was attributed to inaction or worse by a reluctant middleman. Far from sharing any sense of urgency, the Foreign Office procrastinated. A note despatched from the Foreign Office to the British ambassador in Washington, Sir Esme Howard, referred to both apprehension and dislike of the proposed appointment. Howard had an Irish connection, having briefly served as secretary to the Lord Lieutenant of Ireland in 1885, and developed a working relationship with Smiddy countering republican activity in America. He did not anticipate any difficulties working with an Irish legation and did nothing to block or delay the appointment. Frustrated at the slow pace and in an effort to shake things up, FitzGerald announced Smiddy's appointment in the Dáil on 13 June.

The move prompted a flurry of activity in London and Washington. It would require a hastily convened conference in London a week later, on 21 and 23 June, between FitzGerald, Thomas, and officials from the Colonial and Foreign Offices, to iron out the details. Out-manoeuvred, the Foreign Office was unable to delay any further and instead sought to place limits on what the Irish minister could do. It was agreed that Smiddy would not have the status of envoy extraordinary or the power to negotiate treaties. The Foreign Office insisted the Irish legation would represent only Free State interests, with Commonwealth and imperial issues remaining the responsibility of the British embassy. Although the Irish minister would not be subject to the British ambassador's control, it was agreed the two would keep in close touch. In return, the Irish insisted that the countersignature of the British Foreign Secretary be omitted from Smiddy's letter of appointment. The Foreign Office had privately asked the Americans to take the seniority of the dominion into account when determining diplomatic precedence, in the hope that a Canadian minister might appear to save the day. When it became clear this was not going to happen, the number two at the British embassy was promoted so that he would outrank an Irish minister during the ambassador's absence. The negotiations had all the hallmarks of an acrimonious divorce and must have been seen that way by a Foreign Office fretful of where the experiment would lead.

Despite the agreements reached in London, the note to the State Department on 24 June referred to the appointment as a British proposal rather than a decision of the Irish government, prompting disappointment and anger in Dublin. The Americans replied favourably four days later, despite having expressed reservations about the desirability of separate dominion legations, concerns the British had not communicated to Dublin. Having lost the argument, the Foreign Office delayed production of

Figure 7. Timothy Smiddy presenting credentials with J. B. Wright of the State Department, Washington DC, 8 October 1924 (Image courtesy of Library of Congress LC-F8-32727 [P&P])

Smiddy's credentials by a further month. The first fully accredited dominion diplomat, he presented his credentials to President Calvin Coolidge on 7 October without the British ambassador being present, and the Free State office in Washington was upgraded to the status of legation.

The appointment had been secured just in time; the return of the Conservatives to government in London two months later brought a new vigour to British views on the place of the dominions that would have made progress on Irish ambitions harder to achieve. The Foreign Office remained unhappy, predicting the 'experiment, to which we are unfortunately committed . . . is foredoomed to failure'.[60] As if to confirm these fears, the State Department told London in December it would be unable to differentiate between dominion diplomats and those from other countries. The Foreign Office would be proved correct in believing this step in the dark would have repercussions for central control over Empire foreign policy. In 1926, the Canadians followed the Irish lead in opening a legation in Washington and, in the following years, Dublin, Ottawa, and

[60] For Foreign Office views on the appointment of Smiddy, see file at PRO, FO 371/ 1638/3931.

Pretoria opened more missions, challenging the British right to set foreign policy for the Commonwealth. A Foreign Office memorandum reflected on the consequences in 1928:

> What a fatal error it was ever to consent to the Dominions having their own diplomatic representation in foreign capitals. Of course we cannot go back on that, or on the equally foolish step of admitting the Irish Free State to equal status with the Dominions. But we can realise that it means a process of disintegration which we may check but cannot stay.[61]

The first Irish diplomat had been appointed.

The government heralded the Washington appointment as an out-working of the Treaty settlement and proof of the international status the Free State enjoyed. Reaction to the appointment was not uniformly positive, however. Anti-Treaty republicans were dismissive, highlighting the role of the British monarch, in whose name as head of state in Ireland the appointment was made. In the *Catholic Bulletin* J. J. O'Kelly dismissed Smiddy as 'a political sandwich man sent to Washington to advertise the free gifts of England'.[62] Two years later, one of the first election posters produced by the new Fianna Fáil party in 1926 took up the theme: 'Ambassadors—How are you!!' it asked, printing in full Smiddy's letter of credentials from George V to highlight the role of the crown.[63] The first and probably only occasion an ambassador's letter of appointment would receive prominent billing in an Irish election, it was a foretaste of the scrutiny Fianna Fáil would bring to the government's external relations and the role of the British crown when it entered parliament the following year.

Smiddy's appointment encouraged hopes at external affairs that similar steps would follow in Europe. Drawing up the estimates for departmental spending in January 1925, Joseph Walshe hoped it would not be long before closed offices would be reopened. But the estimates as finally approved made no mention of any new appointments and the following year saw yet more closures. Despite the department's hopes, there would be no further openings until 1929. An unlikely exception was the appointment of William Craig Martin as trade commissioner in China in 1924. An insurance-broker in Shanghai who had become friends with the FitzGeralds in Kerry where both families holidayed, Craig Martin had absorbed his friend's nationalist outlook and applied for the job. The

---

[61] Foreign Office minute in dossier concerning appointment of Irish ministers in Paris and Berlin, 28 Sept. 1928, PRO, FO372/2436/10861.

[62] *Catholic Bulletin*, Aug. 1924, p. 663.

[63] Fianna Fáil election poster, NLI ELE/1920–30/2.

Figure 8. Fianna Fáil election Poster, 'Ambassadors, How Are You!' *c.* 1926 (Image courtesy of the National Library of Ireland NLI EPH F 49)

following year, he was confirmed as honorary consul in Shanghai. The building that housed the Free State office still stands at number two Peking Road, amid the banks and trading houses of the historic Bund. Political upheaval in China would see the office close in 1928, as Craig Martin moved his business to Beijing and an Irish consulate general would not open in Shanghai until 1999. His appointment did not, however, signal an opening for Ireland in Asia. A result solely of his friendship with

FitzGerald, it reflected instead the value of personal connections in post-civil war public life. An application by another businessman, William Hickie in Yokohama, to be appointed trade officer in Japan was turned down despite support from the trade ministry, while plans for a trade representative in Argentina were shelved in 1926 following an unfavourable police report (which invariably meant suspicion of anti-Treaty sympathies) on the individual concerned.

A SMALL STATE FOREIGN POLICY?

Although it had been a long-standing nationalist tradition to lament the country's location between Britain and the Atlantic, post-settlement this had become an asset. Compared to most other European states in the post-war years, the Free State was fortunate in its geographical location. Under the terms of the Anglo-Irish Treaty, the defence of Irish coasts was vested in the British navy, until such time as the government acquired the means to take responsibility for its own defence. The Free State was effectively in a British naval exclusion zone. British troops in Northern Ireland and the Treaty ports meant an aggressor could expect a swift British response. With the exception of brief fears of a German or British invasion in 1940, the Free State's security was not at risk. The benefits of the British military umbrella were not only financial. It allowed the Free State to pose convincingly as a pacific country, with a small army for the purposes of defence alone. With the end of the civil war, it was possible to reduce the number of army battalions from twenty-seven in 1924 to five in 1930. The Irish could say they had disarmed, a requirement of League membership, giving them a certain moral advantage. If the new states of Eastern Europe had too many enemies and not enough friends,[64] this was not a problem the Free State shared. Because its security was not challenged, the Free State was freer to pursue a more principled foreign policy than many small countries at the time. As an Estonian government minister noted in 1923, the Free State might not enjoy complete sovereignty, but his own republic's fuller independence was little defence against the intentions of Moscow or Berlin.[65]

This allowed a degree of latitude in Irish thinking on foreign policy. With no immediate threats, it was easy to agree with Desmond FitzGerald's assessment that 'the view of the small nations will always be nearer to the

[64] Sally Marks, *The Ebbing of European Ascendancy: An International History of the World, 1919–1945* (London, 2002), p. 276.
[65] *Studies*, Mar. 1923, pp. 7–25.

Ten Commandments than the point of view of the big nations'. This view was shared on the Labour benches, where party leader Thomas Johnson argued the Free State had taken its place among the nations 'in the hope of playing at least our little part in the formation of world opinion in regard to human progress'.[66] The Catholic *Irish Monthly* hoped Ireland would 'be a beacon shedding the light of holiness' in the world, while the *Church of Ireland Gazette* urged the country 'to forget her own little troubles in contemplation of the vast distress of mankind'.[67] The *Irish Statesman* believed Ireland could become 'the international mediator of the world'.[68] League of Nations enthusiast Bolton Waller argued in a 1928 work that 'if Ireland is to stand high in the eyes of the world it must be by intellectual and moral attainments, by achievements in the spiritual rather than the physical realm', language not far removed from that of the republican Mary MacSwiney during the Treaty debates seven years earlier.[69]

But a tension existed between aspirations towards an independent and principled line in foreign affairs and the need to avoid alienating the British, from whom it was hoped to secure further concessions in the constitutional field. Delegates were told to avoid any suspicion of hostility to the British in interventions at international conferences. This was important for a number of reasons. Apart from the obstacles London could place in the path of Irish constitutional development, as a permanent member of the League council and one of the post-war 'Big Four', Britain was too powerful to have as an enemy. The small states with which the Irish sought to associate would have little to do with it under such circumstances nor would other dominions follow an Irish lead if it were seen to be anti-British. Foreign policy rhetoric still had much of the old nationalist ring to it, and causes were espoused with little thought of the consequences. This doublethink was part of the wider difficulties posed by the transition to independence and it would take time for mentalities to adjust. However unpalatable for some, the new Irish state had interests just like any other.

---

[66] *Dáil Éireann deb.*, vol. 11, col. 1452, 13 May 1925; *Dáil Éireann deb.*, vol. 8, col. 817, 9 July 1924.
[67] *Irish Monthly*, Feb. 1924; *Church of Ireland Gazette*, 2 June 1922.
[68] *Irish Statesman*, 12 April 1924.
[69] Bolton C. Waller, *Hibernia, or the Future of Ireland* (London, 1928), p. 51.

6

The Free State and the Search for European Security, 1925–1926

As the Christmas season approached in December 1923, Michael Mac-White penned a note in Geneva to the editor of *The Freeman's Journal*, Patrick Hooper in Dublin, bemoaning the insular approach to foreign policy of some in official circles at home. 'They can no more ignore their foreign relations,' he mused 'than, say, a farmer can afford to ignore the neighbours on whom he is dependent for the harvesting and the market-ing of his produce.'[1] He may have been prompted to write by the *Free-man's* editorial the previous week warning the government not to neglect the country's foreign relations.[2] The glow of the Free State's entry to the League was beginning to fade and the British had revived efforts at the *inter se* clause. The farming metaphor was apposite. The axiom that good fences make for good neighbours was being tested at home with the Boundary Commission and across the broader front of Irish–British relations.

If arguments in the Boundary Commission centred once again on what Winston Churchill had called in 1921 'the dreary steeples of Fermanagh and Tyrone', on the continent it was the larger challenge of reconciling France and Germany that preoccupied politicians and diplomats. Six years after the end of the war, the search for European security seemed no closer to a solution. Versailles was an incomplete peace. A series of further agreements concluded in the years after adjusted and governed a complex arrangement of reparations payments and military checks and balances, culminating in the Treaty of Locarno in 1925.

The search for European security intruded into Irish politics in the summer of 1924, when the British convened a conference in London to address the issue of German reparations payments. Up to then, the Free State had not been troubled by continental politics. Generally sympathetic to schemes for European reconstruction, it viewed the various proposals of

---

[1] MacWhite to P. J. Hooper, 15 Dec. 1923, UCDA P194/145.
[2] *The Freeman's Journal*, 7 Dec. 1923.

the British and French primarily from a domestic perspective, watchful lest it find itself committed without being consulted to unwelcome obligations or rearguard efforts to circumscribe its international status. The aim of the London Reparations Conference was to stabilize the German economy so that reparations payments could resume. The question of how the dominions should be represented arose when the conference met in July. Faced with French objections to having them at the table, the British government claimed there was insufficient time to reach agreement on individual dominion representation and asked for dominion understanding. The Irish were not pleased at the suggestion they would not be involved in the negotiations. Joseph Walshe's instructions to the high commissioner in London were clear: either the Free State was present or it would neither sign nor ratify the agreement afterwards. Ratification of the Lausanne and Anglo-American liquor treaties had been achieved with difficulty, and the Dáil was unlikely to pass further agreements negotiated in this way.[3] A meeting of the high commissioners with Ramsay MacDonald and the Colonial Secretary at Downing Street on 11 July was unable to reach agreement on British proposals for a form of joint or rotating dominion presence. Both were equally unacceptable to the Irish and Canadians. Dublin was anxious to bring to an end to the practice of being bound by British signatures on treaties it had no hand in negotiating. The government was, nonetheless, sympathetic to the aims of the conference, which gave birth to the Dawes Plan, and did not wish to stand in the way of efforts to secure continental stability. The Free State agreed on this occasion, therefore, not to press for a seat at the table.

The London conference stabilized the economic situation, but did not solve the underlying problem of how to provide security guarantees for the French, Belgians, and others. Following an initiative from the smaller states with the tacit backing of France, the League assembly had recognized in September 1922 the 'indissoluble connection' between security and disarmament. The resolution adopted made a disarmament agreement, something the League was mandated to pursue under article 8 of its covenant, conditional on conclusion of a general defensive pact. It bore fruit the following autumn in a draft Treaty of Mutual Assistance, designed to provide the means to enforce security in the event that a League member was threatened. The powers of the League council were expanded, allowing it to designate an aggressor and decide on the imposition of sanctions, including the direction of military forces. A disarmament

---

[3] Walshe to McNeill, 9 July 1924, NAI DFA D3904.

plan was to follow. The text was presented at the assembly in September 1923, the session at which the Free State joined the League.

The Free State was in favour of the proposed treaty, taking part in the work of the preparatory commission charged with finalizing the text. Dublin could say that it had disarmed, an obligation of League membership largely honoured in the breach by its larger members. Prior to admission, Irish delegates had been required to commit to respecting these limits. National disarmament was in equal measure a political necessity, a financial imperative and an international obligation presented as an act of good faith. The Free State gained credibility through participation, in however passive a manner, at naval and other disarmament conferences for largely constitutional reasons. It was also in the interest of smaller states to constrain the armaments of their larger neighbours.

THE GENEVA PROTOCOL

Despite its origins in Anglo-French discussions, London rejected the draft Treaty on 5 July 1924, unwilling to accept the powers provided to the council or the obligations to take military action enshrined in its provisions. By then the British had conceived of a wider scheme to provide France the security guarantees it sought to enable continental disarmament to commence. Fresh from the success of the London Reparations Conference, Ramsay MacDonald announced his plan for a general scheme for arbitration and disarmament that would build on the commitments contained in the League covenant. Franco-British discussions over the summer resulted in proposals for a 'Geneva Protocol for the Pacific Settlement of International Disputes', unveiled by both premiers at the League assembly in September.

The 'Geneva Protocol' was an attempt to address the conundrum: which should come first, security or disarmament, a question it answered with a triple formula of arbitration, security, and disarmament. It provided an automatic system for arbitration of disputes with failure to accept arbitration one of the tests of aggression. States which signed up to the protocol effectively renounced recourse to war unless with the council's consent or at its behest. Signatories were also required to refer judicial disputes to the Permanent Court of International Justice in The Hague, whose ruling would be final. Non-judicial disputes would be referred to the League council, which, if unable to rule by unanimity, would refer the matter for binding arbitration. Internal, including colonial, disputes were, naturally, excluded; by mutual assent the colonial powers did not wish to bind themselves when dealing with problems in their overseas possessions.

The final piece of the jigsaw was a general disarmament agreement to be negotiated at a disarmament conference planned for July 1925. To ensure that states negotiated this latter element in good faith, the terms of the protocol would not enter into force until the disarmament plan had been agreed.

League members unanimously signalled their assent to the principles behind the protocol in October, but negotiations at Geneva led by the Czech and Greek prime ministers produced a more wide-ranging document than intended by its original sponsors. The French and Belgians signed up immediately, anxious to secure the British military guarantees they had failed to achieve bilaterally. In London, however, the Labour government developed cold feet, concerned at the potentially open-ended implications for Britain's armed forces if called upon to act. The Conservative administration that replaced it in November poured cold water on the whole project, opposed to continental entanglements or anything that might risk conflict with the United States. Geography dictated that this was also a Canadian concern, while the other non-European dominions were equally unenthusiastic about becoming embroiled in disputes in far off places that had little to do with them.

As British difficulties with the protocol became clear, the question of the Irish approach came into focus. Michael MacWhite pressed his superiors to sign up to it in protest at the British note in November which had challenged the Free State's decision to register the Anglo-Irish Treaty. The difference of opinion generated friction between Dublin and London at the time.[4] Calmer heads prevailed in Dublin as the government assessed how to position itself. Earlier that month, FitzGerald had told the Dáil that the government agreed with the goals of the protocol but needed time to study it. The council postponed discussion of the protocol at its December meeting and, as 1925 began, it was increasingly clear that it faced an uncertain future. Austen Chamberlain delivered the *coup de grace* in Geneva on 12 March, having stopped off in Paris to deliver the bad news first. He told a meeting of the League council that neither Britain nor the dominions could accept its terms. The statement was a blow for the countries of central Europe, who received the news like 'a death sentence' in MacWhite's account of the meeting. Requests for clarification on the Irish position had been met with the reply that consideration was still ongoing, and Chamberlain was obliged to indicate he was not speaking for the Free State. MacWhite reported a flurry in the room, as

[4] MacWhite to Walshe, 6 Dec. 1924, NAI DFA 417/105.

a number of delegations assumed this meant the Free State would support the protocol.[5]

However, Dublin was moving in the opposite direction. Two weeks after Chamberlain dropped his Geneva bombshell, FitzGerald told the Dáil on 25 March 1925 that the Free State had not signed up to the protocol and that the British rejection meant he could not recommend its acceptance. In fact, the cabinet had already decided to reject it. An internal memorandum written a week before Chamberlain's Geneva statement had warned that accepting the protocol would increase difficulties with Britain and advised the government to 'reject it for its defects than to consider it for its advantages which will never operate'.

On the face if it, the protocol was in keeping with the Free State's views on disarmament and arbitration as the best means to ensure the security of small states. It was seen this way in the Dáil, where the Labour leader urged the government to sign up to it. While sympathetic to the protocol's aims, the government was concerned about the consequences of being obliged to impose sanctions on Britain if it were the aggressor, or the difficulty of enforcing them against a country should Britain decide not to impose them (a provision for majority voting in some cases raised the possibility of sanctions being imposed in the face of British opposition). Given the level of trade with Britain, imposing economic sanctions on London would be tantamount to 'suicide'. There was unease, too, about the automaticity of sanctions, which might conflict with the rights of the Oireachtas to determine the use of force and continuing concerns about whether the Free State could remain neutral should Britain or one of the dominions become involved in hostilities. In the circumstances, the government concluded that the Free State had 'no choice but to act in solidarity with Great Britain' and reject the protocol.[6]

It was not until two months later, on 13 May, that FitzGerald confirmed in the Dáil that the government would reject the protocol. He set out the reasons why it had failed without making any reference to the constraints on the Free State's freedom of action, imposed by its political and economic relations with Britain. He situated its failure instead in a lack of political will to enforce sanctions against a major power. As the Italians had shown in Corfu, the League covenant could be evaded 'by a quibble' in Joseph Walshe's words. FitzGerald pointed to the

[5] Memorandum by Michael MacWhite on the 33rd Session of the Council of the League of Nations, 17 Mar. 1925, NAI DFA LN87A.

[6] Memorandum on the Protocol for the Pacific Settlement of International Disputes, undated, prob. early Mar. 1925, NAI DT S4040. See Michael Kennedy, *Ireland and the League of Nations*, (Dublin, 1996), pp. 48–52.

contradiction between maintaining the armed forces necessary to impose sanctions and the commitments to disarmament contained in the League covenant. What was needed instead was to 'enhance the moral influence of international conscience'.[7] His announcement was greeted with a chorus of criticism and regret from all sides of the house. He was asked why the Free State was turning its back on an instrument embraced by most other small states and by France, the Labour leader in particular urging the government to reconsider its position

The decision to reject the protocol was not driven solely by the need to manage relations with its larger neighbour. FitzGerald was also concerned that provisions governing inviolability of borders would make it harder to bring into the League states currently outside it. This was a reference not just to Germany but also the United States, which baulked at the prospect of guaranteeing European borders. Borders were also a sensitive topic as the Boundary Commission process moved inexorably towards its disappointing conclusion. The department's finding that the Geneva Protocol was unlikely to gain sufficient support to become operative was proved correct before the Free State had to declare its position, and FitzGerald avoided having to reveal his hand until after Britain had rejected it. A post mortem report found that the protocol had 'come much too early', concluding bleakly that the Free State was 'not an independent state for the purposes of the Geneva protocol'.[8]

THE FREE STATE AND THE LOCARNO SPIRIT

The related problems of security guarantees and the rehabilitation of Germany were resolved later in the year through the Pact of Locarno, negotiated in mid-October and signed in London in December. The pact was in reality a series of treaties, some guaranteed by the British; others, crucially, were not, and each side interpreted the agreement differently. The main text involved a mutual rejection of armed conflict by the French, Germans, and Belgians, and confirmed Germany's western borders but did not seek to fix its frontiers in the east. Although negotiated outside the League framework, the arbitration arrangements created by the pact established a link to the League. As part of the deal, it was agreed that Germany would be admitted to the League with a permanent seat on the council, in keeping with its great power status. The agreements

---

[7] *Dáil Éireann deb.*, vol. 11, col. 1440, 13 May 1925.

[8] Memorandum on the Protocol for the Pacific Settlement of International Disputes, undated, prob. early Mar. 1925, NAI DT S4040. See Michael Kennedy, *Ireland and the League of Nations*, (Dublin, 1996), pp. 48–52.

satisfied the security needs of the French and Belgians largely at the expense of their allies to the east, who were offered bilateral arbitration treaties with Germany that the wartime allies did not guarantee. The Locarno treaties were hailed as bringing an end to the war, prompting, in the words of the *New York Times*, 'an international symphony of praise' in Paris, Brussels, and London.[9] The Eastern Arbitration Treaties offered as consolation to the Poles and Czechoslovaks mainly added to the nervousness of both. Polish anxiety manifested itself in an increasingly uncompromising assertiveness, with demands for a permanent seat on the League council the following year.

The Free State was not party to the military guarantees provided to France and Belgium, Chamberlain had agreed to exclude the dominions from the scope of Locarno fearing the time it would take to secure their acquiescence would fatally delay the negotiations. Despite the machinery in place for keeping the dominions apprised of British foreign policy, they were not consulted in advance or kept informed of progress in the talks, prompting unease about British good faith in Dublin and Ottawa. Speaking in the Dáil in February 1926, FitzGerald welcomed the agreements as 'the greatest step towards the creation of a proper peace spirit in Europe' even if he considered the security fears of the eastern European states to be verging on hysteria.[10] In a departure from the line he had taken when rejecting the Geneva protocol, he argued that the Free State's political and economic relations with Britain made Locarno a matter of interest to the Irish government even if it was not bound by any of the commitments it contained. 'We have always stood on the side of the Ten Commandments,' he told the Dáil, and assured deputies the country's size and location enabled it to support moves for peace 'without loss'.[11] Comment from the opposition benches focused on whether the British could use the Treaty ports in the event of military action, and if Locarno really imposed no obligations on the Free State, questions to which there was no clear-cut answer. In a letter to Smiddy in Washington four months later, Walshe reflected: 'owing to the geographical proximity of the Saorstát and Britain our position in a war might be more difficult than that of the distant Dominions'. This was a situation evident to many and he concluded pragmatically 'it may be as well not to examine the possibilities too closely'.[12]

The Irish response to Locarno was to support Germany's admission to the League and its award of a permanent council seat. This reflected a wish

---

[9] *The New York Times*, 15 Nov. 1925,
[10] *Dáil Éireann deb.*, vol. 14, col. 1866, 26 Mar. 1926.
[11] Ibid., vol. 14, col. 558, 5 Feb. 1926.
[12] Walshe to Timothy Smiddy, 7 June 1926, NAI DFA Letter Books, Washington, 1926.

to a see a normalization of European politics as well as growing economic ties between Ireland and Germany, as witnessed by the role of German companies in constructing the Shannon hydroelectric scheme. The Free State had scrapped reparations taxes on German imports in 1923 and, despite closing its unofficial office in Berlin the same year, the department and members of the Dáil repeatedly made clear the wish to establish relations with what many regarded as the economic power house of Europe. It was Irish policy to encourage universalization of League membership and German reintegration into European diplomacy was seen as an important step in this direction as well as contributing to continental stability. MacWhite passed League documents to the German consulate at Geneva for a year before the country's admission. The Germans lobbied the government in 1924 and 1925 about the heavy burden of disarmament and reparations demanded by the French and the British and found a sympathetic ear.[13] A different wartime experience meant that Irish policy-makers did not share the concerns of continental counterparts about a German resurgence. There was also a tendency to view with sympathy German complaints about the continuing occupation of the Rhineland, a legacy of partition at home. The Locarno treaties could not enter into force until Germany was admitted to the League. But the decision that Berlin would be given a permanent seat set off a messy debate on the composition of the council that would delay German entry by six months and prompt a rethink of Irish policy at Geneva.

GERMANY ENTERS THE LEAGUE

A special session of the League assembly was called for 8 March to make the necessary changes to the Council's composition and admit Germany. The ten-member council was divided between four permanent and six elected non-permanent members. The formula ensured that the smaller and medium sized states were a majority and each member possessed a veto. The addition of Germany would alter this balance, a change many smaller states were willing to accept in the hope of greater European stability.

In the run-up to the session, MacWhite predicted that a permanent seat for Germany would give rise to innumerable complications. The council's non-permanent members were supposed to rotate through election by the assembly. Failure to agree how this should be done meant that no real

---

[13] Mervyn O'Driscoll, *Ireland, Germany and the Nazis: politics and diplomacy, 1919–1939*, (Dublin, 2004), pp. 56–7.

election had been held since 1919 and most members had been rolled over with few additions or changes to the *dramatis personae*. As a result, Belgium, Brazil, and Spain were effectively semi-permanent members and the other seats had been captured for groups: a second seat for the Latin American states (at nineteen, a third of the membership), one for Sweden on behalf of the Nordics and one for the Little Entente (Czechoslovakia taking the honours). This was all achieved through informal understandings and nothing was written down.

Unanimity was required among the council's members to create a new permanent seat and Spain, Poland, and Brazil seized the opportunity to demand permanent seats for themselves. A reaction to the disappointment of Locarno, the Polish move was backed by an embarrassed France (foreign minister Aristide Briand threatened to resign if Warsaw was not compensated), with support from Belgium and France's Little Entente allies. For Spain and Brazil, it was a case of wounded *amour propre* with the latter concerned about a creeping Europeanization of the League. The three dug in their heels, recognizing that the best chance for success lay in linking their demands to the question of German membership.

Dublin was not keen to expand any further than necessary the *directoire* of large states whose permanent council status would make them less likely to heed the wishes of the wider League membership. There was little sympathy for the claims of Madrid, Warsaw, or Rio de Janeiro, which, if granted, amounted to recognizing a new category of semi-permanent member. FitzGerald told the Dáil that the government would prefer there to be no permanent seats but, faced with their reality, believed they should be confined to countries that were 'incontestably world powers'. In the Irish ledger Germany alone met this criterion. MacWhite warned that adding more permanent or semi-permanent members raised concerns about democratic accountability and would be 'a menace to the small states', advice the government accepted, deciding to support German entry and back moves to defer until the autumn any other changes to the council's composition.[14]

It was clear that squaring this circle would be next to impossible. FitzGerald sat on the sub-committee that vetted Germany's application, a straightforward task that was completed quickly. Progress was less smooth in a second sub-committee charged with finding a way to reconcile the competing demands for permanent seats. Sweden acted as cheerleader for a group of small states opposed to creating a new category of middle-ranking powers entitled to a permanent seat. It was egged on by

---

[14] MacWhite to FitzGerald, 13 Feb. 1926, NAI DFA LN1-4.

Britain at first until London reached an understanding with Paris to find a way to accommodate the Poles and Spaniards. The Swedes retreated when they realized their principled stand was holding up not just German entry to the League but the whole Locarno edifice, offering to vacate their seat if it would facilitate a solution to the Polish demands. They were joined by Czechoslovakia, which made a similar offer. The Brazilians were less emolient and used their veto to block German admission in protest at the refusal to grant them a permanent seat or find a formula that would amount to the same thing. The Germans insisted on the agreement reached at Locarno that they alone would receive a permanent seat and refused to countenance any other outcome. With no agreement possible German membership could not be progressed. The result was a decision to defer the matter to the full assembly session in September and establish a commission in the meantime to draw up proposals for council reform.

STANDING FOR A SEAT ON THE LEAGUE COUNCIL

The special commission made up of all council members and a few others including Germany met over the summer to thrash out a compromise. The Poles were bought off with a promise of certain election while the Latin Americans were told a third seat would be achieved through informal means. When it became evident that there was no backing for Spain or Brazil, both gave notice to quit the League in June, making possible a more extensive restructuring of the council.[15] The solution found was to raise the number of non-permanent members from six to nine, thereby maintaining the balance with the permanent members while allowing for wider geographical representation. The package would be put to the League membership to vote on at the assembly meeting in September. If adopted, it was agreed that all non-permanent members would vacate their seats and the assembly would hold a fresh election for nine new members. The election of September 1926 would thus be the first properly competitive contest for non-permanent seats since the creation of the League and the first to take place on the basis of rotation.

The Free State did not take part in the deliberations that produced the reform package and adopted a critical stance when the outcome was published. Although not part of the Swedish-led group the Irish held similar

---

[15] Brazil left for good, but Spain later reversed its position before the two year's notice expired.

Figure 9. Joseph Walshe, Michael MacWhite, and unidentified man at Irish delegation to League of Nations, 43 Quai Wilson, Geneva (Image courtesy of UCD Archives P194/781)

fears that a larger council would be unwieldy, less able to act and more prone to misuse of national vetoes. There was particular disapproval of Spain and Brazil for holding the council hostage in pursuit of national agendas. The Free State was opposed to anything that might weaken the assembly and was unhappy at the minor role it had played in March. As agents of the assembly, Dublin considered the council bound to carry out its wishes, in this case the admission of Germany; the proper response to Brazil and Spain's blocking tactics was for the assembly to exercise its power to dismiss all six non-permanent members en bloc and elect a new council.

As debate on the proposals got underway at the assembly session in September, proponents of the changes argued that expanding the number of non-permanent members made it easier for small states to seek election. In practice however, the creeping practice of allocating seats to informal geographical groupings, even though the covenant made no provision for this, meant it was becoming harder to secure election for those countries that did not belong to one of these groups. The result was that the principles of equal rotation and equitable geographic distribution of seats were being eroded, a development that ran counter to Free State interests and thinking. It would mean a largely formulaic election, with little real choice between slates of candidates agreed in advance by sections of the membership.

Eoin MacNeill had identified the informal group system as a weakness of the League in 1923, but there had been no council election to bring the

Figure 10. Irish delegation to League Assembly, September 1925—Hugh Kennedy, Kevin O'Higgins, Desmond FitzGerald, Joseph Walshe, Michael MacWhite (Image courtesy of UCD Archives P194/785)

issue to a head. The Free State did not consider itself part of any group, even if meetings of Commonwealth delegations at Geneva meant that some League members considered it part of a British group. The suggestion that a sitting council member would be ineligible to stand for re-election unless the assembly voted otherwise by a two-thirds majority was seen in Dublin as a further encroachment on the rights of the assembly to freely elect council members while the absence of any provision to discipline or remove an uncooperative member was a significant weakness in Irish eyes. It meant there was no solution to the Brazilian problem, something Ernest Blythe tried to have changed without success when the proposals were discussed in committee.

This was not the outcome that had been hoped for in Dublin, but there was no alternative on offer and blocking its adoption was not an option. Wishing to register its dissatisfaction, the delegation decided on the spot to stand for election to a non-permanent seat, announcing the bid to a startled assembly on the evening of 14 September, a day before the package was to be voted on and two days before the nine new members were to be elected. Such was the rush that there was no time to seek instructions from Cosgrave in Dublin, who was telegraphed with the news the same evening. The move was being taken 'to assert equal status, as much as to seek election'.[16] At a hastily convened meeting of Commonwealth delegations, FitzGerald explained the reasons for the Irish candidacy. The announcement was greeted with surprise, MacWhite recalling that only the Canadians were supportive. Austen Chamberlain urged FitzGerald to withdraw the bid, arguing that the diplomatic unity of the empire meant only the British could sit on the council. The others claimed their votes were already committed elsewhere. FitzGerald initially yielded to pressure and appeared to say the Free State would not stand. This decision was quickly over-turned under pressure from the rest of the delegation: to have yielded would have been a damaging admission that the Free State was not entitled to the full rights of membership. FitzGerald informed the British and Commonwealth delegates of the final decision by letter that evening. Unhappy at the Irish move, Chamberlain asked the French to persuade Czechoslovakia to run again and a deal was hammered out to support Prague, which entered the race with French and British backing.

A last-minute candidacy was an unusual move and the announcement caused a stir in Geneva. With less than forty-eight hours to the vote, there was little time to canvass for support or to compete with those states who had announced their intention to stand earlier in the year. There was considerable interest in the election, with seventeen states running for nine available seats. FitzGerald's speech when the assembly debated the reform package on 15 September was the only opportunity to set out the reasons for the Free State's move and this he did forcefully and with some eloquence.

He recalled the Free State's record of impartiality and its support for the principles of the covenant, but the focus of his argument was the impact that the changes would have on the rights of small states and the ability of the assembly to hold the council to account. The points MacWhite had made earlier about the democratic principles of the League and the threat to small states featured prominently. FitzGerald called for an effective council, representative of the assembly which elected it, and able to carry out the business of the League. He queried whether a council of fourteen veto-wielding members would meet this standard and, castigating those who had put national interest above the common good, criticized the absence of any provision to remove an obstructive council member. The power of member states to control the council rested in their ability to

---

[16] Walshe to Paul Banim, 15 Sept. 1926, NAI DT S 5166.

elect its members: 'the very essence of voting is choosing' he declared. 'We deny the right of particular groups to be at any time represented [on the Council] in any specified proportion, we deny more emphatically still the right of any group to choose from among themselves a state which the Assembly would be under obligation to elect.' For this reason, the Free State had decided to stand for election as an independent state representing the assembly.[17] A reception later that evening offered a last chance to sway voters.

The question of dominion eligibility to a seat on the Council had arisen from the very early days of the League. The original text of the covenant in 1919 had referred to the right of states, rather than League members, to sit on the council. Having at first objected to the presence of the dominions at the peace conference, Wilson shared the view that council membership should be confined to full states but relented following protest from the dominions. The British were equivocal, contending that they sat on the council representing the empire as a whole, including the dominions. As none of the dominions had so far sought election, the issue had never been put to the test.

MacWhite had been reporting diplomatic chatter about a possible Canadian bid since February. The head of the Canadian delegation to the League, Senator Raoul Dandurand, had told him Ottawa would go forward if new non-permanent seats were created. As rumours of extra seats were already circulating in March, MacWhite wondered if Canada would go forward for one of them. A snap election in Canada meant there was no decision to stand in September and the Canadians confined themselves to a statement that they and the other dominions were entitled to sit on the Council.

The vote took place on 15 September. In the first ballot eight seats were filled by Belgium, Chile, China, Colombia, El Salvador, the Netherlands, Poland, and Romania. The Free State received a respectable ten votes from a total of forty-nine voting states. A run-off was required to decide the ninth seat between Czechoslovakia, Finland, Ireland, and Uruguay. Czechoslovakia emerged victorious, the Free State receiving two votes: its own and Canada's. With Poland, Romania, and Czechoslovakia on the council, France's eastern allies had been accommodated (a seat for Prague also easing guilty minds over Locarno), while the Latin Americans gained their promised third seat and Belgium retained the seat it had held since 1919. The losers were the Nordics who lost their place on the council. The British were relieved not just that the Free State had been unsuccessful, but that the vote had not been close; an uncomfortable situation would have arisen had the bid won broad-backed support but failed through lack of Commonwealth votes.

[17] Desmond FitzGerald assembly speech, 15 Sept. 1925, UCDA P80/540.

The outcome was a verdict on the Free State's position in the wider world; a recognition that it was viewed as much as a small state as it was a Commonwealth member. To persuade nine states to vote for it was no mean achievement after only three years in existence and in the face of British opposition. The arguments used in mounting the bid struck a chord in the assembly: Locarno may have been welcomed in many quarters but it was undeniably a product of the 'old diplomacy' with a League veneer. Small states resented this managing of the international agenda as they did the 'hotel conversations' at Geneva, the handling of the council fiasco, and the attempt to manage the election outcome. The Irish gave voice to this mood in the assembly debate. By standing on the principle of equal rotation irrespective of size or affiliation, the Free State had established a position that would remain central to the Irish approach to the UN and other multilateral organizations. FitzGerald wrote afterwards that the move was not only intended to defend the status of the dominions but also the rights of countries such as Bulgaria and Ethiopia, none of which belonged to informal groups at Geneva, and would have stood aside had another state gone forward on the same grounds.[18]

The announcement had come as a surprise in Ireland, where the goings-on at Geneva did not routinely command front-page attention. *The Irish Times* was said to be flabbergasted. With an imperial conference due to meet in a matter of weeks, it is unsurprising that Irish and British media coverage highlighted questions of status and the rights of the dominions, issues which would shortly be discussed in London. The precedent established would be used the following year by the Canadians in their successful bid for a seat on the council. The contest provided rich material for the political sketch-writers, with one claiming the Irish run was all about showing they had donned 'the long trousers of independence'.[19] FitzGerald believed success would have been possible if the candidacy had been declared earlier. Phelan's assessment was more sober: the Irish bid had come as a surprise in Geneva circles because of the 'rather passive attitude' adopted at previous League meetings. His prescription was simple: if the Free State were more active in Geneva its chances of election would be correspondingly better.[20]

The changes breathed new life into the assembly and also into Irish attitudes towards the League, rekindling hopes that the country would aspire to the kind of active role more in keeping with the ideas of 1919. Domestic preoccupations, the boundary issue in particular, but also a raft of bilateral problems and out-workings of the 1921 settlement had meant

[18] FitzGerald letter, 19 Sept. 1926, UCDA P80/1407.
[19] *The New York Times*, 26 Sept. 1926.
[20] Phelan to Cosgrave, 7 Oct. 1926, NAI DFA S5685.

there was little time to focus on issues of European foreign policy or the opportunities offered by membership of the League. This began to change in 1926, while the end of the boundary issue meant the government had a freer hand when dealing with the British. The trigger for this reappraisal of policy was not a crisis in Irish–British relations but a response to continental politics and the search for post-war security. The Free State had woken up to the League after the false start in 1923.

With agreement on council reform, the way was clear for Germany to enter the League. Recalling the scene in the room, Ernest Blythe, contrasted the mixed reception that greeted the German delegates when they entered the hall (British and French representatives ostentatiously remained in their seats) with that enjoyed by the Irish delegation three years earlier. Stresemann, Briand, and Chamberlain all spoke of a desire to turn a page and consolidate peace and stability on the continent. The Germans were exempted from the requirement to impose military sanctions, recognition of their disarmed status and a concession to the need to maintain relations with the Soviet Union, which viewed the League with suspicion ('a band of robber barons' in Lenin's memorable phrase). A neutrality and non-aggression pact concluded with the Soviets in April was designed to offer further assurances to Moscow.

Germany's rehabilitation was a bitter pill for some, with mixed views as to what it would mean for the workings of the League and the wider question of European security. The first change was that Germany was quickly admitted to the great power gatherings in Geneva hotels at which League business was discussed first in private before being addressed later in public. The British, French, and German foreign ministers met regularly at the quarterly meetings of the council but it was the 'Locarno tea parties' that consummated Germany's return to the European concert. They were also a further undermining of the League. The principal loser was Belgium, which found itself gradually excluded from the *directoire*, although it was invited to be present whenever Germany itself was the topic for discussion.

There was a postscript to the saga of the assembly session. Hopes had been raised that the Locarno spirit would see a speedy start to Franco-German rapprochement when Stresemann and Briand stole away to an inn outside Geneva on 17 September for a private lunch; hopes that were dashed when the meeting ended in recrimination. The following day FitzGerald took lunch at the same hotel, though in the company of a journalist friend rather than a foreign counterpart. The two supped on the same menu the foreign ministers had enjoyed the day before.[21] A spot of

[21] Michael Kennedy, *Ireland and the League of Nations 1919–1946*, p. 90.

harmless tourism, yet having failed to win a seat at the horseshoe table of the council, FitzGerald's trip to Thoiry had the hallmarks of a metaphor: the Free State had not yet made it to the top table in Geneva.

The ink was barely dry on the Locarno treaties when the new order met its first challenge in the form of a border clash between Greece and Bulgaria that broke out in mid-October. In contrast to Corfu in 1923, this time the League council took up the case. After a speedy deliberation, Athens was deemed at fault, fined, and ordered to withdraw its forces. Both sides accepted the ruling, in the spirit of Locarno and the outcome was hailed a success for the League although the fact that neither was a major power nor in favour with one made a solution easier to impose on this occasion. In Ireland, the issue was raised in the senate by Colonel Maurice Moore, the former Sinn Féin envoy turned critic of Cumann na nGaedheal, who viewed the sanctions imposed on Greece as too weak to act as a deterrent to others. Moore was openly sceptical about the Free State's place in Geneva and critical of the 'dirty work' of big power diplomacy (he had voted against ratifying the Lausanne Treaty for the same reason). It was salutary that a country which had chaired discussions on the Geneva Protocol only a year earlier and been itself the victim of aggression should find itself on the wrong side of the League, a measure of the mistrust and instability in Europe's eastern half which Locarno's limited security guarantees did nothing to allay.

CONFERENCE DIPLOMACY

The high profile adopted at Geneva in 1926 marked a sea change in attitudes towards the League. In the preceding years, the country had kept a low profile in the formal workings of the Geneva system, intervening infrequently or not at all at meetings unless to correct British assertions regarding the status of the dominions. Efforts concentrated on using the League machinery to pursue constitutional objectives, most notably registration of the Treaty. The machinery of the League also encompassed an array of technical meetings and conferences held under the umbrella of the League and the ILO that offered avenues for the Free State to assert itself. The country attended fourteen such gatherings in 1925 alone. Unlike assembly sessions, these conferences were open to non-members, meaning the Americans, Germans, and others could take part.

Delegates were to be on guard against British inspired attempts to insert the hated *inter se* clause into League agreements. Dublin felt sufficiently strongly on the matter to warn the British during a conference to limit opium production in November 1924 that it would block any agreement if they insisted on inserting the clause.[22] The negotiations were taking place against a tense backdrop between Dublin and London over registration of the Anglo-Irish Treaty. When the British backed down, Michael MacWhite prompted the Japanese delegation to ask whether the conference outcome would be binding between Commonwealth members, prompting a public admission that it would.

Guarding the country's constitutional flank was not the sole objective behind participation. League gatherings such as the opium conference or negotiations held a few months later in 1925 to limit the arms trade allowed the Free State to support progressive causes in a relatively cost-free way (as it was rarely involved in the practices which these conferences sought to curtail). A number of independent members of the Dáil took an interest in the League's technical activities encouraging the government to play a constructive role. Desmond FitzGerald told the house the Irish position at the opium conference would be 'perfectly disinterested', aiming for the 'good of the people'. Despite this, Michael MacWhite was largely left without instructions when the conference met in Geneva.

The Americans were pushing for a strong outcome from the negotiations, one supported by Japan, China, and many of the smaller states, but opposed by Britain and France, who wished to minimize constraints on production and use. The other Commonwealth countries were content to tow the British line. MacWhite supported the US delegation, led by the chair of the House Foreign Relations Committee, George Porter, earning him praise in the American papers and the opprobrium of the British delegation in almost equal measure. His decision to leak British opium figures to the *Chicago Tribune* caused a storm and provoked a missive from Dublin warning him to avoid tactics that might be considered anti-British. There was no criticism of the position he adopted at the conference or the policy of siding with the Americans.

When the convention was put to a vote, MacWhite was the only delegate to vote against a last-minute amendment to weaken its implementation (by then the Americans had withdrawn in protest at the watering down of their proposals). His stance throughout the negotiations had been to distance the Free State from the Commonwealth group and to prevent any move to exclude the dominions from its terms. In this he had succeeded. A three-way split among Commonwealth delegates earlier in the talks prompted the *New York Times* to question whether fears of a British Empire bloc in the League were credible.[23] Disinterest, self-interest, and a moral stance had combined to advance Irish concerns

---

[22] Michael MacWhite memorandum, c1950?, UCDA P194/681.
[23] *The New York Times*, 2 Dec. 1924.

and the conference outcome would later feature in papers prepared for the imperial conference in 1926.

The Free State took part in negotiations held three months later for a treaty to limit trade in the arms and munitions of war. FitzGerald told the Dáil the government supported efforts to suppress the illegal arms trade. Even if it did not pose a direct threat to the country, he reminded the house it had during the civil war. The independent member, Major Bryan Cooper, encouraged the government to support efforts to reach agreement. MacWhite was again the delegate, but did not play as forward a role in the negotiations as he had at the opium conference, pursuing a position of 'diplomatic reserve' while remaining on the look-out in case the *inter se* clause resurfaced. In the end, it did not, and the Americans pushed to make clear that the treaty would apply to armaments shipped between Britain and the dominions. It was a hollow victory as the convention never entered into force.

It might be asked why the Free State should take part, however marginally, in a conference on issues not directly related to its interests. One of the tenets of the new diplomacy was that states could lend moral weight to the rules-based international order by subscribing to agreements that might not affect them directly, in the hope of influencing the behaviour of others to do the same. By engaging in efforts to curb the drugs trade or supporting calls for disarmament and arms control, the Irish could contribute to strengthening the international order without compromising their own interests.

The Irish calculated that being an international good citizen was an effective defence of their interests (and that backing American proposals would do it no harm, either). It was hoped that this role would bring with it influence—other states would see in Ireland a disinterested and committed member of the international community and therefore seek its counsel on issues which might affect its interests. Not only did this advance Irish interests in general, they also hoped it would make League members more likely to uphold Irish rights should they be seriously challenged by Britain. This reading of the international system dovetailed with a desire to pursue a high profile presence on the world stage to advertise the country's independence and support progressive efforts to improve international life through the technical work of the League. Each time the Irish voted against a British interest, or stood apart from a Commonwealth common position, they illustrated their independence. The Free State could not have used the League to overcome Commonwealth restrictions had it not pursued a high profile policy designed to win approval from the international community. This is where aspirations to a disinterested small state foreign policy underpinned moves to expand the constitutional settlement of 1921.

In a 1926 series of articles for *Studies* on the work of the ILO, Edward Phelan set out the case for Irish engagement in multilateral diplomacy. From his Geneva perspective, he believed League membership provided states with 'international citizenship', which like the individual citizen, entailed both rights and obligations. It followed that the powers of independence were 'given life by use'; if the Free State did not use its sovereignty in the international arena, others would do so for it. Active participation in the organs of the League—its committees and commissions—provided states with a 'new diplomatic currency' which could be traded in pursuit of national interests.[24] In this way, constitutional development would be made both easier and more rapid.

Michael MacWhite shared Phelan's philosophy, but expressed it in blunter terms: 'by obstructing other states, states raise their diplomatic currency,' he argued, and this conviction lay behind his tactics at the opium conference, during the registration of the Treaty and his enthusiasm for the Free State to play a more forward game at Geneva.[25] Phelan shared his ideas with Cosgrave who found them interesting, having followed his advice when registering the Treaty. It is likely that Phelan would have expounded his views on active multilateralism to the Irish delegates when they visited Geneva and it is tempting to see his hand, at least in part, behind the change in gear in Dublin's approach to League engagement in 1926.

The Americans had shown at the opium conference they were willing to engage with the League when it suited them and MacWhite had tried to persuade his fellow delegates of the chance to demonstrate the value of the League by making progress on an issue of interest to Washington. He remained hopeful that the United States might join the League (as did many after the Locarno treaties were signed) but the government took no action to encourage this step. The idea that Irish thinking on global issues might accord with that in Washington was attractive—MacWhite's cooperation with the Americans was motivated as much by a desire to boost the country's status as it was by concern to limit the use of opium. Two years earlier, he had suggested that Irish delegates act as unofficial mouthpiece for the United States at meetings of the League assembly. There is little evidence that this was ever acted on: Washington was able to make its views known without resorting to an Irish spokesperson, and American interests might not always coincide with those of the Free State.

[24] Edward Phelan, 'Ireland and the International Labour Organisation', *Studies*, vol. 15, Mar. and Oct. 1926, pp. 1–8, 381–98.
[25] Michael MacWhite memorandum, 'The Saorstát and the League of Nations', n.d. (1928?), UCDA P194/246.

Just as the post-war international architecture limited international action to bring about disarmament, security, and stability in Europe, the Free State was constrained in its ability to engage on these issues not just by the usual limits faced by small states, but also by the fact that the dominions had not evolved fully as international actors independent of Britain. Like a pebble in a shoe, these constraints were a constant source of irritation, their resolution frustratingly out of reach. Nobody could say, with any certainty, what was the international status of the dominions, or their rights and obligations, a situation complicated by differing interpretations in London and the other dominions. FitzGerald's quip that they were 'adolescent but not entirely adult' came close to the mark.[26] The imperial conference called for the autumn offered an opportunity to come of age.

THE IMPERIAL CONFERENCE OF 1926

The approaching imperial conference and the advances achieved at Geneva meant that the Free State's interests could be pursued by using League and Commonwealth machinery rather than by creating facts on the ground. Such tactics were no longer necessary to promote the Free State's status abroad; indeed, they were counter-productive. In the summer of 1926, representatives abroad were instructed to 'avoid making further endeavours to establish a diplomatic position by precedents. There is no longer any need for indirect methods and they cause unnecessary irritation.'[27]

The imperial conference met in London in mid-October. As in 1923, it was timed for after the League assembly in Geneva, an index of the growing impact of the League on Commonwealth affairs. Much had changed in the three years since the last gathering: the Canadians and South Africans had joined the Irish in appointing diplomats abroad, the right of British negotiators to represent and commit the dominions in treaty negotiations and international conferences had been over-turned and the diplomatic unity of the empire had been challenged at Geneva in the most public fashion by the Free State's council bid. The fact that none of the dominions opted to associate themselves with the Locarno treaty obligations was another straw in the wind.

Having made a splash at Geneva, the Free State was in a confident mood going into the conference. W. T. Cosgrave was present for the start

26 *Dáil Éireann deb.*, vol. 16 no. 2, col. 264, 2 June 1926.
27 Walshe to Count O'Kelly, 26 July 1926, NAI DFA 250.

of the proceedings, but Kevin O'Higgins replaced him as head of delegation for most of the discussions. O'Higgins, who was both justice minister
and vice president of the executive council, was taking a growing interest
in foreign policy. He had caused a stir at the assembly in 1925 when he
corrected a statement by the British representative that he was speaking on
behalf of all the dominions. The arrangement was not to Desmond
FitzGerald's liking, and he complained that O'Higgins lacked a firm
grasp of external relations and was thus easily wrong-footed by the British
who insisted on addressing sensitive issues such as how treaties were
ratified at meetings of heads of delegation. The complaint reflected
FitzGerald's growing insecurity in government following the embarrassing
climb-down over the council election in September.

The outcome of the conference marked a significant step in the development of the dominions with the recognition that they were 'autono-
mous communities within the British Empire, equal in status, in no way
subordinate' to each other or to the United Kingdom. The Balfour
Declaration, as it became known, was hard-won and reflected the growing
assertiveness of the dominions, in particular the Free State, Canada, and
South Africa. The Canadians and the Irish both competed for the laurels
afterwards, claiming they had taken the lead in pushing for dominion
equality in foreign affairs. Who did most of the spadework mattered less
than the outcome, which would not have been possible if both Dublin and
Ottawa, and the South Africans to a lesser extent, had not arrived in
London intent on asserting their equality at the international level.

While much of the agenda dealt with legislative matters, the implications for the international relations of the dominions were far-reaching. It
was agreed that each would be represented solely and exclusively by its
delegate at conferences and treaty negotiations, and the term 'British
Empire' would no longer appear in treaty texts. Each would commit itself
individually through the agency of the king, who would act separately for
each dominion on the advice of its government alone. Each dominion
could decide the extent of the obligations it would assume when agreeing
to be bound by a treaty. The dominions could appoint their own consuls
abroad rather than the previous practice where this was done by London.
The office of the governor general was recognized as representing the king
in each of the dominions and not the British government; communications between the dominions and London would henceforth take place
through direct channels and the practice of using the governor general for
this purpose brought to an end. FitzGerald told the Dáil on return from
London that 'absolute coequality of status' had been achieved.

The insistence on status was not a narrow preoccupation. The power
to conclude separate commercial treaties and appoint trade and

diplomatic representatives was seen as important to economic development. The Farmers' Party brought a ruthlessly utilitarian view to the question of external affairs, asking how much it cost and what was the gain to the economy; Thomas Johnson's retort that the 'trade test is not the best' cut little ice. Mindful of both the bottom line and their constituents' interest, they pressed for an office in Copenhagen citing a need to counter competition from Danish farmers, but were less convinced of the merits in keeping offices in Paris or Brussels. Former unionist and *The Irish Times* called on the government not to overlook opportunities in Britain and the Commonwealth. At one level, Irish foreign policy can be interpreted as an attempt to reconcile political aspiration with economic interests: when external affairs negotiated advances in dominion rights and prerogatives, care was taken to protect the preferential tariffs Irish goods enjoyed in Commonwealth markets. Nationalist economics had assumed growth in overseas markets would follow independence, but the Free State remained overwhelmingly dependent on the United Kingdom for its exports. The high commission in London warned that reluctance to take part in empire promotional events was 'neither good politics nor good business'.[28] The trade commissioner in Britain, Joseph Dulanty, recommended the government avail of advertising for Irish goods funded by the Empire Marketing Board in 1926. Despite the earlier hesitancy about imperial trade organizations, the offer was taken up once the offending legend 'Buy Empire Goods, Ask—is it British?' had been deleted.[29]

The report to the Dáil after the 1926 imperial conference sought to situate the gains in a wider context of the Irish contribution to the development of the dominions, 'our country, considered as a unit, is amongst the smallest in Europe, but it has made a greater racial contribution to the building up of the great new countries of the world than any of our neighbours with the exception of Great Britain'.[30] Sinn Féin propagandists had predicted that Irish diplomats would be listened to abroad, because they would know the mind of official Britain. This proved in part to be true, but not quite in the way anticipated. Much of the importance other states attached to Irish opinions derived from Commonwealth membership. The German and French governments believed the Irish were privy to British policy, an impression in part fostered by Commonwealth meetings at the League, and Irish diplomats exploited this in their dealings with them.

[28] High Commission memorandum, n.d., NAI, DFA D1967.
[29] High Commission memorandum, n.d., NAI, DFA D1967.
[30] Statement on the 1926 imperial conference, 14 Dec. 1926, NLI, mss 21, 817(i).

BUILDING BILATERAL RELATIONSHIPS

The Free State's efforts during this period were almost exclusively devoted
to League and Commonwealth issues, with little opportunity to pursue
bilateral relations beyond contacts at Geneva. The French had made
overtures to the Irish when they joined the League, but Paris blew hot
and cold on relations with the Free State, anxious not to complicate its ties
with Britain. The French were also wary of the dominions' aspirations for
an independent foreign policy role in general, lest this weaken Britain as a
reliable military partner, and took little interest in the Free State at the
League as a result. As the Locarno negotiations were getting under way, the
French consul in Dublin, Alfred Blanche, told Paris it would be a mistake to
overlook a government with a vote equal to that of France at Geneva.[31] In
common with other foreign ministries, the Quai d'Orsay carefully weighed
up the impact on Britain before making overtures to Dublin, and ran ideas
past the Foreign Office first no matter how trivial the matter, such as a
request in 1925 to fix an escutcheon outside the Free State office in Paris.

French diplomats came to see the Free State through the prism of
Franco-German competition. The decision to award the contract to
build the Shannon hydroelectric plant to a German company in 1925
prompted Blanche, to warn Paris 'the Free State is set to become a sort of
German province, a bridge-head in the Anglo-Saxon world'.[32] The
appointment of German academics to Irish universities prompted him
to dismiss the National University as 'a hotbed of ignorance and German-
ism' and he feared the German navy would soon be anchored off the
Atlantic coast.[33] The German vote for the Free State in the council
election in September 1926 did not pass unnoticed in Paris. The French
were also curious to see whether they could induce a more favourable
American attitude by cultivating links with the Free State.

The Americans also paid little attention to the Free State. Smiddy saw
his role in Washington as educating US opinion about the status of the
dominions as a means to establish the Free State's position, a tactic that
brought him into conflict with a vocal segment of Irish-American opinion
opposed to the Treaty settlement and he found himself frequently assailed
in the media. Cooperation between Irish and American delegates at

---

[31] Blanche to Briand, 15 Oct. 1925, Quai d'Orsay, CPC, Europe 1918–40, Irlande,
vol. 13, p. 49.

[32] Blanche to Herriot, 4 April 1925, QO, CPC, Europe 1918–40, Irlande, vol. 15,
pp. 146–52.

[33] Blanche to Briand, 12May 1925, QO, CPC, Europe 1918–40, Irlande, vol. 13,
p. 26.

League-sponsored conferences was not mirrored at State Department level, which evinced little interest in the foreign policy views of Dublin. Despite the opening of diplomatic relations in 1924, the Americans had still not matched the Irish legation in Washington with a similar appointment to Dublin. The State Department worried that an attempt to appoint a minister would open the door to Congress approving an Irish-American hostile to the Free State, an outcome it feared would be embarrassing on both sides of the Atlantic. A Senate resolution calling for a legation in Dublin in January 1925 provoked a sustained lobby from Irish-Americans opposed to anything that would legitimize the Free State. In Dublin, it prompted a reflection on how to deal with continuing anti-Free State activity. Cosgrave took a particular interest. He was anxious to change the way in which American opinion viewed Ireland: 'the time has come for breaking down the tradition of subscription-seeking with which Ireland has so long been associated in American minds', and asked that a cross-party group of politicians visiting the States in September 1925 be briefed on the need for a new narrative in the country's relations with America.[34] Independence had dictated a change in identities: as interests evolved, old images were dropped. One of these was that of the 'fighting Irish', which evoked unpleasant memories of the civil war and clashed with the image of the new pacific Ireland. The government now sought to lose the image of the begging bowl while remaining keen to attract US investment:

> The accepted tradition of a race of starving peasants and needy politicians must be replaced by the realisation of a self-reliant Ireland with great potentialities of prosperity, governing herself with dignity and efficiency, taking her natural place in the commercial arenas of the world, asking no favours, but ready and willing to trade her products.[35]

Curtailing Irish-American financial support for de Valera's republicans was also part of Cosgrave's calculation, although this would prove impossible to achieve.

PROBLEMS WITH FLAGS AND ANTHEMS

Efforts at promotion would only prove partially successful as long as the British foreign service was responsible for Irish representation overseas. Visits by Irish sportsmen to the continent were occasions of vigilance by

---

[34] Michael MacDunphy to Walshe, 25 Aug. 1925, NAI DT S4596.
[35] Ibid.

Irish representatives, lest the British flag and anthem feature on the programme. Here the Free State was at a disadvantage against the superior manpower of the Foreign Office, with British consuls making a point of showing up to local stadiums armed with flag and score. The presence of a Free State representative was not always a guarantee that the correct procedure would be followed, as became clear in April 1926 during an international athletics meeting in Brussels. Things got off to a bad start when the Irish team, accompanied by Minister J. J. Walsh, arrived without prior notification to the trade commissioner in the city, Count O'Kelly. A veteran of the flag wars, he had the foresight to send in advance a tricolour and the score of the national anthem to the organizers. He was somewhat taken aback to see the Union flag and British anthem greet the arrival of the Irish team at the stadium. After much embarrassment on the part of the organizers, the correct flag was found but the music was not. As the Belgian army band did not know the tune, and O'Kelly was unable to hum it, the victorious Irish athletes took their lap of honour to the bars of the Norwegian national anthem, presumably in the hope that there were no Norwegians present to object.[36]

This unedifying episode illustrates the problems the Free State encountered in promoting itself abroad. The name itself was a constitutional mouthful, one indirectly derived from a decision by Sinn Féin in 1917 to use the word 'saorstát' (literally 'free state') to translate 'republic' in Irish in place of the more usual word 'poblacht'. Saorstát appeared on official Dáil documents including the letter paper of the delegation sent to London to negotiate the Treaty with Britain in 1921. In the course of the negotiations, the British seized upon this when naming the new country the Irish Free State.[37] It presented the new state with a challenge in communicating to the outside world. Count O'Kelly put it succinctly when he observed that, whereas 'Ireland' was one of the oldest countries in Europe, the 'Irish Free State' was part of the post-war 'political mushroom growth'.[38]

Steps were taken when circumstances permitted to reinforce the country's image abroad through 'soft' diplomacy. Military visits to foreign academies and the success of Irish equestrian teams all contributed to raising the profile of the Free State in their own way. The League had recognized the Free State as a custodian of Celtic culture, but little was done to act on this: finance officials blocked funds for a Celtic congress in 1925 while doubts were voiced about the pan-Celtic movement lest it

---

[36] Count O'Kelly to Walshe, 13 April 1926, NAI, DFA EA3-1.
[37] Earl of Longford and T. P. O'Neill, *Eamon de Valera* (London, 1970), p. 135.
[38] Confidential report from Count O'Kelly to Walshe, 7 Feb. 1931, NAI DFA EA 231/4/1931.

complicate relations with France. International soccer fixtures presented both opportunities and challenges, given the problems with flags and anthems and the existence of two rival football associations on the island.[39] Efforts were made to promote links with the diaspora through the Tailteann Games, a kind of ethnic Olympiad held in Dublin in 1924.[40] Overseas competitors, including the future Tarzan actor Johnny Weissmuller, were invited to participate in an array of Celtic sports and pageants, which bore little relation to their daily lives back home or with contemporary conditions in Ireland.

Relatively little was done to construct a clear set of images for promoting the country abroad. Uncertainty regarding which version of the national anthem was to be preferred, *Let Erin Remember* or *The Soldiers' Song*, was one obstacle. A lack of publicity materials was another. Michael MacWhite drew attention to the large amount of publicity by the new states of Eastern Europe, and Seán Lester, in his capacity as director of publicity was anxious that the Free State should emulate them. J. J. Walsh put forward plans for a publicity book to coincide with the Tailteann Games and British Empire exhibition in 1924, but a combination of financial difficulties and a dearth of statistics saw the matter shelved until 1929.[41] One of MacWhite's proposals to publicize the Free State included a booklet of Irish versions of town names and using Gaelic script in official correspondence. The cost of equipping ministries with new typewriters put paid to these suggestions, as did the gap between aspiration and linguistic proficiency of many a civil servant.[42]

The situation was also difficult at home. Throughout the 1920s, the government was faced with a low level of engagement on international issues across the spectrum of public life. The Free State was only partially equipped to generate an internal discussion of foreign policy issues, lacking the institutions necessary. Beyond a small circle of opinion in the capital, international affairs were rarely the subject of popular or political interest. The country lacked a publication devoted to the study of foreign policy questions from a national perspective, and coverage of British foreign policy in the media fostered an assumption that international affairs were not an Irish concern, a sentiment which sat well with those whose nationalism came with a home rule flavour, but a source of irritation to government ministers who complained that their foreign

[39] See, for example, Mike Cronin, *Sport and Nationalism in Ireland: Gaelic Games, Soccer and Identity Since 1884* (Dublin, 1999).
[40] J. J. Walsh, *Recollections of a Rebel* (Tralee, 1944), p. 77.
[41] The idea would bear fruit in the beautiful *Irish Free State Handbook*, commissioned in 1929 and published three years later, edited by Bulmer Hobson.
[42] Seán Lester memorandum, 29 Feb. 1924, NA, DF F6/1/24.

policy was misunderstood or simply ignored. *The Irish Times* thought the government was wasting its time on international issues when it should be keeping its head down or following a British lead. The Jesuit quarterly *Studies* provided a forum in which questions of international politics could be examined, carrying an average of two articles per issue dealing with foreign affairs topics throughout the 1920s. Its editor, Patrick Connolly, was a friend of William Cosgrave, and a frequent caller at his home. Horace Plunkett's *Irish Statesman* also took an interest in international news, its editor, the poet and journalist George Russell, receiving background briefing from Desmond FitzGerald.

Overlapping worlds of political, artistic, and intellectual life in post-civil war Dublin meant this conversation was taking place within a small circle. The Irish League of Nations Society was an exception. Founded in 1923 by the civil servant and Church of Ireland minister, Bolton Waller, and Albert le Brocquy, father of the painter Louis, it aimed to popularize the Free State's League membership. The department of external affairs provided background briefings for the society's journal *Concord*, which was launched in 1927. Its editorial line was critical of the level of debate on major international issues, finding the tone in the Oireachtas 'disheartening'.[43]

Efforts to stimulate debate on international issues received a boost in July 1926 when the Women's International League for Peace and Freedom held its congress in Dublin. Louie Bennett was on the League's executive and brought the congress to Ireland. The first major international event to take place in the Free State, it attracted over four hundred delegates from thirty-four countries. W. T. Cosgrave attended an official reception thrown for the gathering (a briefing note prepared for him warned the delegates had 'a great capacity for talking').[44] The League of Nations Society helped organize the gathering, its honorary secretary playwright Sybil le Brocquy providing a link between the two bodies. Divisions within the Irish section of the Women's International League threatened to spill over into the congress, republicans led by Hanna Sheehy Skeffington hoping to embarrass the government, which was forced to issue a press release denying there were political prisoners in Ireland.

There were still those who exhorted the government to use its influence on behalf of this or that cause, or to intervene with the British over colonial transgressions. Questions were asked in the Dáil about the treatment of nationalities in the Empire. The Labour leader, Thomas Johnson voiced the concerns of many when he asked whether

[43] League of Nations Society of Ireland, Leaflet no. 1, 1 Aug. 1923, NA, DFA LN33.
[44] Department of External Affairs minute to Paul Banim, Office of the President, 26 June 1926 NAI DFA GR 393-13.

Commonwealth membership made the Free State 'responsible for misgovernment in Egypt, or in India' or in any other British territory. FitzGerald's view was that the Free State was no more responsible for British injustices than it was for Japanese misdeeds in Korea.[45] He had spoken in support of racial equality at the imperial conference in 1923, but made clear his comments did not imply a right to interfere in the internal affairs of other Commonwealth states, where racial discrimination was a feature of immigration policies. Despite the sincerely held convictions of many politicians, there were too many outstanding issues in Irish–British relations to risk championing the rights of other peoples, although there would be more vocal criticism when Fianna Fáil entered the Dáil in 1927.

Foreign commentators were not always persuaded by Irish claims to a principled foreign policy, despite FitzGerald's assurances in the Dáil that 'we have only one small voice, but I think that among the nations we will use that voice to good effect'.[46] In Alfred Blanche's assessment, the Free State held no firm foreign policy and reacted to events despite a self-generated 'myth of idealism'.[47] Regardless of the constraints on the country's freedom of movement on the international stage, the aspiration towards a disinterested foreign policy was nonetheless sincerely held. Ultimately, however, confusion regarding the status of the Free State, combined with lingering notions that it was still 'a part of Angleterre', complicated efforts to project a distinct image of the country abroad.[48]

The problem was as much one of communication as it was of ambition or the limits of action experienced by any small state. By any measure, 1926 was a successful year for Irish efforts to carve out the space to pursue an independent foreign policy. While much remained to be done, the outcome of the imperial conference and the Free State's respectable showing in the League election marked a qualitative shift in the government's approach to external affairs. To cap a year of progress, Cosgrave received a late Christmas present on 28 December, when Washington decided to reciprocate the move the Free State had taken in 1924 and open a legation in Dublin.[49] Edward Phelan was convinced the decision was a direct result of the imperial conference. As a new year beckoned, Cosgrave's government had much to be satisfied with in its external agenda, but the Free State's gains on the world stage would quickly be put to the test.

---

[45] *Dáil Éireann deb.*, vol. 8, col. 829, 9 July 1924.
[46] Ibid., vol. 16, col. 259, 2 June 1926.
[47] Blanche to Briand, 8 Feb. 1926, QO, CPC, Europe 1918–40, Irlande, vol. 13, p. 57.
[48] Count O'Kelly to Walshe, 3 April 1930, NAI, DFA Paris embassy letter book.
[49] Bernadette Whelan, *United States Foreign Policy and Ireland, From Empire to Independence, 1913–29* (Dublin, 2006), p. 480.

7

'Pious Hopes and Equally Pious Regrets', 1927–1929

Encouraged by the achievements of the previous year, W. T. Cosgrave told the Dublin Chamber of Commerce at the start of January 1927 that the Free State could not live 'in splendid isolation'. It was part of the wider world and must make its way in it. Joseph Walshe was correct to see the imperial conference as a 'turning point' in the country's external relations, but it did not solve all of Dublin's problems and, almost immediately, the government was faced with a new challenge.

While the conference had clarified much of the dominions' international status, it muddied the waters on the vexed issue of whether League agreements would apply between Commonwealth members. The practice had been that such agreements were binding unless they included the contentious *inter se* clause (the clause was needed as the British had failed to uphold the idea that the dominions were not full members of the League). Dublin exerted considerable energy in preventing *inter se* clauses from appearing in conventions negotiated at Geneva while London expended almost equal energy in trying to ensure that they were. The imperial conference effectively ruled that the unpopular clause was no longer necessary as League agreements would not be binding between Commonwealth states. It was a slip-up by the Irish and one that presented the country with a new set of difficulties. From Geneva, Phelan and MacWhite complained that the conference outcome was invalid on the grounds that the League did not recognize different categories of member and that agreements concluded under its auspices must therefore be binding on all. As Phelan observed, the League covenant could not be amended by a gathering of prime ministers in London.

The issue came to the fore in March, when Austen Chamberlain briefed the League council on the outcome of the imperial conference in his capacity, he claimed, as the dominions' representative on the council. The statement took some of the gloss off the imperial conference outcome and could not be left unchallenged if the Free State's status as a full League member were not to suffer. It was decided to respond in a low-key manner, offering London a palatable way to correct the politically unacceptable claim made in the council chamber. The government queried Chamberlain's comments, disingenuously asking the Dominion's Office if a note-taker's error had occurred. Of course, there had been no such mistake in the notes as the League secretary general knowingly confirmed, but the tactic worked and a similar cable from Ottawa saw the offending comment withdrawn by London.

The incident was a sharp reminder of the continuing ambiguities surrounding the dominions' international status even after the imperial conference. The department of external affairs argued that only the election of a Commonwealth member to a seat on the council would put an end to the lingering impression that London represented the dominions at Geneva (an impression which Chamberlain's March comments had been designed to foster). The 1926 reforms to the council meant that elections for three non-permanent seats would take place annually. The Irish contemplated running again in 1927, but decided it would be better to persuade the Canadians to do so. The idea was raised with the Canadian justice minister, Ernest Lapointe, in July during a naval disarmament conference held in Geneva and a series of cables followed from Dublin to Ottawa, each prompting an evasive reply. The secretary of the Canadian foreign ministry, Oscar Skelton, pinned the blame on his prime minister, McKenzie King who, reluctant to rile an imperially minded opposition, rejected the idea while saying nothing about support for an Irish run. As the summer dragged on, the Irish made clear they would stand if the Canadians would not and, in early August, the cabinet backed this stance while making clear they would step aside if Ottawa changed its mind. A snap second election called for mid-September meant the government would have its sights at home if required to act on its pledge to run.

The Canadians arrived in Geneva for the League assembly in September armed with instructions leaving it to their chief delegate, Senator Raoul Dandurand, to make the call. There was an unmistakeable Québec accent to calls for a greater Canadian role in international affairs. This was particularly pronounced at Geneva, where Dandurand had served as assembly president in 1925, while an interest on minority issues made the country popular in Geneva. A combination of conviction and personal ambition prompted Dandurand to announce a Canadian bid for a seat. The decision met with a cool reception from the British but not the outright hostility that had greeted the Irish announcement the previous year.

The Irish cast themselves in the role of midwife for Canada's election and, according to Walshe's personal account, Canadian nerves had to be steadied throughout the campaign.[1] The Canadians succeeded where the Irish had failed, winning election to the third non-permanent seat by three votes. The British media predictably portrayed the outcome as strengthening the British Empire's presence on the council, but Ottawa would follow a principled and independent line at Geneva. But what Walshe called the Foreign Office 'smoke screen' could not disguise the fact that the equal right of a dominion to be elected to the council had been conceded.

PROMOTING DISARMAMENT

The League assembly had instructed the council in 1925 to begin preparations for a general disarmament conference and a preparatory commission was established in December of that year. It met for the first time in May 1926 to draft a treaty covering land, sea, and air forces to be adopted at a conference the following year. The process ran into difficulties over Anglo-French refusal to agree to cuts, insisting instead on defining limits. The Germans, who were already disarmed, wanted reductions rather than limits. Squaring this circle would take several years and the conference would not meet until February 1932, by which time political and economic conditions in Europe were no longer conducive to the difficult decisions required if disarmament were to be achieved. The Free State was committed to supporting efforts to achieve disarmament, while recognizing the political realities standing in the way. As Kevin O'Higgins quipped in 1926, 'Security, Disarmament, Arbitration is a wonderful trilogy, if it didn't mean security in my ill-gotten gains, disarmament for the other fellow and arbitration with the court well-packed'.[2]

In February, the Americans suggested a naval disarmament conference outside the League framework as a follow up to the 1922 Washington treaty. The US aim was not to cut numbers but to limit construction of new vessels and invitations issued to the main high sea powers—Britain, France, Italy, and Japan—who had taken part in the Washington talks. The conference was to meet in Geneva in June and the question arose whether the dominions should be present separately or as a group, under the British. The Americans had not mentioned the dominions in their invitation and the British had replied accepting on behalf of the British government, a fudge which London hoped would get around the issue.

---

[1] Memorandum from Joseph Walshe to Patrick McGilligan on Irish Free State policy at the Eighth Assembly of the League of Nations, 11 Oct. 1927, NAI DFA LN 1/6.
[2] Quoted in Terence de Vere White, *Kevin O'Higgins* (London, 1948), p. 192.

London argued that there should be a single empire delegation, as there had been at the 1922 conference, but was forced to yield when Dublin insisted on its rights or threatened not to take part at all. The initial preference in Dublin was not to attend at all, lest any involvement in discussions on the running of the British navy be used by London to extract a financial contribution. Joseph Walshe was also afraid that if they came to be regarded as 'part-owners' of the British fleet and army, the dominions would 'lose their only influence in the League as small unarmed nations'.[3]

The Free State ultimately insisted on separate dominion representation at the conference. Were agreement to be reached, it would be the first time the dominions would sign in their own right and the first time the British signature would be confined to the United Kingdom and the rest of the empire alone. The mood at the time between Dublin and London on defence issues was tense, the British having rejected an Irish request to take control of the Treaty ports and the Irish having rejected British requests for visits to Irish ports by naval vessels.

With the imperial conference under their belt, it was possible to take a firmer line and officials were instructed to do so. The conference had agreed that the dominions should be represented by their own delegations in negotiations and Dublin insisted on this. The government was no longer prepared to agree to any measure that might create the impression Britain was responsible for the international affairs of the Free State and this found expression in the insistence on a separate Irish seat at the table. Delegates were also told to withhold consent at treaty negotiations, publicly if necessary, until Irish interests had been accommodated, whereas before the practice had been to resolve differences between Commonwealth members in private.

When the conference met in Geneva in June, the dominions were represented separately for the first time at an international negotiation. Irish and British delegates were on an equal footing for the first time, in legal terms at least. The US believed Irish interests at the conference reflected British concerns whereas, in fact, the Irish were motivated by the desire to copper-fasten the gains made at the imperial conference and to force the British to concede that they could only speak for themselves in the proceedings.[4] MacWhite was accordingly instructed to 'act as a silent member' at the proceedings unless the British attempted to speak for the dominions. While Dublin supported efforts to promote disarmament, the

[3] Walshe to O'Hegarty, 8 Mar. 1927, NAI DT S417A.
[4] Bernadette Whelan, *United States Foreign Policy and Ireland, From Empire to Independence, 1913–29* (Dublin, 2006), p. 546.

government recognized that it was not in a position to affect the outcome of discussions on tonnage and cruiser class.

In the end, the conference was unable to agree anything, its only achievement being a further souring of relations between the naval powers. The differences were, in Irish eyes at least, not insurmountable. MacWhite was told to take the floor at the closing ceremony after the British delegate had spoken for the dominions, to express Dublin's regret and expectation that efforts would continue to pursue naval limits leading to ultimate disarmament. The cable from Dublin referred to 'our special interests home and United States' as reasons for taking the floor at this late stage in the proceedings.[5] His remarks raised British eyebrows but had the desired effect, being taken to mean the Free State supported the American proposals and sparked a flurry of press comment. *The Irish Times* spoke of 'pious regrets and equally pious hopes'.[6] But in the words of a Japanese delegate to MacWhite, the conference had been a failure for everyone except the Irish, who had 'used it to assert their international status, in which they have fully succeeded'.[7]

As the naval conference was meeting, a general election at home on 9 June 1927 yielded an upset for the Cumann na nGaedheal government. The formation of Fianna Fáil in 1926 and its decision to contest the election saw the government's majority removed. The shooting dead of Kevin O'Higgins a month later, on 10 July, sent shockwaves through the political system, deprived the government of one of its most able members, and left the department of external affairs without a minister. Fianna Fáil's decision to take its seats in the Dáil in August transformed Irish politics and led to a second general election the following month. When the Dáil reconvened in early October, Cosgrave found himself at the helm of a minority government and facing a genuine opposition in parliament for the first time. Labour's political fortunes had suffered a blow, claiming its party leader Thomas Johnson in the process, while the Farmers' Party's vote collapsed. The opposition mantle passed to Eamon de Valera and his fifty-seven strong Fianna Fáil party. The rhetorical pinpricks of the Farmers' Party might be easily deflected; those of Fianna Fáil hit home more directly. Whenever ministers extolled the advances in dominion status, Ó Ceallaigh reminded the government benches that it was the Free State and not Ireland that had taken its place among the nations.[8] The party argued that the country should admit it was not a full state

---

[5] Telegram from Walshe to MacWhite, 2 Aug. 1927, NAI DFA LN 4/7.
[6] *The Irish Times*, 5 Aug. 1927.
[7] MacWhite to Walshe, 5 Aug. 1927, NAI DFA LN 4/7.
[8] *Dáil Éireann deb.*, vol. 30, col. 809, 5 June 1929.

instead of sending its representatives abroad 'with a lie on their lip', prompting Patrick McGilligan to ask if instead the country's diplomats should be sent abroad to represent 'Ireland minus six counties'.[9] There was a general frustration on the government benches with Fianna Fáil's focus on the Treaty settlement and what one of Cosgrave's lieutenants dubbed its ability to see 'king's heads in every hedgerow'.[10]

Surveying the new political landscape, Joseph Walshe's gaze alighted on de Valera's 'foreign experts', those who had served in the Dáil's foreign service but taken the anti-treaty side. He was convinced (rightly, as it turned out) that de Valera would reinstate them were the party to enter government and feared what this would mean for Irish diplomacy. His verdict on the imperial conference written on the eve of the general election in June 1927—'an Irish Republic could not achieve a position of freedom better calculated to promote in peace our prosperity and our national institutions'—probably said as much about his view of Fianna Fáil as it did dominion evolution.[11]

Sean T. Ó Ceallaigh and de Valera were the principal architects of Fianna Fáil's foreign policy. Other vocal figures included the future taoiseach, Seán Lemass, who was highly critical of the League, a body he believed 'wrapped in utter futility'.[12] An early discussion document advocated a prompt withdrawal should the party enter government, a position Lemass tried to get adopted as policy in 1931. The party voted against the annual budget for the department of external affairs in protest at the government's engagement with the Commonwealth and took a critical view of its foreign policy decisions in general. Anti-imperialist resolutions disappeared from *ard fheis* agendas by 1928 but for some, thinking on foreign affairs had moved little from the Dáil period, prompting John J. Horgan, the *Round Table*'s Ireland correspondent, to observe 'Mr. de Valera's peculiar glasses enable him to see a sinister English plot concealed in every diplomatic document.'[13] A Spartan ethos eschewed the trappings of state functions, including any kind of formal wear, and the parliamentary party boycotted functions hosted by government ministers (an exception was made for the arrival of a papal nuncio in 1930). It was a confrontational atmosphere and, while the government had a slender

[9] Ibid., vol. 30, col. 812–81, 5 June 1929.

[10] Hugh Law T.D., ibid., vol. 30, col. 850, 5 June 1929.

[11] Memorandum by Joseph Walshe on the Department of External Affairs and the Imperial Conference, 1 June 1927, UCDA P80/594.

[12] *Dáil Éireann deb.*, vol. 39, col. 1271, 1 July 1931.

[13] *The Round Table*, Sept. 1928. The Ireland correspondent was the Cork journalist J. J. Horgan.

majority, by-election results confirmed that Fianna Fáil was making advances.

Fianna Fáil faced a formidable opponent in the form of Patrick McGilligan, who took over as minister for external relations following the assassination of Kevin O'Higgins. Another northerner in the Free State administration, the Derry-born 'diamond hard' McGilligan was a popular figure as a result of his role in pioneering the Shannon hydroelectric plant and he retained the role of minister for industry and commerce. A sharp manner and keen legal mind made him a forceful figure in the Dáil and in negotiations with the British and he would play a key role in the final stages of the development of the dominions at the imperial conference in 1930.

'A MISSION OF THANKS': COSGRAVE VISITS THE UNITED STATES

The new American minister, Frederick Sterling, arrived in Dublin in July, shortly after the funeral for Kevin O'Higgins and found the mood sombre. Sterling had served as deputy at the US embassy in London, where he had worked with secretary of state Frank Kellogg, who had been the ambassador at the time. Smiddy hoped the fact that an Irish-American had not been appointed would increase the interest of the 'Hundred per cent American' in Ireland. The government was pleased that Sterling's appointment was followed by a decision to open a trade commission in Dublin even though exports to the US were low (5 per cent of the figure for Northern Ireland) and high American tariffs an obstacle to increasing them.

Cosgrave had initiated a rethink of the Free State's approach to Irish-America in 1925. The emergence of Fianna Fáil lent weight to this exercise. Initially wary of close association with Irish-American organizations, Cumann na nGaedheal now felt a need to engage with them. The legation in Washington made a point of cultivating Irish-American organizations across North America, to the irritation of the State Department which made known its annoyance at what it considered interference in internal American affairs.[14] Radio and Pathé broadcasts also provided a link between the Irish government and the diaspora in the United States. One of the most pressing tasks still facing the legation was the need to establish that it represented a state and not a party. A more engaged

---

[14] Macauley to Walshe, NAI, DFA EA2/225.

approach would be combined with use of the levers of state to receive the official endorsement of the American republic. The means to secure this benediction was an official visit by Cosgrave to the United States.

The agenda for the visit was simple. A memorandum for the cabinet prepared in December 1927 by Joseph Walshe set out the rationale: 'we cannot expect Irish-Americans to take an interest in the Saorstát if we persist in ignoring their existence'. What Irish-America wanted to see was 'tangible evidence of our State's existence and nothing will bring it home to them more definitely than seeing the President ... received by President Coolidge in Washington and honoured by the people who run the United States'.[15] The catalyst for the visit was an invitation by the Irish Fellowship Club in Chicago, a pro-Free State body, which offered to fund a visit to the US by Cosgrave or one of his ministers in 1927. Smiddy had suggested an official visit as early as 1924 and urged Cosgrave to accept the offer as a means of establishing once and for all the legitimacy of the Free State in Irish-American eyes.

Smiddy had also advised Cosgrave that a high level visit would weaken de Valera's influence in the United States.[16] In March 1927, de Valera visited the United States for the first time since the war of independence; his last trip across the Atlantic had been as president of the unrecognized republic. He arrived this time as the leader of Fianna Fáil, and set about fund-raising ahead of the general election scheduled for the summer. His visit took him to Boston, Chicago, and Philadelphia, and to New York where he testified in the court case over ownership of the remaining $2.5 million left from the republican bond drive. Smiddy reported on his movements from Washington, warning the State Department that an invitation to the White House would not be welcomed in Dublin. For his part, de Valera boycotted the Free State legation. Smiddy estimated that the visit had not been the funding success hoped for with elections coming. His comment that 'financial support will come mainly from the servant class', betrayed more than a touch of snobbery towards a section of the Irish community he was supposed to represent.[17] Smiddy's manner and attire were patrician, earning him the opprobrium of Fianna Fáil who questioned his politics and Oxbridge accent in almost equal measure. Despite Cosgrave's claim that his visit was not inspired by party motive, the government was worried about the impact of American dollars on Fianna Fáil's electoral performance in Ireland while Seán

---

[15] Memorandum by Joseph Walshe to Diarmuid O'Hegarty, 8 Dec. 1927, NAI DT S4529.
[16] Smiddy to Cosgrave, 21 July 1927, NAI DFA EA 231/1/1929.
[17] Smiddy to FitzGerald, 5 April 1927, NAI DFA EA 231/1/1929.

Lemass accused him of attempting to 'queer our pitch' in the United States.

There was little over a month between the cabinet's decision to proceed with the visit on 13 December and Cosgrave's arrival in America on 20 January. The speed with which a programme was assembled featuring captains of industry, politics, and the arts, reflected both the influence of the Irish-American organizations and the extent to which Smiddy's efforts had established the Free State. Dubbed by Cosgrave a 'mission of thanks to the American people' for their support for Irish independence, the journey was evocative of de Valera's progress across the States nine years earlier. Smiddy predicted it would be a 'grand triumphant march'.[18] The visit took him to New York, Chicago, Washington, and Philadelphia, with a detour to Ottawa. Cosgrave did not visit that other capital of Irish-America, Boston, on the advice of both the State Department and sympathetic Irish-Americans, who warned a hostile reception was likely. The visit was a whirlwind of meetings and public engagements. Even before his liner had docked on 20 January, Cosgrave had wired a message of thanks to President Coolidge. An editorial in the *New York Times* the following day asked 'what guest could be more welcome to the majority of the American people?'

On arrival in New York, he set off for Chicago by train where he was the guest of the Irish Fellowship Club. He was met on arrival by mayor 'Big Bill' Thompson, whose trademark racoon coat and trilby hat made the local headlines and contrasted with the 'sea of silk toppers' as Chicago society turned out to meet the Irish leader. Among them was a brother of Michael Collins serving in the Chicago police force. The police had prepared for demonstrations but none materialized; the icy January weather was hardly ideal for protesting. Cosgrave used a speech broadcast live from Chicago on national radio to paint a picture of the Free State as a respectable, forward looking European country that had set the divisions of the past behind it. The message was almost entirely economic, emphasizing growth in trade and agriculture, reduction in the national debt and government spending on infrastructure. There was a clear appeal for investment and a call for Irish-Americans to visit. 'Ireland has a big heart for all her children,' he assured his audience, 'she will greet you as a mother.'[19]

Irish-American money paid for the private train carriage that transported the visiting party, giant portraits of Cosgrave that adorned the Chicago streets and the syndicated radio broadcast of his Chicago speech,

[18] Smiddy to McGilligan, 13 Jan. 1928, NAI DT S4529.
[19] W.T. Cosgrave radio address, Chicago, 21 Jan. 1928, NAI DT S4529.

which reached an estimated audience of thirty million Americans. The broadcast was made possible by Owen Young, whose efforts to resolve the reparations problem the following year would result in the Young Plan. The Chicago Irish-Americans even supplied a doctor and dentist to accompany Cosgrave in case of medical emergency. The émigré largesse contrasted with the public messaging of a government and people intent on paying their own way.

Cosgrave called on President Coolidge in Washington on the 23rd and lunched with him the following day. The cabinet and leaders from both sides of the aisle on Capitol Hill turned out for the occasion. A former governor of Massachusetts, Coolidge was no stranger to Irish politics or the weight of the Irish vote. Secretary of State Kellogg also threw a dinner in Cosgrave's honour. He refused to be drawn on the country's prohibition laws, commenting that 'the air here is like champagne'. He was greeted on Capitol Hill as 'America's most welcome guest' and visited both houses of Congress. The Senate was temporarily recessed to enable him to speak and he renewed his thanks, describing his visit as a return for that paid by Benjamin Franklin to the Irish parliament in 1771. The last Irish leader to address the Senate had been Charles Stewart Parnell in 1880. An early morning canter was the occasion for a meeting with Senator William Borah, chairman of the Senate Foreign Relations Committee who had thwarted US ratification of the Treaty of Versailles. The overlapping worlds of Ireland and Britain were evident in a reception thrown by the Cork-born military attaché at the British embassy, Colonel L. H. R. Pope-Hennessy who, a decade earlier, had been a leading light in the Irish Dominion League. In Philadelphia, Cosgrave was presented by the Friendly Sons of St Patrick with a replica of a gold chain given to George Washington made especially for the occasion. In Atlantic City, he toured the famous Boardwalk.

The programme in New York was focused on Wall Street, with visits to a number of banks including the National City Bank that had overseen the Free State's national loan the previous year, a trip to the New York Stock Exchange and a meeting with the *Wall Street Journal*. Several of the banks Cosgrave visited would be among the first to suffer in the financial crash the following year. The government was keen to highlight the sound finances and credit-worthiness of the Free State following reports from Washington that the government's weakened position and the growing strength of Fianna Fáil following the second general election in 1927 had adversely affected the country's credit rating.[20] Fiscal rectitude, market

---

[20] Smiddy to McGilligan, 20 Oct. 1927, NAI DFA EA 231/1/29.

confidence, and financial probity were the watchwords along with an appeal for tourism and investment dollars. Criticism of high American tariffs as an obstacle to Irish exports to the United States prompted Mayor James J. Walker to mention low Free State taxes.

With an eye to the Irish community in the city, Cosgrave was invited to inspect the 'Fighting 69th' Irish American regiment, where the band drowned out a small republican protest. A round of receptions, lunches, and dinners with city dignitaries and Irish-American politicians was capped by a gala Emerald Ball at the Waldorf Hotel. De Valera travelled to the United States at the same time, to raise funds and to mark Cosgrave's cards. Despite staying in the same hotel, he did not attend the ball while Cosgrave appeared only for a few minutes, ostensibly because he was tired but in reality to avoid any unpleasantness should he encounter anti-Free State protesters. Both men avoided meeting and referred only in passing to the presence of the other on American soil.

Cosgrave's visit was choreographed from start to finish to present the best image of the Free State for consumption by the American media. Speeches emphasized the journey the country had travelled since the treaty, the return of internal stability and external respectability. The legation even got in touch with the 'moving picture organisations' to ensure the best shots of Cosgrave would be used in cinema newsreels. If the State Department dubbed it a pilgrimage, it was one performed as much before the altars of the American republic as the shrines of Irish-America: Washington's grave at Mount Vernon, the tomb of the unknown warrior at Arlington, and the battle site at Valley Forge. A call on the elderly Fenian, John Devoy a few months before his death, and dinner hosted by the former judge Daniel Cohalan, who had spear-headed the pro-Free State campaign, paid respect to both sides of the split in Irish-America.

The reception was more restrained but no less warm in Canada, where Cosgrave was the guest of Prime Minister McKenzie King, even if icy weather conditions derailed Cosgrave's train outside Montreal, killing the driver. The travelling party was visibly shaken on arrival in Ottawa while an anxious McKenzie King confided to his diary his fears for the Empire had Cosgrave been killed, leaving the way clear for de Valera to take the helm in Dublin.[21] After paying a visit to the Canadian parliament, he was guest of honour at a state dinner. In Ottawa, too, the financial message was paramount in public, while discussions in private focused on Commonwealth developments and Irish-Canadian cooperation at Geneva.

[21] Diaries of William Lyon McKenzie King, 30 Jan. 1928, pp. 48–9, Library and Archives Canada William Lyon Mackenzie King fonds/January 30, 1928.

If Cosgrave began his American odyssey aboard the *Homeric*, it was somehow fitting that he returned home triumphant aboard the *Olympic*. An airplane escort, gun salute, and fireworks greeted his return to Dublin, providing a welcome lift for a party still bruised from the electoral tribulations of the previous year. The visit surpassed expectations, casting Cosgrave in the role of a statesman received on equal terms in the capital of the most powerful country in the world. Ever-ready to detect a British plot, J. J. O'Kelly used the pages of the *Catholic Bulletin* to accuse Cosgrave of travelling to the United States at London's behest to pacify Irish-America. *The Irish Times*, which generally took a cool view of Irish diplomatic activity, believed relations between America and Britain were better 'because Mr Cosgrave is a prime minister in Dublin'.[22] The visit had also performed an important domestic function, asserting Cumann na nGaedheal's place in what Cosgrave called the 'Irish Mainland' in a St Patrick's Day message two months later.[23]

PREACHING PEACE:
THE KELLOGG–BRIAND PACT

While memories of the visit lingered in Ireland, attention in Washington was focused on the continuing failure of efforts in Europe to achieve progress towards disarmament. The Americans seized the initiative in April, announcing bold plans for a new treaty to outlaw war. The French foreign minister, Aristide Briand, had come up with the idea first, but as a bilateral initiative between France and the United States. Unwilling to be tied into a pact with France alone, lest it prove a backdoor to European security commitments Washington was pledged to avoid, Secretary of State Kellogg recast it as a multilateral peace pact to be signed by the major powers. The United States initially invited only the British to attend, considering the treaty an imperial matter for London to represent the dominions. In keeping with the outcome of the imperial conference two years earlier, London proposed instead that they be invited to sign the treaty individually, in their own right. The Americans acquiesced but did not immediately send an invitation to Dublin, despite Cosgrave's recent visit and Dublin's constructive tone at the naval conference the previous year. Fearing they would appear as adjuncts of Britain, the Irish asked London to solicit a separate invitation. This was quickly forthcoming and the Irish immediately accepted, expressing full support for the American

[22] *The Irish Times*, 21 Jan. 1928.   [23] *The New York Times*, 18 Mar. 1928.

objectives which, McGilligan observed, were in keeping with the covenant of the League, an important point in Dublin if not necessarily so for Washington. The forthright support for the American proposals was published in the press and earned the Free State praise in Washington. The Irish also rejected British proposals to exclude defence of the empire or Commonwealth from the text of the pact.

The Kellogg–Briand Pact, or the 'International Treaty for the Renunciation of War as an Instrument of National Policy' to give it its full title, comprised three brief articles committing signatories to renounce recourse to war but provided no means of enforcement. Self-defence and commitments under existing treaty obligations were excluded from its scope. In addition to the major powers and the dominions, the signatories of the Locarno treaties were also invited to take part in negotiations, fifteen states in total.[24] The Pact was signed at the Quai d'Orsay before the world's press on 27 August. Although other countries sent their foreign ministers, the idea that Kellogg might make a return visit to Ireland after the ceremonies in Paris had been put forward, prompting the suggestion that Cosgrave should sign the pact. McGilligan told Cosgrave it was 'a golden opportunity' for publicity and he agreed: by travelling to Paris he would associate the Free State with the Pact and with the United States.[25] Each of the fifteen signatories signed the pact with gold pens made especially for the occasion. The Irish press noted approvingly that it was the first time the tricolour was flown outside the French foreign ministry. In an echo of the protests outside the League in September 1923, a republican envoy was despatched to Paris to denounce Cosgrave's right to sign for Ireland.

Dubbed an 'international kiss' by one US senator, the pact seemed to revive the flagging Locarno spirit and lifted an international mood deflated by the deadlock on disarmament talks at Geneva. Prior to its conclusion, there had been no mechanism to prevent the United States from coming to the aid of a country that had been declared an aggressor under the League covenant. With the signing of the pact, this situation was rectified and the United States brought a little closer to engagement with the League system, itself an aim of Irish foreign policy. It was the first multilateral treaty negotiated by an Irish government and the first to be separately signed by each of the dominions in their own right. The *Round Table* described it as the Free State's 'first big step' in international affairs.[26] Other countries

---

[24] The Pact's signatories were Australia, Belgium, Canada, Czechoslovakia, France, Germany, the Irish Free State, India, Italy, Japan, New Zealand, Poland, South Africa, the United Kingdom, and the United States.

[25] McGilligan to Cosgrave, 14 Aug. 1928, NAI DFA 27/11.

[26] *The Round Table*, Sept. 1928.

would be invited to accede afterwards, including many of the small states with which the Free State sought to associate itself.

The Pact did not receive an easy ride through the Dáil when it was presented for ratification the following February. Fianna Fáil had tried on three occasions to have it debated in May, before the government signalled its intention to sign, and was in uncompromising mood. McGilligan had told the house it was time the country played its part in promoting peace, and the Labour benches agreed, its leader Thomas O'Connell referring to a small state's 'duty to preach peace'. Speaking for Fianna Fáil, Seán Lemass agreed the Irish were 'a people with a desire for peace deeply ingrained in us to an extent which probably does not exist in any other race', but asked how the country could accept a pact that meant respecting borders while British forces remained in the treaty ports. The party also condemned the lack of a provision outlawing the use of force to defend overseas possessions. 'We would not be true to our history' Ó Ceallaigh argued, by accepting a pact based on such terms.[27] FitzGerald side-stepped the question of the ports, claiming the pact made it less likely they would ever be used while McGilligan appealed to the house to look to the global good: 'we do not believe that the Pact will end war for all time, but we have a right to hope that it may'.[28] Fianna Fáil was not persuaded and voted against, Ó Ceallaigh bluntly stating it would be foolish to give up 'the only means that have yet been used with success to bring that powerful secular enemy of ours to her senses'.[29] The government rushed to ratify the pact when the Dáil resumed on 20 February, in time for Herbert Hoover's inauguration on 4 March. McGilligan took the unusual step of telling the Americans it had been provisionally ratified before the Dáil had even discussed it. Despite the hurry, the Free State refused to allow an instrument of ratification to be prepared beforehand until concerns had been clarified regarding the status of the Council of State vis-à-vis the dominions (George V was ill at the time).

SECRETARY OF STATE KELLOGG
VISITS IRELAND

Cosgrave's visit to the United States had underlined the strong ties of sentiment linking the Free State and the United States and these were now reinforced by Kellogg's decision to visit Ireland on his return to

---

[27] *Dáil Éireann deb.*, vol. 28, col. 285–301, 21 Feb. 1929.
[28] Ibid., vol. 30, col. 809, 5 June 1929.
[29] Ibid., vol. 28, col. 277–320, 21 Feb. 1929.

Washington from Paris. The highest-ranking foreign representative to visit the Free State, his arrival on 30 August generated considerable excitement. Kellogg steamed from France to Ireland on the cruiser *Detroit* with Cosgrave onboard. A victorious James FitzMaurice, fresh from his trans-Atlantic flight (he and his German co-pilots had been feted by Coolidge in May) circled the American ship as it steamed into Dún Laoghaire, while crowds lined the quayside and a twenty-one gun salute rang out. The US navy had to navigate uncertain constitutional waters on the short passage from France: should the ship fly the Irish or British flag on arrival? The navy band opted to play *The Admiral's March* in place of *The Soldier's Song*, claiming they did not have the score (the French army had played *God Save the King* when Cosgrave boarded the ship at Le Havre). It was the first time a foreign vessel had conveyed a dominion premier through British waters and the first military salute for a foreign dignitary performed by the Irish army. The entire cabinet gathered on the waterfront to greet Kellogg, who was awarded the freedom of the City of Dublin. To the evident disappointment of the hosts, champagne bottles were left unopened in a public show of prohibition by the American guests. A call on the governor general and a state banquet completed the official programme. An unusually enthusiastic *Irish Times* hailed Dublin as the 'world's mouthpiece' expressing thanks to the American politician for his work for peace.[30] Speeches emphasized the links between Ireland and America and Kellogg's historic achievement in outlawing war (he was bringing the treaty back to Washington in the ship's safe).The timing of the visit less than three months before a presidential election in November was evident and the American press speculated it would provide a boost to the campaign of Republican hopeful, Herbert Hoover. *The Irish Times* believed the motives for the visit 'need be none the less sincere because . . . it promises material profit', an assessment it was incapable of making of the Free State's own diplomatic efforts.[31]

The issue that dominated the headlines was Kellogg's decision not to visit Britain as well. The British had been expecting him to visit London first, but Kellogg changed his plans and travelled straight to Ireland. An Anglo-French agreement on naval armaments in the summer of 1928 had irritated Washington, which was put out at London's rejection of its proposals at the Geneva naval conference the previous year. President Coolidge accused the British of duplicity and there were rumours of a cooling in relations with London as Kellogg left for the signing ceremony in Paris. Sinn Féin had dreamt of frustrating Anglo-American relations but the Free State found itself unwittingly benefiting from a spat between London and Washington. There was considerable speculation as to why London had not featured in the secretary's travel plans. The official reason given was lack of time, but the three days Kellogg spent playing golf and touring the countryside gave the lie to this argument. A visit to Ireland held out the prospect of votes in the presidential election. The British sought to downplay the incident, but there was a hollow ring to claims that officials were away at their shooting lodges. The Kelloggs and the Sterlings were friends from their days together at the American embassy in London and the programme was largely private; apart from the necessary formalities befitting a visit of such stature, little official business was conducted. Governor General McNeill's brief speech at a private dinner for the visiting party gave the game away: 'Secretary Kellogg has come to Ireland on a mission of peace and it behoves us to give him some.'

DISARMAMENT EFFORTS RESUME

Fresh from the signature of the Kellogg–Briand Pact and Kellogg's much-publicized visit to Dublin, Irish delegates at the League assembly in September sought to inject further momentum into the faltering efforts on disarmament. A flood of petitions from around the world urged governments and leaders to make a leap of faith and call the disarmament conference into being. It was widely believed a simple reduction in armaments would bring greater security and the ability of Geneva to deliver both became elevated in the public mind to a test of the entire League system. These concerns were shared in Ireland, where a petition initiated by the Irish League of Nations Society was taken up elsewhere, tapping into popular concern about the arms race. MacWhite believed the Kellogg–Briand Pact was the most important development in international law since the Versailles treaty, strengthening not just the League's sanctions regime (by denying American support for an aggressor) but European security in general, leaving the 'road to disarmament open', but this would prove an overly optimistic assessment.[32] Criticizing the continuing delay in convening the hoped-for disarmament conference, the Free State called for a deadline in the preparatory commission's work and a date for the conference before the next assembly. Neither was forthcoming and the drift in League efforts continued to the disappointment of all but the main powers.

[32] Memorandum by Michael MacWhite, May 1928, NAI DFA 27/11.

The League had been seeking for some time to establish a security and arbitration framework that would create the conditions for a successful outcome to any disarmament process. With disarmament talks stalled, the League's committee on arbitration and security set to work on a number of model treaties with the aim of advancing international security. Friftjof Nansen had suggested a draft treaty for compulsory arbitration in November 1927 and other proposals followed. All stopped short of the automatic provisions rejected in the Geneva Protocol. Three of these, on conciliation, judicial settlement, and settlement by arbitration, were grouped together in the General Act for the Pacific Settlement of International Disputes. For the Irish, the General Act was a welcome instalment in the League's promise to provide an effective European security architecture. Signatories to the Kellogg–Briand Pact had a duty, McGilligan told delegates, to support the General Act and it was approved by the assembly; even the British agreed despite being unenthusiastic about its content. The Free State also supported Finnish proposals for financial aid to victims of aggression.

The League marked its tenth anniversary in 1929. Hopes were high that a breakthrough could be achieved on disarmament, and Cosgrave called for the 'world movement in favour of peace' to continue in his St Patrick's Day message in March. George Bernard Shaw paid a much-publicized visit to Geneva in September 1928. His impressions of the League appeared in print the following year and were mixed. Highly critical of the League's political record and the quality of debate in the assembly—a 'hot air exchange' where delegates delivered speeches filled with 'Christmas card platitude at best and humbug at worst'—he praised its technical work and the growth of an international public service which, he believed, alone could serve the best interests of humanity.[33]

The Free State remained an ardent supporter of the League, but some of Shaw's criticisms were shared by a department of external affairs frustrated at the ability of the major powers to prevent progress on a range of issues. McGilligan was presented with the outcome of a worldwide campaign for disarmament at the start of the anniversary year, and at the assembly in September lamented that improvements in security 'had not been matched by progress on disarmament'.[34] His call for an immediate meeting of the disarmament conference fell on deaf ears, as did his suggestion that a political discussion was needed and that agreement on

---

[33] George Bernard Shaw, 'The League of Nations', Fabian Tract No. 226 (London, Jan. 1929).
[34] McGilligan speech to League of Nations Assembly, September 1929, NAI DT S8179.

technical details could wait. Unable to influence the discussions (or lack thereof), he opted instead to embarrass others by pointing to the steps the Free State had taken to disarm.

By declaring war 'illegal' as a means of resolving international disputes, the Kellogg–Briand Pact created the conditions to revisit the issue of the Permanent Court of International Justice. Article 36 of the Court's statute (the 'optional clause') gave it compulsory jurisdiction over disputes in which a signatory state was involved. The clause had lain unsigned for a number of years, but a number of states now seized upon it as a means to provide the teeth which the Paris pact famously lacked, pledging to sign the clause at the assembly meeting. How would the Commonwealth react this time?

It had been agreed at the imperial conference in 1926 that Commonwealth members would consult before taking steps to sign the clause. The British had argued against signature at the time, but the return of a Labour government in May 1929 changed things. The new administration decided to sign the clause, but with a reservation excluding disputes between Commonwealth members, and encouraged Dublin and the dominions to do likewise. Ramsay MacDonald travelled to Geneva for the assembly, wishing to deliver a 'joint blow for peace' by announcing Commonwealth support for the optional clause. But the idea of a Commonwealth exception and a British announcement were equally unpalatable in Dublin. A meeting between McGilligan and MacDonald quickly revealed that the British prime minister had not been briefed by his Foreign Office officials on the implications of the proposed Commonwealth reservation (yet again, Cecil Hurst was on hand to confirm the British position that dominion disputes were not international disputes).[35]

The issue of status had reared its head again. Lengthy and, at times acrimonious, Commonwealth discussions in the margins of the League assembly failed to reach agreement while a British proposal to create a special court for Commonwealth disputes if the dominions gave up the right to appeal to The Hague was met with an explanation from McGilligan that theoretical rights had real political consequences for the Irish government at home. In any event, McGilligan had already stated in parliament that the Free State would reserve the right to take Britain to the court in The Hague, even if it would only do so in extremis.

Anxious to quash once and for all the idea that the Commonwealth operated as a diplomatic unit, McGilligan signed the clause without reservation on 14 September, while the other members were still

---

[35] Report by John A. Costello on the Optional Clause, 12 Sept. 1929, NAI DT S4363.

squabbling over the terms on which they would sign. His stated aim was to uphold the primacy of international law and arbitration as the means to resolve disputes. The move generated widespread praise and publicity for the Free State, as did McGilligan's protest at the number of states signing League conventions with reservations that effectively hobbled their application. The other dominions signed the clause with the British reservations, although Canada and South Africa privately supported the Irish position. The only Irish condition was one of reciprocity, although McGilligan conceded in the Dáil that the government viewed the court as a 'last resort' if all other channels had been exhausted.[36] It nonetheless represented a useful alternative to the judicial committee of the Privy Council, whose right to hear appeals from dominion courts the Free State wished to see abolished.

In contrast to its attitude towards the Kellogg–Briand Pact, Fianna Fáil gave the signature a qualified welcome although Ó Ceallaigh was unconvinced that a dispute with Britain could successfully be brought before the International Court. Walshe had clarified the situation in a letter to Smiddy in London a few days after McGilligan had signed the clause: only if the Free State's integrity or status were threatened would the government consider taking Britain to the International Court. The risk of a ruling damaging to the Free State's status was considered too high, however, to make this a realistic prospect for some time.[37] The Free State had reserved the right to independent arbitration even if it might not choose to exercise it, whilst at the same time reaffirming its basic opposition to the practice of signing international treaties with reservations attached. The contrast to the situation in 1925, when the Geneva Protocol had not been signed, revealed the distance the Free State had travelled. Even if McGilligan had been careful not to burn too many bridges, it was a clear Irish interest to establish a legal framework that transcended the obligations of the Anglo-Irish Treaty. As an alternative set of obligations to those incurred under the Treaty, the League maintained its importance. If jurists were undecided as to which set of commitments had supremacy, it was helpful to demonstrate an alternative basis for obligations already existing. McGilligan accordingly told his dominion colleagues the Free State favoured some form of Commonwealth tribunal to hear disputes under its League obligations to arbitration rather than any separate obligation arising from Commonwealth membership.

---

[36] *Dáil Éireann deb.*, vol. 33, col. 893, 26 Feb. 1930.
[37] Walshe to Smiddy, 17 Sept. 1929, NAI DFA 227/80.

Dublin favoured extending the process of arbitration to the maximum extent possible and, by 1929, advances in dominion status and a growing maturity in Irish foreign policy thinking enabled a more forward position to be taken. At the same time that he signed the optional clause, McGilligan also signalled the Free State's intention to sign the General Act, linking it to the Kellogg–Briand Pact and support for the permanent court of international justice. One outlawed war while the other provided for compulsory legal jurisdiction of disputes; the General Act complemented both by providing for arbitration of non-legal disputes. This was again done in advance of other Commonwealth members, which did not sign up until after the imperial conference of 1930. A decision to seek arbitration treaties with France, Spain, Italy, and the United States was also in keeping with support for efforts to promote international arbitration. If the Free State had no axes to grind, presumably it would have no need for arbitration treaties, but Dublin was responding to a growing trend. Thirty bilateral or regional arbitration treaties were registered with the League in 1929, up from fifteen the previous year, and by January 1930 a total of 130 had been registered. Because of pressure of parliamentary business, the General Act was not ratified until June 1931. In the debate that preceded its passage through the Dáil, McGilligan laid out his government's philosophy of international relations. Listing the obligations the country had accepted in the promotion of an international regime for the pacific settlement of disputes, he told the house there was 'no reason why we should stop short' from submitting all areas of the state's international relations to the rule of law.[38]

Although it continued to harbour reservations about the League, Fianna Fáil supported the General Act, acknowledging a 'considerable amount of real belief, if not enthusiasm, in the League of Nations method and machinery'.[39] The party was also willing to give disarmament efforts the benefit of the doubt even if it doubted the sincerity of the major powers in their commitment to actually disarm. The policy of critical support and engagement with the League that it would pursue in government gradually asserted itself over the more isolationist ideas of some in the party who favoured more traditional nationalist concepts of the country's place in the world based around the global Irish race. Fianna Fáil took a different view on security policy, however, contending the government should seek to establish grounds for neutrality in the event of war rather than trying to avert the possibility itself.[40]

---

[38] *Dáil Éireann deb.*, vol. 39, col. 1141, 1 July 1931.
[39] Ibid., vol. 39, col. 1141, 1 July 1931.
[40] Ibid., vol. 27, col. 447–8, 21 Nov. 1928.

ECONOMIC DISARMAMENT

If the Free State supported international efforts at arms control and disarmament, it was less comfortable with moves in the direction of tariff reduction. A World Economic Conference in Geneva in May 1927, called in part as a response to the growing US share in world trade at Europe's expense, produced a series of resolutions intended to liberalize trade and promote tariff reduction, but progress would be slow in implementing its findings (the first convention would not be adopted until two years later).[41] With some forty-seven states represented, over half by ministers, it was the first international conference since the war that gathered the principal powers including the United States and the Soviet Union. The conference represented both a challenge and an opportunity. MacWhite told Dublin the 'leading men in industry and commerce throughout the universe' were in Geneva, making the conference a chance to promote the Free State's economic policies and attract investment.[42]

The challenge lay in the growing mood that tariff reduction was the answer to Europe's economic woes. The Free State welcomed the removal of tariffs as a source of international friction—in the jargon of the day, 'economic disarmament' would parallel the League's efforts at actual disarmament—but was concerned that blanket elimination would disadvantage smaller, under-developed economies such as Ireland. The question of tariff reduction and protection had arisen during Cosgrave's visit to the United States in January 1928 and, at the League assembly that September, Ernest Blythe rejected any obligation on states to move towards tariff reduction, asserting that the onus should fall on those with high tariffs to take the first steps. Free State tariffs were low by comparison with other European states and the country sought a balance between protectionism and free trade.

Deepening agricultural recession and the beginning of economic slowdown in Europe kept the focus on tariffs. It was a formula that appealed most to industrialized economies but not to countries like the Free State that were trying to nurture indigenous industries behind tariff walls. The 1929 assembly reviewed recommendations for further reduction leading to a 'tariff truce', proposals Health Minister John Marcus O'Sullivan dismissed as an 'invitation to commit economic hari kiri'. The Irish feared this would retard efforts at industrial development in less-advanced economies to the benefit of the industrialized nations. McGilligan, who was

---

[41] Patricia Clavin, *Securing the World Economy: the Reinvention of the League of Nations, 1920–1946*, (Oxford, 2013), pp. 42–5.
[42] MacWhite to FitzGerald, 6 may 1927, NAI DFA LN30(b) ML03/0226.

also trade minister, asked the League if it was prepared to take action on other forms of economic nationalism but received no answer.

At home, the government had decided the answer was to negotiate a series of commercial treaties with the main economies in Europe and the United States, as a means of securing market access for Irish exports at favourable rates. Agreements would soon follow with Germany and France, although negotiations in Washington ran into difficulties. Fianna Fáil welcomed the announcement, but nonetheless accused the government of neglecting trade concerns, Lemass in particular believing the work of industry and commerce had suffered while McGilligan, who held both portfolios, was 'gadding around international conferences in Europe'.[43]

It was a crowded international agenda and the Free State struggled to manage the range of issues that affected its interests. The infrastructure at home was unable to keep up (the industry and commerce department almost sent no one to the World Economic Conference) and the scattering of officials abroad was overstretched. It was time to look at the meagre resources devoted to pursuing the government's external relations.

DIPLOMATIC EXPANSION

The French consul in Dublin believed Cosgrave had developed a taste for grandeur as a result of his transatlantic tour in 1928.[44] What he did return with was a renewed appreciation for the role that foreign policy could play in promoting the country's interests and prestige, and a determination to expand the country's diplomatic network in Europe. One of the conclusions drawn from Canada's election to a seat on the League council the previous autumn was that the time had come to expand the Free State's presence in Europe as a further means of demonstrating the country's separate status from the Commonwealth. Joseph Walshe argued that such a step was also needed if Irish trade with the continent was to be increased.

The Free State's own candidacy for a council seat in 1926 had highlighted weaknesses in the department of external affairs, which was ill equipped to cope with the responsibilities a successful bid would have entailed. Even without an international role, the limits of the existing system were becoming apparent. Advances at the 1926 imperial conference had been achieved by dropping other business. As the Free State's external interests and commitments grew, the risk grew also of a precedent

---

[43] *Dáil Éireann deb.*, vol. 30, col. 800, 5 June 1929.
[44] Blanche to Briand, 3 Sept. 1928, QO, CPC 1918–40, Europe, Irlande, vol. 14, pp. 39–50.

being established to the detriment of the country's status or of a ball being dropped. 'Our missions abroad have been left entirely to their own devices,' Walshe explained to ministers. 'Our activities in our relations with Great Britain, the Dominions and nations external to the Commonwealth have been almost entirely confined to preventing the establishment of precedents likely to be used against us in the course of our constitutional development.'[45] With Fianna Fáil snapping at its heels, the implications of a constitutional setback and the attendant domestic political costs were readily understood. Hopes had been raised that foreign affairs would assume a higher priority when Kevin O'Higgins was appointed external affairs minister in the cabinet reshuffle that followed the June 1927 general election. Desmond FitzGerald moved to the defence portfolio but would remain a regular figure on delegations at Geneva and imperial conferences in London. Implementation of the imperial conference report, the general elections of 1927, and the death of Kevin O'Higgins meant that it was not until 1928 that the government turned its attention to an overhaul of the foreign ministry.

A report prepared by Walshe in July that year concluded that the existing system was inadequate and an overhaul required. W. B. Yeats described the new Free State coins that entered circulation that year as 'silent ambassadors on national taste', but there were few ambassadors of the flesh and blood kind. Five years after the Free State's creation, its overseas network extended to offices in London, Geneva, and Washington, trade commissioners in Brussels and New York, and a handful of staff working at headquarters. Finance minister Ernest Blythe had returned from the 1926 League assembly convinced of the need for a higher international profile and believing the country had reached a watershed in its League policy—either it should push forward and make the most of the opportunities of membership or it should give up—in his mind there was no halfway house between the two. Opportunities had been wasted, but the September assembly election convinced Blythe that, with suitable preparation and investment of resources, the Free State could aspire to a role similar to that played by Norway and the other Scandinavian countries.[46]

Blythe was encouraged in his thinking by MacWhite in Geneva and by his childhood friend and fellow northern Protestant, Seán Lester, head of the League section in Dublin. His support would be crucial in overcoming objections from officials at the department of finance. A cabinet

[45] Joseph Walshe aide memoire, 2 Nov. 1928, UCDA, P24/5621C.
[46] Ernest Blythe memorandum to the Executive Council, 20 Oct. 1926, NAI DT S8176.

sub-committee comprising Cosgrave, McGilligan, Blythe, and agriculture minister, Patrick Hogan, was set up in early December to finalize plans. Despite his experience as foreign minister, Desmond FitzGerald was not involved in the deliberations. In a short memorandum prepared for the cabinet, Walshe concluded that, despite advances in dominion status, European governments still did not fully regard the Free State 'as a unit in international affairs in no way subservient to Great Britain'. The only way to correct this would be to open legations in European capitals.[47]

The final complexion of the new service emerged in early January 1929. A decision was taken to establish full diplomatic relations with France and Germany and to open legations in Paris and Berlin. Cosgrave had raised with Aristide Briand the question of an Irish legation while in Paris for the signature of the Kellogg–Briand Pact. McGilligan justified the new offices in terms of trade, prestige, and historic ties. Ottawa was added to the list, in view of cooperation on Commonwealth issues and at Geneva. The network in the United States was also to be extended, with more staff for the Washington legation and a new consulate general in New York that, in 1930, assumed responsibility for consular services previously handled by the British. At first, it was proposed that League affairs would be handled by the new minister in Paris (widely rumoured to be Michael MacWhite), a practice followed by many small states at the time but, on reflection, it was decided to keep a full office in Geneva. The Ottawa office was dropped and would not open until 1939, a decision taken partly for reasons of cost, partly because Irish constitutional advances were no longer directly dependent on Canadian practice. These changes were complemented at headquarters by the appointment of a legal adviser and a restructuring of the department into divisions dealing with Commonwealth affairs, the United States, the League of Nations, and Northern Ireland. Altogether, the estimated cost of these changes was £25,792, a considerable investment at the time.

As in 1924, negotiations with the British were required before the offices could be opened, and these began in August. Changes wrought by the imperial conference of 1926 meant the procedure used when Smiddy had been appointed was no longer valid. Appointments were now made on the advice of the dominion government and no longer required the counter-signature of the British Foreign Secretary, while the dominions were jointly responsible for imperial affairs with the British. These were important gains, but the Irish wished to further dilute the Commonwealth connection involved in making the new appointments.

---

[47] 'Memorandum by External Affairs', 5 Nov. 1928, NAI DFA D1983/4.

McGilligan told London in August 1928 that he wanted to end the require-ment for consultation with British embassies and was unhappy with refer-ences to the diplomatic unity of the Commonwealth. The Canadians were also considering overseas appointments and shared some of the Irish concerns.

The Foreign Office remained un-reconciled to the growing dominion competency in foreign affairs, fearing the move away from diplomatic unity of the empire would result in a reduction in British influence abroad. If there was little it could do to halt a process that had acquired a momentum of its own, as Lord Cushendun observed while acting foreign secretary in the second half of 1928 (Chamberlain had collapsed in July from overwork), 'we should surely do our best to discourage and delay it'.[48] Cushendun's unionist background would not have endeared him to Dublin's efforts in particular and the Foreign Office believed the Dominions Office softened the tone of dispatches to placate the Irish.[49] The minuet between the Foreign and Dominions Offices would thus continue as the Irish and others capitalized on the gains won in 1926 to increase their international profile.

The Foreign Office was aware that Cosgrave's government wanted to make speedy appointments for domestic reasons, and replied at the end of September, warning that Canadian appointments would proceed faster as they had raised fewer objections.[50] Discussion between Dublin, Ottawa, and Pretoria yielded a compromise by June: the Irish conceded some mention of diplomatic unity whilst references to consultation were kept to a minimum. The British had already conceded the point in the Kellogg–Briand Pact. In addition, there would be no formal endorsement from the British government. The path was thus cleared for the Foreign Office to approach the French and German governments about the appointments.

Despite the agreement in London, the British ambassador in Paris, Sir William Tyrrell, wrote to the Quai d'Orsay on 13 June stating that the new Irish minister was being appointed 'under instructions of HM Principal Secretary of State', instead of providing the verbal intimation of London's acquiescence in the appointment he was supposed to deliver. The reply from the Quai d'Orsay agreeing to the appointment ambigu-ously referred to the wish of the 'gouvernement royal' to open an Irish legation in Paris, which a furious Dublin interpreted to mean the British rather than Irish government. Despite assurances from the Dominions

[48] Acting Secretary of State (Lord Cushendun) memorandum, 8 Oct. 1928, PRO FO 372/2439/10861.
[49] Foreign Office minute, 17 June 1929, PRO FO 627/9/388.
[50] McGilligan to Passfield, 19 Sept. 1928, NAI, DT S5736A; Batterbee to Murphy, 29 Sept. 1928, NA, DT S5736A.

Office that this was not the case, a formal complaint was lodged, McGilligan insisting that the documents be withdrawn and re-issued to make clear the appointment was being made solely at the decision of the Irish government. If the Dominions Secretary, Lord Passfield, was not prepared to do so, McGilligan warned he would bypass the British entirely and write directly to the Quai, a threat the Foreign Office seemed to take seriously as the documents were reissued without the offending reference to the foreign secretary. Dublin had successfully used the Dominions Office to enforce the correct procedure on the Foreign Office.[51]

The French and Germans responded positively to the overture and announcements were made in July. The Brussels office was closed and Count O'Kelly moved to Paris to open the new legation there. The difficulties he had experienced through lack of a formal diplomatic status in Brussels (he had found his dealings with the British embassy particularly difficult, a situation not eased by his penchant for taking initiatives to assert his status without sanction from Dublin) were no longer an issue in Paris. The Count's instinct to jump in and ask questions afterwards was not so readily resolved (his proposal that the British embassy in Paris should be renamed to remove reference to 'Irlande' resulted in the setback of a less welcome reference to 'Irlande du Nord' on the brass plate), although he would prove a valuable networker in 1930 during the Free State's bid for a seat on the League council. A UCD law professor, Daniel Binchy, was appointed minister in Berlin. A former student of Joseph Walshe, Binchy was no stranger to international affairs, having attended the League assembly in 1926. In contrast to other Free State representatives, he had not played a part in the campaign for independence. A detached academic outlook combined with thinly veiled sympathies for Cumann na nGaedheal meant he quickly found himself a 'fish out of water' in the diplomatic world and he quit the ministry in March 1932, weeks after Fianna Fáil entered government, although his views may well have seen him recalled.

MacWhite was offered the Washington post, where he would remain until 1938. His influence on the Free State's policy towards the League had been considerable, as was his understanding of how the League could be used to roll back the Treaty settlement and secure an international status and profile for the country. His grasp of this important fact was firmer than Joseph Walshe, who did not fully understand how the League worked. The head of the League section at the Foreign Office, Sir Alexander Cadogan, found MacWhite 'tortuous' to deal with while

[51] McGilligan to Amery, 14 Aug. 1929, UCDA, P24/188; McGilligan to Passfield, 4 Oct. 1929, NAI, DT S5735A; Passfield to McGilligan, 14 Nov. 1929, NAI, DT S5735A.

Cecil Hurst, architect of the *inter se* clause, told him at a Washington garden party in 1930 'you tried to get things over at Geneva but you didn't always succeed'. His views coincided with those of McGilligan on many issues and were all the more influential as a result. A list of recommendations for the Free State's League policy he prepared in 1928 had all been acted on by the time of his departure from Geneva: seek to replace Canada on the council in 1930 with an early declaration of candidacy; take a firm line on arbitration, the 'bedrock' of the covenant; sign without reservation the optional clause of the statute of the permanent court of international justice; adopt a strong attitude on disarmament issues; and champion humanitarian issues including drugs and human trafficking.[52] His move to Washington was a loss to the Free State's League policy but his successor, Seán Lester, quickly made himself at home in the world of gossip and corridor intrigue that was Geneva. Speaking French with a noticeable Ulster accent, he was a more than able replacement and quickly developed an impartial international outlook.

The French government welcomed the establishment of diplomatic relations, despite having entertained doubts that separate dominion representation in Paris would complicate relations with Britain, a perennial French concern. The French consul in Dublin had been pressing for a legation ever since the Americans upgraded their representation in 1926, and objections from the French embassy in London were over-ruled by the Quai d'Orsay.[53] Count O'Kelly presented his credentials to President Doumergue on 20 October 1929, and the French government undertook to reciprocate by raising its consulate general in Dublin to legation status. Events progressed more smoothly in Berlin. The German government agreed to the opening of a legation in late November 1928 and announced that they would reciprocate the move. Binchy presented his credentials to President Hindenburg six days after O'Kelly, on 26 October.

The transfer of MacWhite to Washington should have been a routine matter of ascertaining whether he would be *persona grata* with the American government, yet even this did not proceed as planned. The illness of George V meant his letter of credentials had to be issued by the Council of Regency. Having asked the Dominions Office to approach Washington, news leaked to the press, possibly deliberately, and Dublin received a direct agreement by cable from Washington. MacWhite presented his credentials to President Hoover on 14 March 1929, the first foreign envoy

---

[52] Michael MacWhite memorandum, 'The Saorstát and the League of Nations', 14 April 1928, NAI DFA LN 1/7.
[53] Raoul de Warren, *L'Irlande et ses Institutions Politiques* (Paris, 1928), p. 406.

to do so. Hoover's reference to the 'unusually friendly relations' between the Free State and the United States may have been prompted in part by the positive effect on the Republican vote of Kellogg's visit the previous year.

Reaction in the Dáil was more favourable than in 1924, although Fianna Fáil reminded the government that the new offices would represent the Free State rather than Ireland as a whole.[54] Press reaction was also broadly positive, despite complaints from *The Irish Times* about wasting money on 'national luxuries'. Convinced the government's sights should be kept closer to home, it intoned 'Donegall Square [in Belfast] is infinitely more important than either the Wilhelmstrasse or the Quai d'Orsay'.[55] The move was opposed from an entirely different quarter, by the underground 'republican government' of the rump Sinn Féin, which sent letters to Paris, Berlin, and Rome repudiating the newly appointed Free State envoys.[56]

In May 1927, London severed relations with Moscow in protest at alleged communist funding of labour unrest in Britain. A consequence of the move was to release the Free State from the terms of the 1921 Anglo-Russian treaty of commerce, the agreement that had put an end to hopes for an understanding between Sinn Féin and the Bolsheviks six years earlier. Dublin was consequently free to consider its own trade arrangements with the USSR. The Soviets approached Michael MacWhite in Geneva in August, suggesting trade in fish and followed up on 29 November, when assistant commissar for foreign affairs, Maxim Litvinov, met MacWhite, to propose the opening of trade links and a trade commission in Dublin. The Soviets were willing to undertake not to cross into Northern Ireland or enter Britain without permission from London.[57] MacWhite was reasonably positive, believing an arrangement could be reached that would enable a commercial treaty to follow. The Russians followed up again in February and, the following month, he again urged Dublin to consider the proposal, believing the British were looking for ways to restore relations and would not object.

Even if there might have been doubts about MacWhite's assessment of Stalin as an opportunist who accepted Marxism was a failure, discussions continued until the middle of 1929 about the possibilities of opening trade in fish, with most concern centring on the risk of non-payment.[58]

[54] *Dáil Éireann deb.*, vol. 30, col. 785–895, 5 June 1929.
[55] *The Irish Times*, 22 Nov. 1928.
[56] J. J. O'Kelly, *The Republic of Ireland Vindicated* (Dublin, 1931), p. 14.
[57] MacWhite to Walshe, 30 Nov. 1927, NAI DFA EA 104(b).
[58] MacWhite to Walshe, 7 Mar. 1928, NAI DFA 107/2.

The prospect of a centre for communist propaganda was viewed less favourably and, having consulted London unofficially, the government decided against taking up the Soviet proposal. Nevertheless, interest remained in reaching some form of commercial arrangement. There was some sympathy for the Soviet Union in labour circles, a consideration the department had in mind when instructing its new ministers to Paris and Berlin to pay the customary courtesy call on the Soviet ambassador. Few were as supportive as the Cork Fianna Fáil deputy, Thomas Mullins, who told the Dáil in late 1928 that a trade representative in the 'Eastern democracy' would be money better spent than offices in Paris, Brussels, and Geneva combined.[59]

The initial proposals for an expanded overseas network did not include a legation at the Holy See, but the government decided in the spring of 1929 to formalize relations with the Vatican, which had remained undeveloped since the Luzio affair. The motivation for the decision was domestic and political: Fianna Fáil's growing electoral fortunes were causing unease for many in Cosgrave's party. An official channel to Rome would trump the lines of communication between Fianna Fáil and John Hagan at the Irish College, who remained unsympathetic to the Free State and kept Ó Ceallaigh informed of Vatican thinking towards Ireland until his death in 1930. The government also hoped to derive a strengthened hand in dealing with republicanism and increased legitimacy at home and abroad. There was also a sense that, as a predominantly Catholic country, Ireland should be represented and respected in Rome.

Patrick McGilligan confided to Leopold Amery, the Dominions Secretary, in March that the government was keen for political reasons to show 'in some public way that the existing regime in the Free State is recognised by the pope'.[60] Appointing an envoy to the Vatican was one way to do this, and McGilligan sought advice on how this could be achieved without a nuncio being appointed in Dublin. Joseph Walshe travelled to London on 5 April to prepare this 'urgent matter of internal politics', but the British were reluctant to become involved, fearing the Vatican would raise the question of appointing a nuncio in London, something the British government wished to avoid.[61]

The government hoped a nuncio would be installed in Dublin in time for celebrations marking the centenary of Catholic emancipation, which

[59] *Dáil Éireann deb.*, vol. 27, col. 474, 21 Nov. 1928.

[60] Foreign Office minute of Amery–McGilligan discussion, 25 Mar. 1929, PRO, FO 627/7/176.

[61] Foreign Office minute of Amery–Walshe discussion, 5 April 1929, PRO, FO 627/7/199.

were due to begin on 19 June. This did not leave much time to complete the necessary diplomatic formalities. Walshe travelled to Rome to initiate *pourparlers* on 12 April and, as a measure of the importance attached to a speedy exchange of relations, McGilligan joined him there four days later. The government was prepared to send a letter from Cosgrave to Pius XI, if necessary to secure agreement, which would have created problems with the British. At a meeting with the Vatican secretary of state, Cardinal Gasparri, on 18 April, agreement was reached to exchange representatives. Walshe had separately received what he understood to be an assurance that a nuncio would be quickly announced and, believing arrangements would be in place in time for the emancipation ceremonies, McGilligan announced in the Dáil that a nuncio would arrive in Dublin by 24 June.[62] This proved to be an embarrassing miscalculation. The Vatican had not decided whom to appoint to Dublin, and proposed instead to send a papal legate, a representative to the Irish church alone, for the emancipation celebrations. The Holy See had its own reasons for wanting a representative in Dublin but it was in no hurry, and the Foreign Office was not prepared to intervene to extricate the Irish from what it considered an 'act of some inexperience'.[63] To Dublin's disappointment, the new minister to the Holy See, Charles Bewley, did not present his credentials in Rome until three days after the celebrations in Dublin had ended. 'Whose history can show greater devotion to the cause of Christianity than ours?' asked Bewley, a convert from Quakerism, when meeting Pius XI.[64] But the Vatican would not be rushed and there the matter rested for the summer.

The delay in appointing a nuncio was embarrassing for the government. Under pressure in the Dáil, McGilligan went so far as to offer to water down demands at the forthcoming Commonwealth conference in London if the British would put pressure on the Vatican to make an appointment. The Foreign Office declined, citing the government's claim that securing a nuncio was an internal Irish affair.[65] A more sympathetic Dominions Office tried unsuccessfully in late October and November to persuade the Foreign Office to change its mind, with the result that the British envoy at the Vatican, Sir Henry Chiltern, was told to do whatever he could to assist as long it would not create problems for London. With an eye on the barometer of ecclesiastical opinion at home, Walshe attributed the delay in part to opposition from Irish bishops uneasy at the prospect of

[62] Dermot Keogh, *Ireland and the Vatican* (Cork, 1995), p. 39.
[63] Foreign Office minute, 6 June 1929, PRO, FO62/7/10/348.
[64] Charles Bewley report, 27 June 1929, NAI DFA 217/15.
[65] Record of McGilligan–Attorney General conversation, PRO FO627/10/631; Foreign Office minute of discussion, n.d.1929, PRO, FO 627/10/631; Mounsey to Batterbee, 18 Nov. 1929, PRO, FO 672/10/653.

a nuncio becoming involved in the affairs of the Irish church. The Vatican finally named its envoy in Malta, Paschal Robinson, as nuncio on 27 November. Robinson, who was born in Ireland but raised in the United States, was received in Dublin with considerable pomp the following January. In keeping with the mood of the time, the ecclesiastical ceremonies of his appointment were conducted before those of the state.

As 1929 drew to a close, the Free State had taken a major step in its relations with the outside world. The number of its overseas offices had doubled and, while still small when compared to other similarly sized European countries, it led the pack among the dominions in projecting an independent and principled line on matters at the League, consistent with the expanding field of dominion prerogatives. The two American visits of 1928 and the Free State's growing profile at Geneva added to the sense of an evolving foreign policy, while the new diplomatic offices emphasized the country's European connections. The imperial conference in 1930 would complete the work of asserting the equality of the Commonwealth members in international affairs. What remained was to complete the unfinished business of 1926 and secure election to a seat on the League council. McGilligan used Commonwealth discussions on the optional clause to announce the Free State's intention to run for election to the council the following year. The Australians indicated that they, too, were considering a run—as the second oldest dominion they saw it as their right to succeed Canada on what they clearly regarded as a dominion seat. The Free State view was rather different: it would run again as an independent member state for one of the three seats up for election. Opposed to informal groups in general and the notion of a Commonwealth one in particular, it did not accept an automatic right for one dominion to succeed another on the council. It would run and be judged on its own merits. The diplomatic agenda for 1930 had been set.

8

'A Policy of World Peace and World Economic Development', 1930–1932

The long, dark decade of the 1930s began two months early, in late October 1929, when the stock market collapsed on Wall Street. The financial turmoil unleashed sent stock prices and financiers tumbling. The governments they funded would not be long in following them as politics and economies spiralled out of control. Across the continent unemployment bit deep, placing societies and the democratic principles that underpinned them under strain. Nervous electorates and volatile markets left their mark on the political and diplomatic landscape. In the Free State, however, continuity was the order of the day, as Cosgrave's government entered its eighth year in office.

The reverberations were slow to be felt in Ireland but the country was not immune. A year into the financial crisis in November 1930, Cosgrave told international audiences that the country would pursue 'a policy of world peace and world economic development' while hoping the Free State's 'more pastoral life' would insulate it from the worst of the shocks.[1] Policy-makers were slow to respond to the shifting winds, while international obligations entered into in better days fell to be implemented in more troubled times. As the global economy tipped into recession, the Free State expanded its diplomatic network, broadened its trade agreements and committed to running for a seat on the League council.

The calmer years of the late 1920s were giving way to a more turbulent international politics. Within a year of the economic crisis, the international system would face its first major challenge. Even before the Japanese invasion of Manchuria in late 1931, the League was showing signs of fatigue, unable to make disarmament a reality. Its heyday over, the

---

[1] Cinema newsreel speech by W. T. Cosgrave, 11 June 1931, NAI DT S2366. The Free State's predominantly agricultural economy left it less exposed to the effects of the depression than more industrialized countries. This was seen at the time as a reflection on its relative lack of economic development since independence. See Patricia Clavin, *Securing the World Economy, the Reinvention of the League of Nations, 1920–1945* (Oxford, 2013), p. 78.

League was at the start of a decade of disappointment and decline as the Free State set its sights on a seat at the top table. The campaign would be a test of Dublin's standing at Geneva and a measure of how it was seen by other states. European, Commonwealth, and diaspora identities would all come into play, as would the extent of the dominions' development towards equality on the world stage. On the Commonwealth front, an imperial conference beckoned at the end of 1930, at which the British would finally concede the full equality and independence of action for the dominions internationally. As the year began, the strategy followed by Cosgrave's government over the past eight years was months away from being achieved. Two years later, it would be abandoned when Fianna Fáil displaced Cumann na nGaedheal in government at the start of 1932. All of these issues will be explored as we look at where the Free State sought to position itself a decade after independence.

WINNING A SEAT AT THE TOP TABLE

The main international issue on the government's agenda at the start of 1930 was securing election to the League council. Three non-permanent seats were due to be filled in September when Canada, Cuba, and Finland stepped down. The group arrangements against which the Free State had set its face in 1926 meant that two of these seats were foregone conclusions. Guatemala was the South Americans' choice, while Norway was tipped to take the second seat for the Nordics. For all the semblance of an open and free election, there was effectively only one vacancy—the seat occupied by Canada. The Free State faced two major obstacles in its bid for election. It would have to overcome perceptions that it represented the dominions or that its election would copper-fasten a dominion seat on the council, reducing yet further the space for other countries to win a place at the League's top table. It also faced two strong rivals in China and Portugal.

Count O'Kelly began canvassing the Paris diplomatic corps in December 1929, before an official declaration had been made that the country would stand as a candidate. The Free State was popular, he reported, but the idea of a dominion right to a seat was not. Seán Lester had drawn similar conclusions from his contacts in Geneva. The Irish decided to campaign on their record as an independent small state committed to fulfilling the obligations of League membership, and on an anti-group ticket—the same platform as in 1926. Since then, their internationalist credentials had been burnished by signature of the optional clause, support for the General Act, and their status as a founder signatory of the

Kellogg–Briand Pact. The country's support for disarmament, the codification of international law, and implementation of League commitments meant that its profile as a good international citizen was clear. Frequent references to its global connections through the diaspora reminded others of an intangible influence in the United States, an impression that it was increasingly important to foster given Washington's support for League efforts to achieve disarmament.

Belief in an Irish desire to pursue a disinterested agenda was widely held. The League secretary general, Sir Eric Drummond, told Lester in 1929 he felt the Free State could play a 'distinctive part' at Geneva greater than its size might indicate and, on the eve of Cosgrave's visit to the United States in 1928, the *New York Times* had asserted 'in any conference of nations Ireland is sure to have a greater influence than most states of four million'.[2] Lester followed his predecessor, Michael MacWhite, in detecting a tendency amongst Geneva delegates to 'have a confidence in the Saorstát representative in a way that they withheld, perhaps naturally, from others'.[3] The problem was that the Free State was a founder signatory of the Kellogg–Briand Pact and the London naval treaty because of its Commonwealth status and not because it was a small European state. How to manage this dual identity was the challenge.

The Free State's Commonwealth status was a stumbling block for a number of reasons. Australia had also indicated an interest in running and those who set store by such things considered it should take precedence. The problem was resolved when Canberra decided not to seek election. The path now clear, by the end of April the support of the other dominions had been secured for the Irish candidacy, but this created its own problems. The Free State campaigned on its reputation as an independent and responsible League actor; any attempt to cite dominion endorsement would undo efforts to disassociate its candidacy from the Commonwealth grouping. As Ernest Blythe commented, the Commonwealth link 'cut both ways'.[4]

There were other problems. The League secretariat saw the Canadian vacancy as a last opportunity of keeping an open seat on the council and Eric Drummond asked Dublin to defer its bid until the following year. His preference was for China to be re-elected, as he explained to Lester, in the interests of strengthening the League in Asia (ironically, as it would turn out, in view of the League's response to Japan's invasion of Manchuria the following year). Drummond also approached Edward Phelan with

[2] *New York Times*, 19 Jan. 1928.
[3] Lester to Walshe, 23 April 1929, NAI, DFA 217/44; *The New York Times*, 8 Jan. 1928.
[4] *Irish Independent*, 7 Oct. 1930.

his concerns, confident that they would be relayed to Dublin.[5] Patrick McGilligan was unhappy with these reports, but decided not to do anything as long as Drummond did not encourage anyone to vote for the Chinese, a line the secretary general was careful not to cross.

Similar considerations were influencing British thinking on the Irish bid. Although Arthur Henderson had said London would support the Free State if the Australians decided not to run, Canberra's decision not to seek election did not trigger the anticipated British commitment. In London, a committee charged with deciding how to react to the Irish bid recommended in May to keep all options open until nearer the election in September. The main reasons for waiting were concern about the situation in China and possible consequences for British interests in the Far East, although this was not conveyed to the Irish.[6] High Commissioner Smiddy was convinced the Foreign Office opposed the Irish candidacy, believing they would sacrifice British interests to advertise their independence if elected. The Dominions Office was also unenthusiastic, hoping the Irish would wait a year to avoid the appearance of a dominions group with a right to a seat on the council.

The situation was little better in Paris or Berlin, where voting intentions were unclear despite the direct diplomatic channels that now existed. Following signature in mid-May of a commercial treaty with Berlin, Daniel Binchy was asked to approach the foreign ministry for German support even though he believed this was doubtful. Count O'Kelly met Aristide Briand in Paris a month later to discuss the election but received an evasive reply. As the summer break approached, the Free State was unsure of support from any of the five permanent members of the council. Most embarrassing was the inability to indicate whether it had Britain's support. Concerned at London's prevarication and rightly suspecting the reason was China, Patrick McGilligan wrote to the Dominions Secretary, J. H. Thomas, in June formally requesting British support. The arguments he advanced could have been written ten years earlier. Describing the Free State as 'one of the most ancient of the civilised countries of Europe' whose status as a mother country in the Commonwealth afforded it a special role, McGilligan reminded the British that the diaspora was an important factor in US–Commonwealth relations—in particular the power of Irish-American channels, which he implied Dublin could

[5] Lester to Walshe, 13 Feb. 1930, NA, DFA 26/95; Passfield to McGilligan, 3 June 1930, NAI, DFA Paris Embassy 109B.
[6] Michael Kennedy, *Ireland and the League of Nations, 1919–1946, International Relations, Diplomacy and Politics* (Dublin, 1996), p. 135.

influence.[7] He wrote to the Colonial Secretary, Lord Passfield, the same day, rejecting British assertions that the Free State candidacy could be seen as establishing a dominion group. Making clear his view that the situation in China had no place in the election, he questioned what the Chinese could contribute to the work of the League if they could not even pay their League contributions (the country was in arrears to the tune of eight million gold francs). Asking for British solidarity, he stopped short of suggesting that bilateral relations would suffer if this were not forthcoming.[8]

Concerns about Britain's voting intentions or the creation of a dominion seat were taking their toll elsewhere, the Irish receiving professions of goodwill but no firm commitments. The thorough ventilation of the dominion group issue in the British press did not help matters in Dublin, which attributed Fleet Street interest in the subject to Foreign Office prompting. In an effort to draw a line in the sand, McGilligan issued a statement in late August denying the Free State was a Commonwealth candidate and recalling its opposition to group seats. Privately, he believed it was better to lose than win on a dominion ticket.

The department of external affairs initially viewed the Chinese candidacy as posing the greatest threat to Irish hopes, but as sentiment shifted against China at Geneva over the summer, the danger posed by Portugal came into focus. A staunch opponent of the group system, which it saw as blocking its own advancement in the League, the Portuguese bid aimed to block what is saw as a Commonwealth claim to the last 'free' seat on the council. Overtures by the South Americans in Geneva for a voting pact between Dublin and Lisbon were vetoed by McGilligan, who considered the Norwegians to be better League members and friends of Ireland. Piqued, the Portuguese mounted a negative campaign, claiming a vote for the Free State was a vote for a dominion seat.

By the start of September, the Free State had secured the support of the four dominions and three South American states; forty-five countries had been canvassed. With little prospect of the Chinese securing sufficient support to stand for re-election, Britain confirmed it would back the Irish a week before the vote. Drummond advised the Chinese to withdraw, but they refused, hoping the Free State would leave the field. For Dublin its international standing and its Commonwealth policy were at stake and resources were thrown at the bid. Count O'Kelly and Daniel Binchy were despatched to Geneva for the last push and Michael MacWhite would also

[7] McGilligan to Thomas, 18 June 1930, NAI DFA 26/95.
[8] McGilligan to Passfield, 18 June 1930, NAI Paris Embassy 109B.

have been diverted too, had he not been aboard a liner sailing for New York.

The implications of the National Socialists' success in the German general election three days earlier were still being digested across Europe as the election took place on the morning of 17 September. There were four candidates, the assembly having ruled against China's bid. Guatemala was elected first with forty-one votes, followed by Norway with thirty-eight. The Free State took the third seat with thirty-six votes from a total of forty-eight while Portugal trailed with thirty. Commonwealth votes had decided the Free State's win. At a council meeting immediately after the vote, Ernest Blythe took the Irish seat. The outcome was, he said, a tribute to the Irish race at home and abroad. *The Irish Times* described the result as a 'signal honour for the youngest dominion'. Its earlier doubts forgotten, the *Irish Independent* also welcomed the election, which *The Star* saw as a 'striking testimony of the international esteem' the Free State enjoyed.[9] Reacting to the announcement in Dublin, Patrick McGilligan pledged Irish support for disarmament, 'the real and immediate task of the League' and called for the disarmament conference to meet as quickly as possible.

Securing a seat at the League's top table was something many of the new states in Europe and some of the older ones had yet to achieve. The Free State was more successful than Hungary, Bulgaria, or the Baltic States, all of which, for various reasons, were unable to make a mark at Geneva. The Portuguese had mounted a negative campaign, describing an Irish seat as another vote for Britain on the council. Their fourth place indicated the extent to which this was no longer believed. The candidacy had provided an opportunity to break out of the Commonwealth shadow, whilst still retaining the advantages of membership. The empire journal *Round Table* had suggested that the 'blend of the idealist and realist' characteristic of Irish politicians 'may now prove a valuable contribution to world politics from a nation which is both European and detached'.[10] That assessment would now be put to the test. Before the Free State could turn its attention to its duties on the council, however, there was an imperial conference to get through.

THE IMPERIAL CONFERENCE OF 1930

Patrick McGilligan had not travelled to Geneva for the election because of preparations for the conference, which opened in London two weeks later

---

[9] *The Star*, Oct. 1930.   [10] *Round Table*, Dec. 1929.

on 1 October. It was the Free State's third imperial conference. Much of the groundwork had been carried out the previous year by a Committee on the Operation of Dominion Legislation and its report, published on 3 February 1930, formed the basis for the conference. The Committee was essentially an imperial conference in miniature, with a substantive political agenda of its own. As Harkness rightly points out, much of the constitutional arcania it did away with was of concern to the older dominions rather than the Free State but the Irish nonetheless took a close interest in its work on the grounds that strengthening the other dominions' sovereignty would enhance the status of the dominions as a whole. The issue that received the greatest attention was disallowance and reservation of dominion legislation by the British parliament. No such provision existed in the Free State constitution, but the Irish regarded its continuing existence as an affront to dominion sovereignty. The related issue of whether dominions could alter their constitutions was also affirmed. This was mainly a concern of the other dominions whose constitutions had been laid down by acts of the British parliament (the Irish did not regard the provision that their constitution should conform to the Treaty of 1921 a limitation so much as an undertaking that they should not breach its terms). These hangovers from an earlier period in Commonwealth development were removed. Limitations to the territorial application of dominion legislation were also cleared up.

The Committee took up the question of nationality at Dublin's instigation, which was already preparing its own nationality legislation. Issues relating to succession and royal titles would henceforth be a matter for all Commonwealth parliaments to agree on and not just Westminster, the crown becoming 'the symbol of free association of the British Commonwealth of Nations'. It was also resolved that the dominions would be responsible for regulating their own merchant shipping—henceforth Irish ships would fly the Irish flag. No agreement was reached on the question of judicial appeal to the Privy Council, however, which was held over to the imperial council to consider. It was clear that implementation of these recommendations would require a substantive piece of British legislation—an 'act of renunciation' in Patrick McGilligan's words—and it was agreed that this would be in place by 1 December 1930. In the meantime, the imperial conference would discuss those issues on which agreement had not been found.

The Free State delegation was among the most experienced at the conference and found itself frequently correcting British experts and ministers on the minutiae of Commonwealth practices. Arriving in London as an elected member of the League council also strengthened its hand. Preparation for the conference absorbed considerable time and political attention, while the growing strength of Fianna Fáil at home raised the political stakes for Cumann na nGaedheal to deliver.

In the foreign policy sphere, the main concerns for Dublin revolved around treaty making. The continuing existence of the *inter se* clause and the insertion of accession clauses in British treaties implied the right to act for the dominions, as did the granting of privileges and assumption of obligations for all British subjects. Direct communication between the dominions and foreign governments via British diplomatic missions instead of passing through the Foreign Office was also considered desirable on grounds of principle, presentation, and efficiency. Dublin complained that it took months for documents to be delivered or responses received believing its requests were left to gather dust in Whitehall. As the liberal government of Mackenzie King in Ottawa had been replaced by one of a conservative hue under R. B. Bennett (who regretted the loosening of imperial ties pursued by his predecessor), the Irish had lost their main allies in pushing back the boundaries of dominion competence. An effort was therefore made to recruit the South Africans behind Dublin's agenda.

For the first time there was also a substantive economic agenda. The deepening global recession prompted champions of empire to demonstrate that the Commonwealth was not preoccupied solely with its own organization, but could also contribute to growth and recovery. The Labour government's preoccupation with economic slowdown and industrial unrest in Britain was a further reason. Desmond FitzGerald believed the British government was in an impossible position on both economic and constitutional fronts, unable to meet domestic expectations or those of the dominions, and found British ministers irritable and ill-prepared. As the conference opened, *The Irish Times* pointed to the 'paramount question of imperial trade;' but for McGilligan, it was constitutional issues that were paramount and their resolution (along lines acceptable to Ireland) would allow time to devote to economic issues. With its overwhelming dependency on the British market, the Free State was not in a position to take the lead on economic issues and would have to follow the lead from the large trading dominions.[11]

Yet despite its initial promise, the conference achieved little in the constitutional sphere beyond what had been agreed by the Committee on the Operation of Dominion Legislation. It delegated entirely on the economic side to a conference that would not gather in Ottawa until July 1932. The stumbling block was abolition of appeal to the Privy Council, which the Free State pressed for vociferously and which the British resisted

---

[11] D. W. Harkness, *The Restless Dominion* (London, 1969), p. 186. Harkness's account of proceedings remains authoritative.

just as forcefully. The Canadians had come to London looking for measures to increase inter-Commonwealth trade. Disappointed at the lack of traction for their ideas, they supported the Irish on the constitutional side, while the new Australian government proved equally cooperative in pushing for fuller dominion autonomy.

For the Free State, however, the conference was a success and the culmination of Cumann na nGaedheal's policy of hollowing out Commonwealth status from within. Its outcome was formalized by the Statute of Westminster adopted in December 1931, which revoked British claims to superiority over the dominions in any area of their internal or external affairs. Even this formalization evoked drama, with a last-minute attempt by Conservatives to amend the Statute in the Houses of Commons to give the British parliament the right to govern implementation of the Anglo-Irish Treaty. Cumann na nGaedheal could not afford any retreat from the gains of the imperial conference nor any suggestion that the Treaty settlement could be undone from London and told London the amendment was unacceptable. Although the move was seen off, it was a reminder that the legacy of 1921 remained a raw issue on both sides of the Irish Sea. In a press statement issued following its adoption, McGilligan heralded the Statute as ushering in a 'new epoch' in relations between Britain and the dominions. The 'act of renunciation' he laboured to achieve confirmed the Irish government's view that only the Treaty of 1921 governed the relationship between the Free State and Britain. With a general election a matter of weeks away, he claimed it as vindication of the government's constitutional policy and, by implication also, Cumann na nGaedeal's interpretation of what the Treaty meant.

Despite the gains at the imperial conference, the Irish remained on the lookout for British backsliding. As Europe slid towards recession, Joseph Walshe was increasingly concerned with the minutiae of daily diplomatic life as a means to assess whether British officials were observing dominion prerogatives abroad. Constantly taking the temperature of the relationship with London, his appetite for reports on interaction with British diplomats betrayed a lively preoccupation with what the British thought of the Free State. He was convinced it would take at least a generation before British officials would be able to treat their Irish counterparts with anything approaching equality. Seán Lester put it more bluntly, telling Walshe 'every British Secretary of State for Foreign Affairs has to learn that Ireland is not a "dummy" at the League'.[12]

---

[12] Lester to Walshe, 5 Mar. 1932, NAI DFA 27/18A.

Discussions continued between Commonwealth delegations at League assemblies and conferences, despite concerns that this blurred the Free State's image. Walshe remained wary of British attempts to draw the Free State into any coordination of foreign policy positions, believing too much discussion in a Commonwealth format would result in a 'hen and chickens' attitude, and efforts were made to minimize formal meetings or discussions; maintaining a reserve was the only way 'to form independent judgments in keeping with our historical background and our own present needs'.[13] The approach to the dominions was 'wholeheartedly friendly' with the aim of winning their support when dealing with the British. The desire to avoid too close an association with the Commonwealth created problems in places such as Paris and Berlin. In both capitals the Free State could carry greater weight in political circles because of its Commonwealth membership. How to exploit this without blurring the country's identity was a challenge for the Free State's European diplomacy.

TIES WITH GERMANY AND FRANCE

By the start of 1930, the Free State had diplomatic relations with more states than any other dominion and Dublin hosted the largest diplomatic corps of all the dominion capitals. The opening of legations in Berlin, Paris, and the Holy See had been an element in the preparation for the council bid, putting in place the mechanism by which to canvass as much as a statement of the country's European identity. But on arrival in Berlin, Binchy found an attitude of 'uninformed sympathy' towards Ireland. The Germans did not open a legation in Dublin until summer 1930, almost a year after his arrival in Berlin and only then following pressure from Dublin. Binchy hoped to consolidate a relationship typified by German involvement in the Shannon hydroelectric scheme and the transatlantic flight of Captain James FitzMaurice and his two German co-pilots in 1928. He also hoped to achieve the biggest impact in the political sphere, addressing Berlin audiences on the twin subjects of Irish and Commonwealth constitutional development. This was where his work was cut out for him.

Binchy believed the Free State's position in the Commonwealth was not understood on the Wilhelmstrasse.[14] One of his tactics to correct this was to fly the tricolour over the Irish legation on the king's birthday to

[13] External Affairs circular letter to overseas offices, May 1930, NAI, DFA GR310; Walshe to O'Kelly, 24 June 1930, NAI DFA 19/7.
[14] Binchy to Walshe, 27 May 1930, NAI, DFA EA 231/4.

stress the multiple nature of the crown, which he did with the support of McGilligan and Walshe. In Paris, the Irish anthem was played during the royal toast at official events, again to emphasize the fact that the crown acted solely on the advice of the Irish government. While this was constitutionally correct, it clashed with the image of separateness that was being constructed at the same time. Fianna Fáil had a point in contending that such 'nice judicial points' were not always understood and confusion regarding flags and anthems continued to be a feature of Free State public events, such as a rugby international in Paris in January 1930. As none of the other dominions had a mission in the German capital, Binchy described the Irish legation as strengthening relations between Germany and all the states of the Commonwealth when he presented his credentials to President Hindenburg. His remark attracted wry comment from the British ambassador in Berlin, Sir Horace Rumbold, who complained to London that this was the very passage Dublin had sought to remove from the letter of credentials.[15] Against the backdrop of growing political instability, it was difficult to make progress in developing relations with Germany. Nevertheless, a commercial treaty was concluded in 1930 and McGilligan visited Berlin the following year. As economic collapse exacted its political toll, Binchy's reports to Dublin chronicled the demise of Weimar democracy as the National Socialists moved towards their shock advance in the German election on 14 September 1930. He heaped blame on the Centre Party, 'a rudderless boat' since Stresemann's death, for its inability to see the threat posed by Hitler's potent mix of economic rhetoric and nationalism.

Paris was a different story. Count O'Kelly experienced none of the problems that had marred his dealings with the British embassy in Brussels. He regarded his role as being largely publicity in nature, though the importance of France in League and international affairs meant it was valuable to have a direct channel to the French government. Relations between France and the Free State were largely shaped by trade concerns and a French desire to avoid injuring relations with Britain: overtures continued to be run past the Foreign Office. If the Quai d'Orsay did not share its consul's assessment of German influence in Ireland, it was nonetheless keen to increase the share of government contracts awarded to French companies.[16] The main outstanding issue of tariffs on French wine imports was resolved in 1929 with the signing of a commercial treaty. On arrival in 1930, the new French minister in Dublin, Charles

---

[15] Rumbold to Henderson, 17 June 1929, PRO, FO 372/9/388.
[16] De Margère to Briand, 16 July 1928, QO, CPC 1918–40, Europe, Irlande, vol. 14, p. 26.

Alphand, nevertheless accused both his predecessor and the Quai of neglecting French interests in Ireland. Believing France had a role to play in 'Europeanising' the Free State, he maintained the Irish would be receptive to an extension of French influence.[17]

PLANS FOR EUROPEAN FEDERAL UNION

The extent of France's Europeanizing vocation had been demonstrated the previous September, when Aristide Briand made his dramatic plea for European integration at the League assembly in Geneva. It was as unexpected as it was unprecedented, and was greeted by a marked lack of enthusiasm in the chancelleries of Europe. His proposal for 'some kind of federal bond' was designed to create a framework for economic cooperation to counter American economic domination.[18] It was, in Briand's words, necessary to unite in order to survive. The plan was a response to deepening economic recession in Europe and failure to resolve the nexus of disarmament and security that plagued French policy-makers. The assembly gave the idea a lukewarm welcome, the East Europeans being most enthusiastic given their own pervasive sense of insecurity. Paris followed up with a detailed memorandum in May 1930, in which political objectives trumped the economic concerns they were in theory designed to advance. A conference of European states was proposed (those who were League members, leaving out the Soviet Union), serviced by a standing political committee and a secretariat. The conference would meet in Geneva but would be separate from League structures. Effectively a grand customs union scheme, it would have provided for a mixture of protectionism and some tariff reductions.

The Free State replied to the proposals two months later. Dublin accepted there was a 'natural bond' between European countries 'tending towards a closer association' for political and economic purposes, but history and experience meant this was not felt 'so forcibly' in Ireland. While couched in the quieter tones of government communication, the response echoed the Dáil declarations of a decade earlier. It situated the Free State as both a European and a mother country, for whom ties to the diaspora were a 'bond or moral union in no degree less binding' than those with Europe. An emphasis on Australia in addition to North America

[17] Alphand to Briand, 1 Sept. 1930, QO, CPC 1918–40, Europe, Irlande, vol. 20, pp. 11–14.
[18] Zara Steiner, *The Lights that Failed, European International History, 1919–1933* (Oxford, 2005), p. 584.

was new: a reflection of closer cooperation in a Commonwealth context. No mention was made of the Commonwealth itself or the obligations arising from membership. The message was clear: arrangements that did not take account of the Free State's extra-European connections would 'only partially express the true orientation of Irish political consciousness'.[19]

While avoiding detailed comment on the proposals, Dublin suggested the initiative stood a better chance of success if pursued under a League umbrella, with individual countries free to determine the extent of cooperation. The truth was, however, that the Irish doubted whether a mood for intra-European cooperation existed; a judgement quickly proven correct as European governments pursued unilateral remedies to the depression, mostly at their neighbours' expense. There was a very real concern about the potential impact on the League or the need for new international structures. Better instead to implement existing League commitments, a prescription McGilligan would repeat to the assembly in September.

French arguments for a customs union scheme caused unease in Dublin, where the government was keen to protect the economy from debilitating economic undertakings. Proposals for tariff reductions were unwelcome even if the scheme would have involved some protectionism as well. Unsurprisingly for the leadership of a newly independent state, they were also reluctant to embrace proposals that were not based squarely on freedom of association and national sovereignty: 'no country so situated could reasonably be expected to make economic sacrifices for the establishment of a common market in Europe, before it felt assured that it was in a position to secure its due participation in that market' (a position that had been recognized by the League's Economic Consultative Committee). Not wishing to appear unconstructive, however, the Irish proposed the idea be taken forward within the League and pointedly called for dialogue with other states before embarking on new structures and commitments in Europe.[20]

The Irish were not alone in their lack of appetite for Briand's proposals, which were equally indigestible elsewhere, and the assembly kicked them to touch in September, voting to establish a commission of enquiry. In a sop to Paris, the ailing Briand would chair its work. The commission made little progress, hampered by a deepening recession that fuelled a growing antagonism among European governments. The sense among delegates was that none would live to see the plan become reality. Briand died the following December and the idea was buried with him. The desire to do

[19] Irish response to the French Government plan on Federal European Union, 16 July 1930, NAI DFA Paris Embassy 109B.
[20] Ibid.

something about the deepening recession did not. The Free State was present at tariff truce conferences held in March and November 1930 and in March 1931. Only Albania did not attend. Dublin's objective was to preserve complete tariff autonomy and it therefore rejected the Tariff Truce Convention that emerged from these meetings. The convention turned out to be a failure, unable to go far enough in either direction to satisfy differing views on free trade and protectionism. Fianna Fáil opposed Irish participation in these conferences, *The Irish Press* warning in November 1931 that free trade would impose the 'yoke of serfdom' on the Irish people.[21]

LOOSE ENDS AT GENEVA

The remainder of the 1930 assembly was taken up with efforts to strengthen the League's security and arbitration framework. At the beginning of October, the Free State signed a Finnish-sponsored convention to provide financial assistance to the victims of aggression. A British insertion meant it would only become operational when a general agreement on disarmament had been reached which effectively amounted to an indefinite postponement. In a sign of the changing international mood, Germany, Italy, and Japan declined to sign up. It also argued against efforts by the main powers to shelve work on the codification of international law on the spurious grounds that more time was needed to review the subject material. Ernest Blythe warned the assembly of growing disillusionment at the lack of progress on disarmament, which was undermining public confidence in the League itself.

The League was also hampered by a low rate of ratification by its members of the conventions they had signed up to at Geneva. The Free State was no exception. A letter from the secretary general in April 1928 had revealed a patched record in enacting the provisions of League conventions into domestic law, including the opium convention the Free State had played a role in bringing about. McGilligan had pledged back then to do better, with an eye to the council election the following year but also from a conviction that strengthening the League and international law was an Irish interest. He had lectured delegates in 1929 on their responsibility to ratify conventions even when the subject was not of direct concern to them, and without nullifying reservations. The following March, the cabinet forwarded a batch of nine conventions, seven of them

[21] *The Irish Press*, 6 Nov. 1931.

from the League, to the Dáil for ratification and the process was completed by June in good time for the council election. By the end of 1930, the Free State stood third in the list of states ratifying ILO conventions.

Perhaps unsurprisingly given its size and limited resources, the Free State was unable to follow every issue at the League. There was a tendency to pursue thematic issues and take a lower profile on country-specific issues. This was because issues such as the jurisdiction of the permanent court were linked to the question of status, while disarmament and the codification of international law were clear small state interests. It was also because the 1920s were a relatively calm period in European relations. Irish diplomats and policy-makers were mostly able to avoid involvement in out-of-area problems when there was no discernible Irish aspect to their resolution. For example, Joseph Walshe advised against supporting League membership for Iraq when the British mandate in the territory expired in 1930, on the grounds that it might prejudice negotiations with London. It was better not to become involved in 'questions in which we are not very directly concerned'.[22]

The definition of matters of concern included the rights of Christians in Iraq, which Lester was told to raise if it did not complicate efforts to end the mandate.[23] The issue had arisen in the middle of the Free State's council campaign in 1930 and, wth an important imperial conference scheduled for the end of the year, it did not wish to rock the boat. Similarly, Cosgrave declined to receive Gandhi when a visit to Ireland was mooted in 1931, citing lack of notice (in the end, the visit did not go ahead).[24] This did not mean the Free State was unwilling to oppose the interests of larger states. On the contrary, it did so by insisting on the continuation of work on codification of international law and by its support for disarmament (which accorded with the rhetoric but not always the interests of the major powers). In general, however, until its election to the council in September 1930, the Free State tended to approach League issues from an abstract perspective of the rights and protections of League members, in particular smaller states. Its attention had been focused on events in Europe and America, where it had diplomatic representation. But council membership inevitably widened the scope of international affairs to which the Free State would be exposed.

---

[22] Walshe to O'Kelly, 6 Aug. 1930, NAI DFA Paris Embassy 109B.
[23] Cremin to Lester, 2 Feb. 1930, NAI, DFA S2/25A.
[24] O'Hegarty to M. F. Woods, 30 Sept. 1931, NAI, DFA 35/35. See, also, Kate O'Malley, *Ireland, India and Empire: Indo-Irish Radical Connections, 1919–64* (Manchester, 2008).

FIRST STEPS ON THE LEAGUE
COUNCIL, 1931–1932

All the issues of international life, major and minor, passed before the horseshoe table of the council. As Seán Lester told Dublin, election would see the Free State 'enter international life to an infinitely greater extent than at present'. With more than an echo of MacWhite's earlier warnings, he cautioned that prestige for a small state 'can only be won by arduous continuous labour directed by a wise and consistent policy . . . [it] is not merely an intangible contribution to a sense of patriotic gratification: it means security'.[25] The first twelve months of the Free State's council membership were relatively uneventful. The Irish strove to further the twin goals of international arbitration and disarmament that they had advocated before election. This was, in Blythe's estimation, the whole point of Irish participation at Geneva. With this in mind, McGilligan travelled to Geneva for the January meeting of the council, where he once again pressed for the disarmament conference to meet. Reflecting his legal background, he set as priorities the codification of international law and efforts to reduce Polish–German tensions over Danzig. It was decided not to support German calls for revision of the Treaty of Versailles until the Free State had greater experience of the workings of the council, an astute decision given Anglo-French opposition. As a deal on disarmament was unlikely without some change to the Versailles settlement's limits on German armed forces, this nettle would have to be grasped at some stage.

There was little scope for the Free State to play an active role on a council whose permanent members conducted business among themselves before proposing solutions to the rest. In March 1931, the Free State voted with the rest of the council to refer to the International Court German proposals for a customs union with Austria (the Geneva protocol of 1922 had safeguarded Austrian economic independence). It was the most sensitive issue to cross the council table thus far in the Free State's tenure, provoking fears in France and Czechoslovakia of *Anschluss* by stealth. As newcomers, the Irish were entrusted with the role of rapporteur on health issues and child welfare, which came as a disappointment to Dublin and afforded little opportunity for profile building. Much of the work was left to Lester as permanent representative to the League. McGilligan found himself more and more occupied in Dublin as 1931 progressed and the economic and electoral situation deteriorated at home.

---

[25] Lester to Walshe, 22 Mar. 1930, NAI DFA 26/95.

It was a frustrating time for Lester, who frequently found himself without clear instructions and was forced to abstain on votes as a result. Despite this, at the end of its first year on the council, the Free State was keen to be appointed rapporteur for more weighty subjects and Lester was asked to see if a role might be possible dealing with Danzig, disarmament, or economic issues.

THE WORLD DISARMAMENT CONFERENCE

The prospects of a country with the Free State's record of support for disarmament being charged with guiding the council's work in this area were remote, however. Two months after the Irish had joined the council, the impasse on efforts to agree a draft disarmament convention was finally overcome in November 1930, paving the way for the preparatory commission charged with drafting the text to resume its work after an eighteen-month gap. The Free State had not been a member of the commission, but was included now by virtue of its council seat. The problem for Dublin was that the main contours of the draft had already been fixed, leaving little scope to influence the text. Discussions in the commission were protracted and heated; as Lester observed 'one was close to the bitter realities of European antagonisms'. A month of discussions produced a draft convention in which political, military, and financial considerations were bound up with one another. Having laboured long and hard, the outcome was disappointing: the text contained blank tables of reductions with the difficult decisions on numbers left to the conference. Despite Dublin's interest in disarmament issues, Lester lacked clear instructions. Having played no real part in its negotiation and unhappy with its content, he considered it prudent to distance the Free State from the draft convention and, when it was published on 6 December 1930, the Free State was joined by Norway in doing so.[26]

Some progress towards disarmament had been achieved earlier in the year, but not in a League setting, with agreement at a conference in London on a new naval reduction treaty. It was hoped that this agreement, which replaced the Washington Treaty of 1922, would bring fresh momentum to discussions on general disarmament at the League. Where the Geneva conference of 1927 had failed, the London conference of 1930 succeeded in bridging the gap between British and American ambitions for naval reductions. But only at the cost of French and Italian

[26] Lester to Walshe, 16 Dec. 1930, NAI DFA LN 4/9.

support, who failed to sign up to the new treaty. As in 1927, the dominions were present in London but apart from general support for naval reductions and disarmament more generally, the Free State did not play a prominent part in the discussions. The resulting London Naval Treaty was not a major concern for the Irish government until autumn, when the Americans pressed Dublin to ratify it so that it could enter into force.

The United States wanted the treaty in place before the final meeting of the League's preparatory commission on disarmament began on 6 November 1930, so that it would have a freer hand to urge agreement on limitation of land forces. The problem for Dublin was that parliamentary approval was needed and this could not be arranged in time. Moves to ratify without Dáil assent were abandoned in the face of a Labour party refusal, the government fearing a vote of no confidence should it press ahead. The administration's weak position in parliament was beginning to affect its ability to conduct policy while the opposition was unwilling to offer the government a free pass even on an issue related to disarmament. In Fianna Fáil's view, the Free State had no business being at the London naval conference in the first place. The issue was unresolved by the time the preparatory commission met, prompting MacWhite to warn of possible friction in the bilateral relationship if the issue was allowed to drag on for much longer. The situation was embarrassing in light of the Free State's support for disarmament and its election to the council. The Naval Treaty passed both Houses of the Oireachtas on 11 December, after the disarmament commission had finished its work. In an effort to avoid further delay, it was ratified using the United Kingdom seal as the new Free State one was not yet ready.

Following publication of the draft disarmament convention, in January 1931 the council finally announced a date for the long-awaited world disarmament conference but decided another year was needed for preparations. Talks would not begin until 2 February in Geneva. No decisions were taken about what these preparations would entail or who would chair the conference. Addressing the council on 20 January, McGilligan had labelled the draft convention a starting point that required much improvement, urging the powers to improve the international atmosphere so that progress could be achieved. Otherwise he predicted the conference would amount to little and the rest of the League's activities, however admirable, would 'serve only to screen warlike preparations'.[27] Given that the Free

---

[27] McGilligan speech at 62nd session of the Council of the League of Nations, 20 Jan. 1931, NAI DFA LN 80/1.

State was already effectively disarmed it is unlikely his arguments cut much ice with the major powers.

In an effort to prod the British and French into action, and perhaps also to repair the damage with Washington over the delay in ratifying the Naval Treaty, Lester had been instructed to propose an American chair for the disarmament conference at a secret meeting of the council on 22 January. There was no time to consult the Americans in advance, with the result that Michael MacWhite raised the matter in Washington on the same day that Lester had tabled the idea in Geneva. Secretary of State Stimson told MacWhite he appreciated the proposal but wished to keep his hands free. The European powers were unenthusiastic about a US chair for different reasons, fearing it would pressure them to make greater cuts than they were prepared to agree.

The conference would have implications for the Free State's defence arrangements. A department of defence paper in February 1931 described the Free State as the most disarmed country in Europe and warned that, unless decisions were made on the country's future defence needs, the disarmament conference would fix an allocation at what was considered the low level pertaining at the time.[28] A further factor was the need to keep in mind defence provisions of the Anglo-Irish Treaty, which had set limits for the size of the Free State's armed forces. Consultations between the departments of defence and external affairs aimed to thrash out these difficult questions. McGilligan told the cabinet the Free State should play a 'reasonably prominent' part at the conference, in keeping with the country's policy of support for disarmament, and a cabinet committee was established on 4 May comprising Blythe, FitzGerald, and McGilligan to determine the approach it would take.[29] This would not be just a matter of abstract principles and obligations under the League covenant: for the first time decisions about Irish security needs would be made in a multilateral setting.

Cosgrave described disarmament as the 'principal plank' of Irish foreign policy in a message to the United States at the end of May. Cinema messages recorded for broadcast in Britain and America in June stressed the need for a successful outcome at the disarmament conference while officials in Dublin believed it would be the most important diplomatic gathering since the Treaty of Versailles.[30] The Free State's position was

[28] Department of Defence memorandum on the British Cabinet Committee on the Disarmament Conference, 25 Feb. 1931, NAI DFA 11/3.
[29] 'Draft memorandum on Disarmament Conference by the Department of External Affairs for the Executive Council (Secret)', 20 April 1931, NAI DFA 11/3.
[30] Memorandum by the Department of External Affairs on the Irish Policy at the League of Nations, n.d. 1931, but probably written March–May, NAI DT S2220.

not finalized until the start of 1932. A meeting of the cabinet committee on 2 January accepted the draft convention as a basis for the conference. It was recognized that discussion would be difficult, involving not just complex negotiations over naval tonnage, force size, and disposition, but also sensitive political issues including revision of the Treaty of Versailles if Germany's demand for equal treatment were to be met. The committee also decided that the Free State should seek the upper limits provided for under the Anglo-Irish Treaty (article eight of the Treaty set the maximum size of the Irish armed forces according to the population ratio with Great Britain). A considerable increase in the country's armed forces would be needed to reach these limits but, even then, the Free State would still have been below most other European countries.[31] It was also decided to seek a naval allocation, even though the Free State had no navy at the time, in order to preserve the option to develop one should agreement be reached with London under article six of the Treaty to assume responsibility for defence of the Irish coast.[32]

TIES WITH THE UNITED STATES

The government continued to regard bilateral relations with the United States as a priority for domestic reasons and on account of the growing US role in efforts to pursue disarmament. When Michael MacWhite was transferred to Washington in January 1929, Joseph Walshe told him he was getting 'the very best post in the gift of the Saorstát'.[33] Walshe saw a link between the growth of the Free State's standing abroad and the increase in influence of the Irish community in America, telling Mac-White there was a strong interest in developing Catholic influence in the United States. Walshe believed American public opinion had been central to the achievement of independence, and that maintaining a well-disposed American public opinion was a sensible insurance policy.

The importance of the diaspora is evident from the allocation of diplomatic resources: the Free State had three offices in the United States by 1932: a legation in Washington, and consulates in New York and Boston. Additional consulates were opened in the following two years, in San Francisco and Chicago. These offices had multiple objectives—

---

[31] As the article referred to Ireland and Great Britain rather than the Irish Free State and the United Kingdom, the exact figures were open to interpretation.

[32] 'Draft memorandum on Disarmament Conference by the Department of External Affairs for the Executive Council (Secret)', 20 April 1931, NAI DFA 11/3.

[33] Walshe to MacWhite, 20 Dec. 1930, UCDA P194/139.

influencing opinion in favour of the Free State, countering anti-treaty propaganda, and trade and economic work. They were also sources of income from passport and visa fees. Agreement on the assumption of a consular function by the dominions cleared the way for these consulates, bringing the Irish state into direct contact with the diaspora in new ways. A belief that the Irish could influence American policy, a legacy of the Sinn Féin period, persisted despite indications to the contrary. The idea of Ireland as a bridge between Europe and the United States remained a feature of speeches and publications, including during the campaign for a seat on the League council.[34] Cumann na nGaedheal politicians tended to be more circumspect than others, experience having illustrated the limited sway an Irish government could hope to wield in American political circles. But politicians of all hues continued to make claims in the Dáil about the increased weight of Irish influence provided by the diaspora.

As the global political and economic situation became more difficult to navigate, Dublin changed gear in its approach to the United States in 1931, downplaying efforts to interact with Irish communities in favour of greater engagement with the administration in Washington. There was a shift from publicity to diplomatic work, with particular emphasis on efforts to understand the Hoover administration's foreign policy—especially as it affected Europe. The legation was nonetheless asked 'are the Catholic Irish holding their own?' a perennial concern for Walshe.[35] MacWhite approvingly reported Secretary of State Stimson's description of the Free State in September 1931 as 'the one bright spot they had to deal with, and the country that gave them the least trouble', but this did not mean the relationship was without its difficulties.[36] Efforts to negotiate a commercial treaty were broken off in November over the issue of tariffs. The Americans were unwilling to offer the level of preferential treatment sought by Dublin for Irish goods, while, as mentioned, the slow pace with which the Free State ratified the London Naval Treaty caused irritation in Washington and cut across its disarmament agenda. The Americans had been flattered but not helped by the Free State's decision to suggest an American chair for the disarmament conference without first checking whether the administration would welcome such a move. It was, nonetheless, a valued and valuable relationship, which Dublin made strenuous efforts to cultivate, even if it was difficult to recapture the level of US attention the Free State had briefly enjoyed in the high-water year of 1928.

---

[34] See, for example, Elliott O'Donnell, *The Irish Future* (London, 1915), p. 40; Raymond Regnault, *Le Courroux nationaliste en Irlande* (Paris, 1932), p. 34.
[35] Walshe to MacWhite, 20 July 1931, NAI DFA 9/2.
[36] MacWhite to Walshe, 22 Sept. 1931, NAI DFA 19/2.

REPRESENTING FAITH AND FREE
STATE IN ROME

If relations with Washington provided the Free State with a secular seal of approval, the government was equally desirous of receiving the imprimatur of the Holy See. With a legation in place, a long-standing ambition to represent in Rome the interests of the Irish race abroad and of English-speaking Catholics more generally became possible. In contrast with other European capitals, Bewley believed the Free State's constitutional position was well understood at the Vatican and advised Dublin that the Vatican's primary interest in Ireland was its position within the Commonwealth—'a Roman Catholic force in the English-speaking world'.[37] Walshe took a close personal interest in policy towards the Vatican and saw in the legation a means to consolidate the Free State's place in Rome as 'the most Catholic state in the world' and a defender of Catholic values. He assumed the Vatican would also see things the same way.[38] He took an abiding interest in titbits of clerical gossip, which Bewley supplied him from his conversations with members of the curia or the Irish religious communities in Rome, and was pleased with the friendlier attitude of the Irish College following the death of Monsignor Hagen in March 1930.

Walshe saw in the advancement of Irish clergy a reflection of the Free State's own standing and a means to increase its visibility in Rome. It was also a means to further Irish interests in countries such as the United States. When it came to his notice in 1931 that German clerics were being appointed to American bishoprics, he asked Bewley to make discrete enquiries to see if Irish clerics could be appointed instead.[39] At Geneva, the Free State voiced concerns about the position of the Christian minority in Iraq and the Holy Places in Palestine. Bewley was instructed to impress on Vatican contacts the Catholic nature and legislation of the Free State, and cited censorship laws and the lack of divorce as evidence not just of the country's Catholic persona but also its difference from Britain. Walshe believed all overseas offices had a role to play, expecting them to 'emphasise our separate language, our Catholic religion, Catholic history, everything, in fact, that makes us different from England'.[40] The department was quick to draw Vatican attention to resolutions in parliament, such as that passed by the senate in April 1928 condemning persecution of

---

[37] Bewley to Walshe, 1 July 1930, NAI DFA EA 23I/4.
[38] Walshe to Bewley, 23 July 1931, NAI DFA 19/1B.
[39] Walshe to Bewley, 18 Aug. 1931, NAI DFA EA 23I/4.
[40] Walshe to O'Kelly, 30 Dec. 1930, NAI DFA EA231/4/1931.

the Catholic Church in Mexico. MacWhite had proposed a similar course of action for different reasons—as a means of distancing the Free State from Britain, which had not issued a condemnation. The senate took a similar step in 1930 in condemning religious persecution in the Soviet Union, and called upon the Dáil to do likewise in the name of 'god-fearing' Ireland.[41] By demonstrating Free State activity on issues in which the Holy See took a close interest, Walshe hoped also to increase the country's standing with other states, particularly Catholic ones, many of whom Dublin looked to for support in its bid for a seat on the League council.

The Vatican had hinted to Bewley in late 1929 that Dublin might raise with London its concerns in Malta, when relations became strained over demands by the administration on the island that clergy provide affidavit evidence of information obtained from the confessional. In the hope of inducing the Free State to intervene, possibly at the forthcoming imperial conference, Bewley was passed a Vatican file on the affair and suggested to Dublin that raising the Vatican's concerns would earn the Holy See's appreciation. The issue had potential constitutional implications. As none of the other dominions were represented at the Holy See, in the event of a diplomatic rupture between London and the Holy See the Free State could find itself representing Britain and the Commonwealth in Rome. By remaining accredited to the pope in the name of the king, the severalty of the crown would be strikingly demonstrated. Ordinarily on the lookout for opportunities to advance the Free State's standing and independence, Walshe sounded a note of caution on the grounds that a rupture between Britain and the Vatican 'might not be for the good of religion in general', and was unwilling to raise the matter with the British, hoping that 'other more suitable occasions will arise' instead.[42] The Maltese affair dragged into 1930, without any Irish action on the Vatican's behalf.

Intervening in a dispute between Britain and the Holy See over a colonial possession might not have been good for religion but would certainly not have helped Irish–British relations either. To have become involved would have run counter to the established policy of avoiding unnecessary antagonism or confrontation with London except on issues of vital national interest. The government had enough on its plate managing an increasingly broad agenda of issues where Dublin and London disagreed on Commonwealth matters without adding to the list. Importing a religious dimension would further complicate relations with a Foreign

[41] *Dáil Éireann deb.*, vol. 30, col. 821, 5 June 1929; *Seanad Éireann deb.*, vol. 10, col. 398, 25 April 1928; *The Irish Times*, 13 May 1930.
[42] Walshe to Bewley, 24 June 1930, NAI DFA 231/4.

Office already wary of Vatican ambitions to capitalize on the presence of a nuncio in the Irish capital to push for one in London.

Pursuing an overtly Catholic foreign policy was not without risks closer to home. While the Northern Ireland Government, and Ulster Unionism more generally, showed little interest in the Free State's foreign policy, the decision to open relations with the Holy See can only have confirmed a view held by many north of the border that the Free State was a confessional state.

Walshe's interest in the standing of the Irish clergy and the Catholic interest more generally in the United States had the potential to complicate relations with Washington. A waspish State Department wary of outside involvement in the affairs of the Irish-American community would not have shared Walshe's assessment of Catholic interests (the reluctance to see an Irish-American appointed to the American legation in Dublin may have been inspired on similar grounds). Linking Irish and Catholic interests in the United States risked furthering the perception of involvement in domestic American affairs.

Singling out the Maltese affair in particular, the French minister in Dublin warned his superiors to take note of Irish aspirations to be considered a semi-official spokesperson for Anglophone Catholics in the Commonwealth, a view shared by his Vatican colleague.[43] Paris suspected the nuncio in Dublin would keep Rome briefed on Irish-American and Anglo-American relations.[44] In the end, the British did not break off relations with the Vatican but downgraded the level of their representation, with the result that Bewley was more senior. This more comfortable outcome for Dublin was put to good use demonstrating the Free State's independence and also its role as a Catholic leader in the Commonwealth, such as when Bewley presented the Australian prime minister to Pius XI during a visit to Rome in October 1930. Whatever aspirations may have been held to speak for Anglophone Catholicism had to be squared with other priorities, in particular relations with Britain and the Commonwealth.

The Vatican legation was also used as a channel for conveying Walshe's and the Irish Government's *desiderata* regarding the position of the Catholic Church at home. At various times, Bewley was instructed to emphasize the desirability that any future nuncio should be Irish or of Irish descent, to enquire about the prospects of the archbishop of Dublin

[43] Alphand to Briand, 12 Dec. 1930, QO, CPC 1918–40, Europe, Irlande, vol. 19, p. 21; Gentil to Briand, 27 Aug. 1931, ibid., p. 47.
[44] Alphand to Briand, 12 Dec. 1930, QO, CPC 1918–40, Europe, Irlande, vol. 19, p. 21.

being promoted to cardinal and to ask whether a red hat was envisaged for the nuncio.[45] The choice of Dublin to host the international Eucharistic Congress in the summer of 1932 provided an opportunity to highlight the Free State's Catholic credentials and the country's global connections. Walshe took a close interest in preparations, keen to ensure the Vatican selected a papal legate who would have the interests of the Free State government at heart. Establishing the identity of the legate occupied an increasing amount of Bewley's time in the first half of 1931, as rumours circulated that various clerics judged unsuitable by Walshe were under consideration. As the year progressed, however, the government became increasingly concerned that its efforts to showcase the Free State's progress and stability would be undermined at home by the stirrings of armed republicanism and the first signs of possible communist agitation in Ireland.

THE SOVIET UNION AND THE 'RED SCARE'

The emergence of communist activity across Europe in the wake of the depression prompted the government to ask its missions on the continent to collect information on conservative political parties and their policies. As Joseph Walshe explained, 'the Communist menace is making such movements a matter of primary state interest'.[46] Cumann na nGaedheal feared proximity to Britain with its large working class and a Soviet legation in London made the Free State vulnerable to communist agitation, while any combination of communism and extreme republicanism was seen as particularly threatening.[47] There was also a strong Catholic impetus to concerns to counter communism and the risk it posed to the moral health of the country. The intellectual environment was receptive to conspiracy theories. The Jesuit writer, Edward Cahill, published a best-selling diatribe in 1929 depicting an international anti-Christian movement led by Protestants, Freemasons, and Jews challenging the values of Catholic Ireland.[48] It also targeted the League and was received as unquestionably reliable by many in Ireland. *Studies* reported repeatedly on conditions in the Soviet Union the following year while the

---

[45] Walshe to Bewley, 12 May 1931, DFA 19/1B.
[46] Walshe to O'Kelly, 6 Nov. 1931, NAI, DFA Paris embassy 48.
[47] Fighting Points for Cumann na nGaedheal Speakers and Workers, (Dublin, 1932), pp. 139–40.
[48] Edward Cahill, *Freemasonry and the Anti-Christian Movement* (Dublin, 1929), pp. 247–50.

Figure 11. Cumann na nGaedheal election poster 'We want no "reds" here!', 1932 (Image courtesy of the National Library of Ireland NLI EPH F 54)

anti-communist campaign of another Jesuit, Richard Devane, received considerable publicity.

It was against this backdrop that the Free State's relations with the Soviet Union returned to the fore. The decision of the Labour government in Britain to restore relations with Moscow in June 1929 had quickly led to a commercial agreement with the Soviet Union the following spring which would apply also to the Free State should the Irish government so wish. Dublin was unwilling to accept a treaty negotiated in the name of the British government, deciding instead to seek its own arrangement with Moscow pending negotiation of a separate commercial treaty in April 1930, on grounds of status as much as a desire to facilitate trade. There was genuine interest in establishing a basis for trade to facilitate the export of tractors from the Ford factory in Cork. Joseph Walshe downplayed the issue of communist propaganda, telling Count O'Kelly in May that the government knew this was already happening. It was more important to ensure the Free State's relations with Moscow were no worse than those of Britain.[49]

The Soviets forwarded the text of a commercial treaty to Dublin for consideration in July 1930 and moves were made to begin talks. The question of opening a trade office in Dublin arose again. Although a police report had found no evidence of Soviet activity in Ireland the last time this had been proposed in 1927, by late 1929 potential communist agitation had become a concern in some quarters.[50] The government considered a Russian trade office in Dublin would make it easier to monitor communist activities, but changed its mind as concerns grew about possible Soviet influence over the IRA. Cosgrave blocked Trotsky from entering the Free State in September, telling the trade unionist William O'Brien the Russians had never done anything for Ireland. His office circulated government departments with reports of religious persecution and Soviet-backed agitation abroad.[51] Against this background, the negotiations were broken off and no reply was provided to the Soviets. The shooting of a witness by the IRA, amid fears over the summer of 1931 of growing communist influence over the IRA, convinced the government to take action.

It was hoped to use the Vatican to enlist the Irish bishops as agents of the state in combating the menace of armed republicanism. In early September, Bewley raised government concerns in Rome regarding an upsurge in republican violence and communist influence—including the emergence of Saor Éire—with Cardinal Pacelli, seeking a condemnation by the bishops. He was concerned to learn that the nuncio had not reported to the Holy See on the issue, an omission Walshe attributed to an uneasy relationship between the nuncio and the Irish bishops.

---

[49] Walshe to O'Kelly, 23 May 1930, NAI DFA 107/2.
[50] Eunan O'Halpin, *Defending Ireland, The Irish State and its Enemies Since 1922* (Oxford, 1999), pp. 71–5.
[51] Cosgrave memorandum, 6 Sept. 1930, NAI, DT S2430; Diarmuid O'Hegarty circular, 9 April 1930, NAI, DT S6004.

Confidential government memoranda prepared for the Irish bishops on the activities of Saor Éire and the IRA were passed to the Vatican by Bewley, who attributed the trouble to a 'small but determined minority, under communist influence, but masquerading as Irish patriots'.[52]

Over the summer of 1931, evidence that the IRA was influenced by Soviet-style communism prompted fears of a 'red scare' in Ireland. The government contemplated special legislation to deal with the threat, inserting provisions of the Public Safety Act into the constitution.[53] Walshe asked Bewley to brief the Vatican in early October on the measures being taken in defence of both state and religion and to raise again the question of a condemnation by the Irish bishops. The government's efforts to persuade the bishops to act bore fruit in the form of a joint condemnation of communism and republicanism on 18 October. Special powers entered into force three days later and a crackdown ensued. Pius XI told Bewley on 10 November that he approved of the government's efforts to curb extremist violence and did not criticize the measures taken.[54] Bewley in turn assured the pope that the government had been largely successful in restoring order and that the communist influence in Ireland was on the wane.

THE MANCHURIA CRISIS

It was just as the red scare was reaching its height in Ireland that events in East Asia cast a shadow over world affairs. Far from the improvement in the international climate that McGilligan had hoped for at the start of the year, the League was plunged into crisis in September 1931 when a skirmish at a railway junction outside the Manchurian town of Mukden was the pretext for a Japanese invasion on the evening of 18 September. Hostilities had already begun as the Irish statement was being delivered in the assembly hall in Geneva. It was the first major crisis to face the League and the post-war order. The Free State had been on the council exactly a year and a day. Three days later Britain announced it was leaving the gold standard as the financial crisis in Europe deepened, sending shockwaves through the world economy. A banking collapse in Germany in July and widespread fears of contagion meant minds were elsewhere.

[52] Bewley to Walshe, 5 Sept. 1931, NAI, DFAP4/4/42.
[53] Dermot Keogh, *Ireland and the Vatican, The Politics and Diplomacy of Church-State Relations, 1922–1960* (Cork, 1995), p. 82–4.
[54] Bewley to Walshe, 10 Nov. 1931, NAI DFA 19/1B.

In Ireland, the government's emergency legislation in response to the red scare was being rushed through the Dáil as the council met in Geneva to decide what to do. The first signs of difficulties with British legislation enacting the outcome of the imperial conference were prompting concern in Dublin. The Free State adopted a general approach of good will towards both China and Japan, although relations were not particularly developed with either. Lacking interests in the region (its trade office in Shanghai had closed in 1928) the only significant encounter with China had been the council election in 1930, when diplomats had sympathized with the country's desire to be free of outside interference. The Japanese had a consulate general in Dublin and contact was made at numerous League conferences.

Like other council members, the Free State was uncertain how to respond to the Japanese invasion. As Michael Kennedy rightly observes, the crisis exposed the limits on Irish diplomacy, or that of any small state at the time.[55] While it was clearly a breach of the covenant, there was a limit to what a small and unarmed League member could do in the absence of leadership from one of the major powers. This was conspicuously absent. McGilligan, who was in Geneva for the assembly, took little interest and left the running to Lester who quickly became convinced the League was facing a serious challenge. A month into the crisis, on 20 October, the Free State sent demarches to the Japanese and Chinese governments, using the new machinery of direct access to British diplomatic missions agreed at the imperial conference. The government recalled the obligations of both Japan and China under the Kellogg–Briand Pact and the League covenant and urged restraint on both sides. But as the matter was before the council, there was no condemnation of the Japanese invasion.[56]

Although formally on the council agenda, discussion had quickly become diverted to a committee of its permanent members. Lester wanted to challenge what he saw as moves towards a two-tier council membership, but was told by Dublin he could only do so in private. When he did raise the matter the French and British backed down. Unwilling to speak up themselves, the Poles and Yugoslavs thanked Lester for doing so. Two days later the council passed a resolution calling on Tokyo to withdraw. As the Japanese exercised their veto it would have no force. Believing the

---

[55] For a comprehensive account of this episode, see Michael Kennedy, 'Principle well seasoned with the sauce of realism: Seán Lester, Joseph Walshe and the definition of the Irish Free State's policy towards Manchuria', *Irish Studies in International Affairs*, vol. 6 (October 1995), pp. 79–94.

[56] Telegram from the Department of External Affairs to the British Ambassador in Tokyo and the British Minister in Peking, 20 October 1931, NAI DFA 27/18.

Japanese would take steps to withdraw, the council broke without any attempt to put the 'committee of the five' on a formal footing.

The silence of the other non-permanent members suggested a calculation of the limits within which a small state could realistically act. McGilligan approved of Lester's action to preserve the principle of equality among council members in general, a position in keeping with the Free State's views on equal status in all areas of the League's work, but did not believe this amounted to having equal weight in determining what the council should do. The Free State was not in a position to judge events on the ground in China, nor would its interests be affected were sanctions to be agreed. Given the issues at stake it was unsurprising that Dublin should adopt a cautious line.

The council was due to meet again in mid-November. Lester believed the Free State could play a prominent role, but McGilligan was tied up in Dublin handling problems in London surrounding the Statute of Westminster. When the council met in Paris on 16 November, he proposed requesting a map showing Japanese positions as a means of establishing what everyone suspected, that the Japanese had not withdrawn. The initiative met with an immediate cable from Dublin to do nothing. Two days earlier Walshe had written to Lester setting out McGilligan's views on the conflict, which boiled down to a pious hope that the authority of the League and Japan's interests in China could somehow be reconciled. For Walshe, as for many at the time, there was a certain amount of admiration for Japan's role as the 'outstanding factor making for stability, progress and civilisation in the Far East'.[57] Behind minds in Dublin was a fear that unrest in China would provide fertile ground for the spread of communism. The preferred outcome was a negotiated settlement, however unlikely this seemed. Lester was disappointed, believing the Free State should uphold the obligations of the covenant, which the Japanese were flouting. Far from preventing the growth of communism in China, he believed Japanese actions would hasten its spread: 'to reduce the League is to weaken the world's shield against Bolshevism'.[58]

The council was faced with a choice of admitting it could not act or of bringing the question under article fifteen of the covenant. The latter option did not require the assent of the parties to the conflict, thereby getting around the Japanese veto, but it raised the prospect of sanctions. The major powers hesitated, as did China, which feared the imposition of sanctions against Japan could lead to all out war. Lester told Dublin that Britain and France would prefer 'a lifeless institution at Geneva' if faced

[57] Walshe to Lester, 14 Nov. 1931, NAI DFA 27/18.
[58] Lester to Walshe, 16 Nov. 1931, NAI DFA 27/18.

with the choice of economic or military sanctions against Japan.[59] It was a realistic assessment, adding to concerns in Dublin that nothing be done that might result in the League's sanctions machinery being invoked.

McGilligan's overarching concern was to avoid the Free State being either the instigator of sanctions or bound to implement them in the absence of consensus on the council or between the major powers. Walshe told Lester on 20 November that McGilligan believed the League was 'stronger as a court of conciliation than as an engine of coercion' and did not favour a rush to impose sanctions.[60] This was consistent with the Irish approach to the League, which emphasized conciliation and arbitration over recourse to sanctions. The Free State would not block a move towards sanctions but it would not initiate them either.

A suggestion from Tokyo for a commission of enquiry to investigate the situation was seized upon, even though it meant accepting the status quo while it carried out its work. The Japanese played for time, delaying agreement on the commission's terms of reference for three weeks while its military consolidated its hold in Manchuria. The Lytton Commission was established by the council on 10 December, charged with reporting on all the circumstances of an international character which threatened peace and good relations between China and Japan but, crucially, not with drawing up proposals for a resolution to the conflict.

The Free State voted to establish the commission in keeping with Lester's instructions to support proposals based on conciliation, even if he harboured personal doubts about the motivation behind the idea. This time, Lester did not push the issue of a non-permanent member on the commission, leaving it to Spain and Panama to object. Back in Dublin, the government faced an increasingly difficult political situation in the Dáil. The Statute of Westminster received royal assent as the council entered its second week of deliberations in Geneva. Preparations for the disarmament conference also weighed on minds even if the conditions for holding it seemed to grow bleaker by the day.

Lester was convinced that action by the smaller states on the council, unfettered by interests in the Far East, could have influenced the major powers to take a firmer line towards Japan. He complained that his instructions had reduced him to the role of spectator as the council went about its final business of the year. Authorized to speak at the last meeting, he decided instead to maintain a policy of 'silence in good company' with Norway and Yugoslavia as the council approved the Lytton Commission's terms of reference.

[59] Lester to Walshe, 12 Nov. 1931, NAI DFA 27/18.
[60] Walshe to Lester, 20 Nov. 1931, NAI DFA 27/18.

Edward Phelan wrote to McGilligan over the Christmas break urging the government to take a firmer line. 'We have a good name at stake,' he warned, and a duty to those who voted for the Free State 'on the grounds that we were under nobody's thumb and that precisely in such a crisis as this we would be free to take an independent League stand'.[61] But McGilligan was unwilling to sanction a more active stance at Geneva while the Lytton Commission was at work. The crisis had now lasted three months and the League had suffered a marked loss of prestige. The commission was not constituted until early January 1932, its members drawn exclusively from among the major powers, and did not leave for the Far East until the beginning of February. In the interim, the Japanese occupation was complete, a puppet administration installed and, by the end of February, Tokyo separated Manchuria from China and declared the independent state of Manchukuo.

As the disarmament conference gathered in Geneva in early February, the crisis in China entered a new and dangerous phase as fighting spread to Shanghai. The Dáil had been dissolved on 29 January and the country was in the midst of a closely fought election campaign. It might be possible to ignore what was going on in Manchuria but the economic interests of the western powers were directly threatened by events taking place within view of the international concessions in Shanghai. China requested a special meeting of the assembly under article 15 of the covenant following Japanese military action in Shanghai. Lester was told not to intervene in the debate unless absolutely necessary and then to seek instructions first. The department reiterated its position on 17 February that any move towards sanctions must come from states that would have to implement them; the Free State could only support sanctions on the basis of consensus 'no matter how unwarranted the actions of [Japan] may appear to be'.[62]

Before the Manchurian episode had reached its climax or the disarmament conference got down to work, Fianna Fáil defeated Cosgrave's Cumann na Gaedheal in a general election on 16 February and formed a new government three weeks later. Eamon de Valera took office on 9 March, opting to be his own foreign minister. His programme of removing the royal oath and halting the payment of land annuities set Dublin on a collision course with London, over-turning Cumann na nGaedheal's policy of engagement in Commonwealth matters.[63] There would be

[61] Phelan to McGilligan, 6 December 1931, UCDA P35B/121.

[62] Telegram from Department of External Affairs to Lester, 17 Feb. 1932, NAI DFA 27/18A.

[63] For a detailed account of de Valera's policy on the commonwealth, see Deirdre McMahon, *Republicans and Imperialists, Anglo-Irish Relations in the 1930s* (New Haven & London, 1984).

greater continuity at Geneva, where de Valera pursued a high-profile policy of criticism at the failure of the major powers to uphold the obligations of the Covenant.[64] The election result came as a surprise to many in the external affairs ministry, accustomed to working to a Cumann na nGaedheal agenda. Joseph Walshe had been anxious to complete the expansion of the foreign service before a Fianna Fáil government could take office. The legation in Washington reported in detail on de Valera's fund-raising visits to the United States and Walshe instructed MacWhite to pass information to the American press to counter what he called the opposition leader's 'gyrations' in the United States.[65] Walshe was not alone in wishing to see de Valera remain in opposition. Daniel Binchy was more pronounced in his political sympathies, having argued against a council bid in 1930 for fear of handing a seat to Fianna Fáil. Believing strongly in the Free State's Commonwealth vocation, he confided to the government deputy Michael Tierney in early 1931 that he would resign, using as much royal terminology as possible should Fianna Fáil enter government.[66] Ironically, Binchy's was one of the voices that persuaded Cosgrave to call the early election that brought de Valera to power. Despite his apprehensions, Walshe came to a speedy and fruitful understanding with de Valera (MacWhite dubbed him the 'leopard who changed his spots') when he held on to the external relations portfolio on entering government. Binchy made good on his pledge and resigned.

---

[64] See Kennedy, *Ireland and the League of Nations*, , in particular pp. 189–222.
[65] Walshe to MacWhite. n.d. (marked 1931), UCDA P194/300.
[66] Binchy to Tierney, 2 Jan. 1932, UCDA, LA30/406; Binchy to Tierney, 7 April 1931, UCDA, LA30/448.

Conclusion

First of the Small Nations?

The opening chapter in the story of Irish foreign policy was written before independence. A set of ideas and aspirations that took form in the first two decades of the twentieth century subsequently shaped the development of independent Ireland's early foreign policy. These ideas emerged from the imaginings of those who pictured an independent Irish state taking its place among the nations, the role it should play in world affairs, or indeed if it should involve itself at all. Many of these ideas were impractical, some even naive. To an extent, they were bound up in the very idea of separateness, an element in the articulation of a political future different to home rule.

The aspiration to a principled and disinterested view of the world has a long pedigree. It formed a part of how Irish nationalists imagined their country's place in the world. Because the Irish regarded their predicament as unique, they envisaged for themselves a unique international role, as bridge builders and honest brokers, free from the pursuit of selfish national interests to speak honestly on the international issues of the day. Eoin MacNeill told the Dáil in 1923 it was the country's destiny to be a teaching nation, setting an example to the rest of the world with 'our ancient ideals, faith, learning, generous enthusiasm, self-sacrifice—the best things calculated to purge out the meanness of the modern world.'[1] We might dismiss such ideas as over-blown romanticism, but they had a wide currency both before and after independence. Combined with a conviction that Ireland's historical experience, as nationalists saw it, should incline it to a compassionate and principled stance, the contours of Irish aspirations begin to emerge.

Over the two decades before the declaration of independence in 1919 and during the key years leading to the establishment of the Free State in

[1] Quoted in Brian Farrell, 'MacNeill and Politics', in F. X. Martin and F. J. Byrne (eds), *The Scholar Revolutionary* (Dublin, 1973), p.79.

1922, the ideas and aspirations were laid down that would shape the development of Irish foreign policy. Independence accelerated this process, as ministers were faced with the need to produce an Irish position on issues that had until then remained abstract. How to translate aspiration into activity confronted Irish leaders, and their efforts during this period can be divided between a need to preserve and advance the new state's position, and an attempt to strengthen a national identity through the elaboration and performance of international roles. As we have seen, Irish scope for action on issues of substance was limited, not only by the incomplete nature of independence, but also by the constraints imposed on the freedom of action of any small state. The former could be gradually removed in the course of Commonwealth evolution and, naturally enough, this was a priority. The latter, a function of the small state situation, could not so easily be resolved.

Speaking on the eve of independence in 1922, George Gavan Duffy had claimed that 'no country started its international career with a better potential than ours after the war.'[2] The ambitions from the Dáil period were lowered because of the civil war, the cost of building a new state and the transition from revolutionary movement to statehood. But the story of Ireland in the world was not diminished before it had properly begun, as he had once feared. A decade later, much had been achieved: the Irish Free State was an established element in the European system and a member of the League of Nations. It had blazed a trail in asserting the rights of the dominions to their own foreign policy, in the process establishing full diplomatic relations with the United States, France, Belgium, Germany, and the Holy See. It was concluding its own political and commercial treaties and using the apparatus of international relations to pursue its interests. It had received the accolade of election to a non-permanent seat on the council of the League of Nations and asserted its full equality with Britain and the other dominions within the Commonwealth. This was a remarkable and fascinating transformation; one achieved almost against the odds when set against the Free State's complex and contested birth.

We might expect a newly independent state to assert its existence by creating a foreign policy, particularly when not only the fact, but also the form of independence was unclear. Early Irish foreign policy can also be seen as an attempt to develop an international identity through the elaboration and performance of international roles. A primary ambition was to make the Free State a respected international entity. International role-playing can be seen as compensating for problems of legitimacy

---

[2] 'Confidential Memorandum by the Outgoing Minister of Foreign Affairs on the Position of Ireland's "Foreign Affairs" at date of General Election', June 1922, DFA, p. 3.

abroad, and as a means of bolstering sovereignty at home. The Irish Free State's efforts were sometimes successful, often not, and it was not able to live up to hopes of being the first of the small nations. But it was perhaps more successful than the country's small size and resources might have suggested.

By the start of the 1930s, the main tenets of an Irish foreign policy had been established with features that we might recognize today. Its main themes were a commitment to multilateralism and the rule of law, disarmament and the arbitration of disputes, and the protection of minorities. Above all, the Irish espoused the right and obligation of all states to play a part in international affairs regardless of size or means. The philosophy laid down has proved remarkably resilient in the decades since. In forging its foreign policy, the Free State drew on its European identity, its status as a mother country, its membership of the Commonwealth and a belief that it could act as a bridge between Europe and America. It was this multiple identity that enabled the Irish to aspire to a principled approach to foreign policy.

The espousal of open diplomacy and of values, honesty, and disinterest was both modern and historically grounded. It grew out of a sense of Ireland as a place outside of time, untouched by the failings of the modern world. For nationalists this was the quality that equipped Ireland to practise a new form of international politics, unsullied by association with the pre-war order or its collapse. Irish internationalism and Irish nationalism were thus intimately bound together. This was accompanied by a tendency to conflate the Irish and international cases, making Irish independence a 'test case' for the emerging liberal internationalism. It was mirrored in James Connelly's celebrated belief that the causes of Labour and Ireland were the same. For Eamon de Valera it was broader still: Sinn Féin stood not just for Irish freedom, but the freedom of mankind. Irish internationalism thus quickly took up the idea of the League of Nations and its transformative agenda, seeing in it a path to security and equality as well as a vehicle for a better world it believed could be created if the old ways of big power rivalry could be set aside. This attraction manifested itself in the imagining of Ireland as a seat for the League and, more practically, in an active engagement at Geneva which came to characterize the Free State's policy from the middle of the 1920s.

If some of the language used by nationalists conveyed the impression of a country outside the European mainstream, this was not the case. The influence of international currents can be seen in the ideas circulating in Ireland in the years before independence—nourished, in part, through exposure to trans-national movements at gatherings of stateless peoples during the pre-war years. Networks of Irish men and women were influenced by the currents of nationalist and internationalist thought shaping wider European discussion on the role of the nation and the state; their relationship with each other and their rights and obligations as members of a newly conceived international community of states. The international suffrage movement exposed Irish women and some men to broader currents of thought. Catholic internationalism, whether fuelled by a missionary impetus or a preoccupation with countering the spread of communism, was also a shaping factor for many, evident in the views and decisions of policy-makers and those who sought to influence them.

The Free State was an enthusiastic advocate of the codification of international law throughout the inter war years. In this it had a dual objective: the successive definition of international law strengthened its status as a sovereign state, as well as that of other small states. It also strengthened its hand in constitutional negotiations within the Commonwealth. Irish politicians were also committed to a pacific approach to conflict resolution, upholding the principle of League arbitration of disputes. This was also a small state interest. The ability to invoke League opinion in its support was important as the Free State pushed the boundaries of dominion status. The business of the League also provided a forum in which to establish precedents that would aid the country in its constitutional development. The desire to support international arbitration as a small state interest dovetailed with the need to demonstrate the country's independence through alternative mechanisms to Commonwealth membership. In this sense, multilateral foreign policy also served Irish interests in the narrower field of Irish–British relations.

The League assisted Irish efforts to carve out a foreign policy, as it did other small states, by providing a framework and rulebook and by creating a level playing field, however circumscribed and notional. As Michael MacWhite observed, one member was as good as another at Geneva and efforts were concentrated there.[3] The Geneva insider, Edward Phelan, regarded the League as crucial not only to the young state's foreign policy, but to its constitutional status as well. In his view, 'the work at Geneva has been in a way as important as the Treaty itself. In fact, without it the Treaty would never have any real operation.'[4] The League focus accelerated with membership of the Council from 1930 until the collapse of collective security under the strains of the pre-war years.

Never far behind was a commitment, carefully phrased, to dominion status, as that was the bedrock upon which the country's status was based. At times it suited the Free State to insist upon correct constitutional usage,

[3] MacWhite to Smiddy, 28 July 1924, NAI DFA Berne Embassy papers.
[4] Phelan to MacWhite, 4 Mar. 1929, UCDA P194/139.

at others it was in Irish interests to elide the Free State and Ireland. Anomalies abounded, and even when they had been cleared up, the impression persisted that they remained. Efforts to push back the frontiers of dominion sovereignty were not an academic exercise. The conviction that the formal equality of states should characterize international relations was a provision by which successive Irish governments set store. As Patrick McGilligan told the Dáil in 1931, 'we are recognised at Geneva as one of the main upholders of the complete independence of the smaller states'.[5] There was, of course, a narrow interest behind this enthusiasm, as the evolving definition of international law strengthened the Free State's juridical status as a sovereign state in its own right, independent of its membership of the Commonwealth. It was also in the country's interest to mitigate the effects of anarchy in the international system. It could be argued that the Free State was not in a position to conduct its relations on any other basis; lofty ideals would thus come easily. But this does not detract from the sincerity with which this conviction was held.

Was the Irish Free State a dominion or a European small state? The League of Nations Society journal, *Concord*, asked itself just this question in 1928, concluding that the country had a foot in both camps.[6] Addressing League enthusiasts the following year, Patrick McGilligan affirmed his belief that the role of the small state in international affairs was growing. Increasingly, Irish foreign policy came to presuppose the country's identity as one of these small states, though with the shadow of the diaspora and Commonwealth membership ever present in the background.

There was a tension between the different spheres of Irish diplomatic activity. At times, the Free State was able to play off its League and Commonwealth memberships, seeking to portray itself as the only dominion that did not espouse British interests and the only European state with an insight into Commonwealth affairs. Election to a non-permanent seat on the League council in 1930 demonstrated that it had succeeded in this (so much so that the British were concerned about what an Irish seat would mean for their interests). This multiple image corresponds to the dichotomy between the country's identity as both English-speaking and European. Politicians and diplomats sought to combine and transcend these different identities and aspirations. The Free State's response to the French proposals for European integration in 1930 captured its multiple identity; the diaspora constituted 'a moral union in no degree less binding than that which exists between this country and the other European states.' Reflecting a long-standing duality in nationalist thinking, for the

---

[5] *Dáil Éireann deb.*, vol. 39, col. 128, 1931.   [6] *Concord*, Feb. 1928.

Irish government, any European scheme could 'only partially express the true orientation of the Irish political consciousness'.[7]

Once independence was achieved, the cares and concerns of the outside world faded in significance as more pressing demands closer to home occupied policy-makers. The proposition that Ireland should not have a foreign policy at all, however briefly held, was as much an expression of Irish exceptionalism as the belief that the country should pursue an external policy based on exclusively principled or even transcendental lines. Each was equally impractical of being pursued once a state had been established. Proponents of both viewpoints relied on the notion of Ireland being a country apart, but states do not live apart and each would prove as unrealistic as the other.

Asserting the right to conduct a foreign policy was an integral element in building the Irish state, particularly given the incomplete constitutional evolution of the dominions at the time. W. T. Cosgrave came to understand that the state's internal structures could only be ensured if its external consolidation was also taken in hand. Speaking at his party's *ard fheis* in 1927, he outlined his belief that 'no nation can be free to work out its destiny at home unless its international status and integrity are safeguarded'. For that reason, he viewed the department of external affairs as 'one of the most important elements in our State system'.[8] Despite this, the foreign ministry remained a marginal branch in the early Irish administration, a reminder of the political divisions of the civil war, remote from the pursuit of everyday concerns, its internationalist mission neither understood nor appreciated elsewhere in government.

The Free State was able to benefit from a benign geopolitical setting compared to its small state counterparts, even if continuing friction in Irish-British relations served as a reminder that this had not always been the case. Reflecting on this from Danzig as League high commissioner in 1935, Seán Lester wrote to Ernest Blythe 'life between the frontiers in north eastern Europe does make one appreciate some of our geographical advantages at home'.[9] A stable and secure backyard made it easier to pursue a principled approach and to develop a tradition of international good citizen or 'international citizenship' as Edward Phelan dubbed it.

There was a level of outside interest in developing ties with the Free State, but this was limited when compared to other European small states

---

[7] 'Response of the Irish Free State Government to a Memorandum of the French Government on European Federal Union', 17 July 1930, NAI DFA S2/25(a).

[8] William Cosgrave, *The Policy of the Cumann na nGaedheal Party* (Dublin, 1927), p. 11.

[9] Lester to Blythe, 30 April 1935, UCDA P24/1556.

for whom history, geography, and economics prompted the development of a larger diplomatic infrastructure to manage relations with their neighbours. There were a number of reasons for this. If the development of ties between countries entails a mixture of push and pull, in the Free State's case it was more a question of push from Dublin than pull from abroad. The Irish had to push against the considerable weight of British power and the imperial edifice. What pull there was from abroad was frequently attenuated by fears of alienating London.

The small size of the Free State economy, the dominance of its agricultural sector, and an overwhelming dependence on the British market meant there was little pressure from industry to open diplomatic missions or trade offices in foreign markets. Commercial treaties could be negotiated without a direct diplomatic channel owing to the agreement that the dominions could use British missions. The expense of maintaining an expansive infrastructure of legations and consulates was thus avoided. Instead, the idea was established that relationships with other countries could be managed through participation in multilateral frameworks, be it the League of Nations or the Commonwealth, rather than through direct and formal diplomatic relations. By contrast, the only European countries with which Finland did not have diplomatic relations by 1939 were Albania, the Holy See, and Ireland.

As in other areas of national life, the ambitious rhetoric of pre-independence Sinn Féin was not easily matched after 1923. No real attempt was made to act upon the pledge made at Geneva to protect or promote Celtic culture abroad, much to the lament of scholars and language activists, although it is difficult to see what the Free State could have achieved with its limited resources. Civil servants were quick to dismiss Gaelic League links with Breton nationalists in 1928 as 'Gaelic blather', and intervened to put a stop to them.[10]

Irish independence arguably represented a strengthening of the principle of self-determination that, previously, had been applied on the territory of defeated states or collapsed empires. Yet despite this, and in contrast to Irish governments' support for decolonization in the 1950s and 1960s, the Free State did not pursue an identity based on support for self-determination. Having secured independence, it made little sense to become a cheerleader for the cause of others, whatever the personal sympathies of many Irish men and women at the time. The unresolved situation in Northern Ireland was perhaps another reason, Cosgrave and

[10] P. S. O'Hegarty to W. T. Cosgrave, 19 Oct. 1928, NAI DFA Paris embassy P19/11.

his ministers believing partition would be resolved over time between the two parts of Ireland and not through agitation at Geneva or elsewhere.

There were also limits to the extent that what was then called a race-based policy could be pursued. Government ministers made regular reference to the overseas Irish in the Dáil and at Geneva. A defence report submitted to the cabinet in 1925 even envisaged using the diaspora for propaganda and sabotage in the event of war.[11] But the Free State made little effort to engage its diaspora, relying instead on the potential for influence and the memory of mobilization during the campaign for independence. This had a certain convenience: the actual strength of this supposed influence was never tested, nor was its utility as a foreign policy tool. Only as propaganda at election time, or as a rhetorical device at international gatherings, did aspirations to a race-based foreign policy approach reality.

This was combined with projecting a folksy image of the state and its people, derived from a mixture of romantic nationalism and Celtic history that cultural nationalists had popularized, and which the tourist board inherited from them. Tourist posters of misty Connacht hills by Paul Henry were characteristic of efforts to portray the country abroad, as were those designed by Seán Keating in 1929 to advertise Irish dairy produce in Britain. Featuring a group of almost Iberian-looking peasants surrounded by hens and ramshackle farmyard buildings, the campaign was juxtaposed against the image of modernity and financial probity that Irish leaders sought to portray abroad.[12]

The men who shaped this first foreign policy—and they were men: however limited it may have been, female involvement in the Dáil's diplomacy became an early victim of 'normalization' after the civil war—reflected the mostly conservative nature of the nationalist revolution. Unlike their counterparts in almost every other diplomatic service at the time, none were men of means. Michael MacWhite's office in Geneva doubled as a family sitting room by evening; dinner invitations had to be declined for lack of funds to reciprocate, and Professor Smiddy complained of being unable to compete when the wealthy businessman Vincent Massey arrived in Washington as Canadian minister in 1926.

Unsurprisingly, they were predominantly Catholic; Joseph Walshe and Vaughan Dempsey had been clerical students. Seán Lester was a Protestant and both he and Michael MacWhite had worked as journalists, as had Desmond FitzGerald. Most had studied at University College Dublin,

---

[11] 'Request for Direction on Defence Policy—Submission by the Defence Council to the Executive Council', 1925, p. 7, MA, DOD 4./1478.

[12] For a photograph of the poster, see file at NAI, DT 55 1981.

although two of the most accomplished diplomats from the period— Lester and MacWhite—had no formal education. A majority came from Munster, closely followed by Ulster and Leinster, with Connacht under-represented. Until the first recruitment was held by public competition in 1929, its staff was drawn from the ranks of those who had been active in secondary positions in the Sinn Féin movement's overseas activities. While Seán Murphy and Osmond Grattan Esmonde came from promin-ent home rule families, the sons and daughters of those who expected to govern in a home rule Ireland did not make their way into the early department of external affairs.

Nor did the nationalist movement attract Irish staff from the British Foreign Office; only James McNeill had anything approaching a comparable experience, in the colonial service in India. There was thus no transfer of experience or know-how to the nascent Irish foreign ministry. The suspicion that greeted Irish people who had worked for the British state, particularly in those institutions most closely associated in nationalist eyes with the imperial and unionist traditions, meant that any who may have been tempted to seek a position would have been unwelcome. The experience was rather different in Norway, where the former permanent under secretary of state in the Swedish foreign ministry, Thor von Ditten, played a leading role in setting up a Norwegian foreign service after independence in 1905.

Prior to independence, nationalism was unburdened by the actuality of statehood or any realistic estimate of what it might entail. Once estab-lished, the Free State had interests like any state, the protection of which on occasion constrained its freedom to pursue a principled line. The Irish might not have selfish international aims but their larger neighbours did and keeping Britain onside was a policy priority for as long as the constitutional agenda remained open. Many at the time had fluid under-standings of the limits of state action or of what constituted national interest. There were those who exhorted the government to use its influence on behalf of this or that cause, or to intervene with the British to rectify colonial transgressions. This was unsurprising as the nationalist movement accommodated itself to the reality of government. If in the clamour for independence the idealists held sway, once it had been achieved the voice of the realists was heard more clearly.

The Irish Free State espoused a modern understanding of foreign policy that went beyond the promotion and protection of interests to encompass values and ideals. Why is this significant? Because it is an early example of an independence movement using disinterest to argue for independence, and of a state seeking to espouse a foreign policy based on values. Equally modern was the attempt to create an international rationale for Irish independence by arguing that it would be in the interests of the international community, itself a concept that was new at the time. While these ideas have become commonplace today, in the early years of the twentieth century they were relatively unknown. In its mastery of the press release and the publicity stunt, Sinn Féin was also ahead of its day, recognizing the potential power of international public opinion if properly organized.

The politician and polemicist Conor Cruise O'Brien was probably right when he suggested that foreign policy was unlikely to make the rafters ring in Roscommon. But there was nonetheless a level of interest extending beyond the external affairs department. The fact that both Cumann na nGaedheal and Fianna Fáil used foreign policy in their electoral campaigns (if only to demonstrate their respective versions of the Free State's true constitutional status); the stirrings of civil society evident in the work of the League of Nations Society, the international disarmament petition and the congress of the Women's International League for Peace and Freedom, it is necessary to at least reconsider the view that the Free State in the 1920s was an introverted place unaware of its surroundings or unwilling to contribute to them.

What outlet or in which direction might Irish nationalism and its foreign policy have taken had it not been absorbed with consolidating and expanding the settlement of 1921? The British may have been wiser to cut the Free State adrift, an entity it would have found easier to dominate as an isolated state than as a Commonwealth member. While the direction of constitutional development within the Commonwealth was perhaps inevitable, the pace at which it was achieved was not. The Canadians and South Africans were supportive of steps to flesh out dominion rights in the external arena, but it is possible to imagine a more gradual and less contentious evolution in a Commonwealth without Ireland.

For all the bitterness of the civil war divide, a certain consensus existed regarding the international values to which an Irish state should aspire, even while the form of the state and the means through which policy should be pursued were contested. The change of government in 1932 was thus marked by a combination of continuity in League policy and change on the Commonwealth front, as Eamon de Valera set about dismantling much of the Treaty settlement and, with it, Cumann na nGaedheal's policy of critical engagement with the Commonwealth. Even if Cosgrave's government had been returned, it is possible to imagine Irish positions diverging by ever-greater degrees once the goal of equality within the Commonwealth had been achieved.

There was a further motivation behind the desire to create an Irish foreign policy. The Irish wished to have their voice heard, and believed they had something worth saying. Arthur Griffith maintained that the British had built a paper wall around Ireland. On the inside they painted what they wanted the Irish to know about the rest of the world; on the outside what they wanted the rest of the world to know about Ireland. The notion of breaking through that wall, as much as the pursuit of national self-interest and the desire to complete the unfinished business of December 1921, motivated Irish attempts to forge a foreign policy in the first years after independence. As Patrick McGilligan explained a decade later, 'we are telling the world something worthy of ourselves at last'.[13] Reflecting on the changes that had occurred in the country's relationship with the outside world, Hugh Law pictured a scene from his constituency in the south of Ireland:

> In a small neighbouring farmhouse a boy has just installed a wireless set, and that even in this most remotest corner we can hear the chimes of Big Ben, have the latest news of the English markets, discuss the doings at The Hague, and follow with interest and pride the speeches of our representatives at Geneva. For good or for evil (doubtless for both) the old isolation is at an end.[14]

[13] *Dáil Éireann deb.*, vol. 39, col. 128, 1931.
[14] Hugh Law, 'The Irish Free State in 1929', *Review of Reviews* (Sept. 1929), p. 194.

Bibliography

1. ARCHIVES

Dáil Éireann Papers
Department of Defence
Department of Finance
Department of Foreign Affairs
Department of the Taoiseach
Dominions Office
Foreign Office
Government and Executive Council Minutes
Governor General files
Military Archives, Dublin
Ministry of Foreign Affairs, Paris

2. PRIVATE PAPERS

Ernest Blythe	UCDA
Erskine Childers	TCD
Liam de Róiste	Cork Archives Institute
Eamon de Valera	UCDA
George Gavan Duffy	NLI and NAI
Desmond FitzGerald	UCDA
Michael Hayes	UCDA
Thomas Johnson	NLI
Hugh Kennedy	UCDA
Louis le Brocquy	NLI
Seán Lester	UNOG
Joseph McGarrity	NLI
Patrick McGilligan	UCDA
Kathleen Napoli McKenna	NLI
Michael MacWhite	UCDA
Colonel Maurice Moore	NLI
Art O'Brien	NLI
Seán T. Ó Ceallaigh	NLI
Count Plunkett	NLI
Austin Stack	NLI
Michael Tierney	UCDA
Bolton C. Waller Memorial Fund	NAI

3. NEWSPAPERS AND CONTEMPORARY PERIODICALS

Catholic Bulletin
Church of Ireland Gazette
Concord
Irish Freedom
The Irish Independent
The Irish Statesman
The Irish Times
Nationality
New Ireland
New Ireland Review
The Round Table
Scissors and Paste
Sinn Féin
The Star
Studies
United Ireland
United Irishman

4. BOOKS AND ARTICLES

aan de Wiel, Jerome, *The Irish Factor, 1899–1919, Ireland's Strategic and Diplomatic Importance for Foreign Powers* (Dublin, 2008).

Andrews, C. S., *Dublin Made Me* (Dublin, 1979).

Andrews, C. S., *Man of No Property* (Dublin, 1982).

Barton, Robert, *The Truth about the Treaty and Document No. 2* (Dublin, 1922).

Bennett, Louie, *Ireland and a People's Peace* (Dublin & London, 1918).

Bewley, Charles, *Memoirs of a Wild Goose* (Dublin, 1989).

Birmingham, George, *An Irishman Looks at his World* (London, 1919).

Boyd, Ernest, 'Ireland, Resurgent and Insurgent', *Foreign Affairs*, vol. 1, no. 1 (September 1922), pp. 86–97.

Brennan, Robert, *Allegiance* (Dublin, 1950).

Briscoe, Robert, *For the Life of Me* (London, 1958).

Brown, Stephen, 'Catholic Internationalism', *Studies*, no. 13 (September 1925), pp. 474–9.

Cahill, Edward, *Freemasonry and the Anti-Christian Movement* (Dublin, 1929).

Campbell, Malcolm, *Ireland's New Worlds: Immigrants, Politics and Society in the United States and Australia, 1815–1922* (Madison, 2008).

Carroll, Francis, *American Opinion and the Irish Question, 1910–23* (Dublin, 1978).

Casement, Roger, *Ireland, Germany and the Next War* (Belfast, 1913).

Childers, Erskine, *The Framework of Home Rule* (London, 1911).

Childers, Erskine, *Is Ireland a Danger to England?* (Dublin, 1921).

Clavin, Patricia, *Securing the World Economy, the Reinvention of the League of Nations, 1920–1945* (Oxford, 2013).

Collins, Michael, *Free State or Chaos* (Dublin, 1922).

Collins, Michael, *The Path to Freedom* (Dublin, 1922).

Comerford, R. V., *The Fenians in Context* (Dublin, 1985).

Coogan, Tim Pat, *De Valera, Long Fellow, Long Shadow* (London, 1993).

Cosgrave, W. T., *The Policy of the Cumann na nGaedheal Party* (Dublin, 1927).

Coxhead, Elizabeth, *Daughters of Erin* (London, 1965).

Cronin, Michael, 'The League of Nations Covenant', *Studies*, vol. 8 (March 1919), pp. 19–34.

Cronin, Seán, *The McGarrity Papers* (Tralee, 1972).

Davies, Richard, *Arthur Griffith and Non-Violent Sinn Féin* (Dublin, 1974).

Davis, Troy D., 'Diplomacy as Propaganda: The Appointment of T. A. Smiddy as Irish Free State Minister to the United States', *Éire-Ireland* 31 (Fall/Winter, 1996), pp. 117–29.

Dawson, Richard, *Red Terror and Green, the Sinn Fein-Bolshevist Movement* (London, 1920).

de Blácam, Aodh, *Towards the Republic* (Dublin, 1919).

de Valera, Eamon, *Eamon de Valera States his Case* (Boston, 1918).

de Valera, Eamon, *Ireland's Case Against Conscription* (Dublin & London, 1918).

de Valera, Eamon, *A National Policy* (Dublin, 1926).

de Valera, Eamon, *Fianna Fáil and its Economic Policy* (Dublin, 1928).

de Vere White, Terence, *Kevin O'Higgins* (London, 1948).

Devoy, John, *Recollections of an Irish Rebel* (Shannon, 1969).

Dryhurst, N. F. (ed.), *Nationalities and Subject Races, Report of a Conference held in Caxton Hall, Westminster, June 28–30, 1910* (London, 1911).

Duffy, Colm Gavan, 'George Gavan Duffy', *Dublin Historical Record*, vol. 36, no. 3 (June 1983).

Duffy, George Gavan, *La République d'Irlande et la Presse Française* (Paris, 1919).

English, Richard, *Radicals and the Republic: Socialist Republicanism in the Irish Free State, 1925–1937* (Oxford, 1995).

Escoufflaire, R. C., *L'Irlande ennemi?* (Paris, 1918).

Fanning, Ronan, *The Irish Department of Finance, 1922–58* (Dublin, 1978).

Fanning, Ronan, 'Irish Neutrality–an Historical Review', *Irish Studies in International Affairs*, vol. 1, no. 3 (1982), pp. 27–31.

Faucon, Guillaume, *Le statut de l'Etat Libre d'Irlande* (Paris, 1929).

Figgis, Darrell, *The Gaelic State in the Past and the Future* (Dublin & London, 1917).

Figgis, Darrell, *The Historic Case for Irish Independence* (Dublin, 1918).

Figgis, Darrell, *Recollections of the War in Ireland* (London, 1927).

FitzGerald, Desmond, *Memoirs of Desmond FitzGerald, 1913–1916* (London, 1968).

FitzGerald, Garret, *All in a Life* (Dublin, 1991).

FitzGerald, Garret, *Ireland in the World, Further Reflections* (Dublin, 2005).

FitzGerald, William G., *The Voice of Ireland* (Dublin & London, 1925).

Fitzpatrick, David, *Harry Boland's Irish Revolution* (Cork, 2003).

Foley, Tadhg and O'Connor, Maureen (eds) *Ireland and India, Colonies, Culture and Empire* (Dublin, 2007).

Foster, R. F., *The Story of Ireland* (Oxford, 1995).

Fraser, Major Gen Sir Thomas, *The Military Danger of Home Rule for Ireland* (London, 1912).

Gaffney, Thomas St John, *Breaking the Silence* (New York, 1930).

Gallopin, Roger, *Le conflit anglo-irlandais* (Paris, 1935).

Garvin, Tom, *Nationalist Revolutionaries in Ireland, 1858–1928* (Oxford, 1987).

Gay, Francisque, *L'Irlande et la Societé des Nations* (Paris, 1921).

Ginnell, Lawrence, *The Irish Republic. Why?* (New York, 1919).

Glandon, Virginia, Arthur *Griffith and the Advanced Nationalist Press in Ireland, 1900–1922* (New York, 1985).

Gnathaí Gan Iarraidgh (Ernest Augustus Boyd), *The Sacred Egoism of Sinn Féin* (Dublin & London, n.d.).

Golding, G. M., *George Gavan Duffy, 1882–1951* (Dublin, 1982).

Green, E. E. R., 'The Fenians Abroad' in T. Desmond Williams (ed.), *Secret Societies in Ireland* (Dublin, 1973).

Griffith, Arthur, *The Resurrection of Hungary: a Parallel for Ireland* (Dublin, 1904).

Griffith, Arthur, *The 'Sinn Féin' Policy* (Dublin, 1905).

Griffith, Arthur, *When the Government Publishes Sedition, Tracts for the Times No. 4* (Dublin, 1915).

Gwynn, Denis, 'The Grand Orient in France', *Studies*, no. 14 (June 1925).

Gwynn, Denis, *The Irish Free State, 1922–1927* (London, 1928).

Gwynn, Stephen, *The Case for Home Rule* (Dublin, 1911).

Gwynn, Stephen, *The Irish Situation* (London, 1921).

Gwynn, Stephen, 'Ireland since the Treaty', *Foreign Affairs*, vol. 12, no. 2 (January 1934), pp. 319–30.

Harkness, David, *The Restless Dominion* (London, 1969).

Harkness, David, 'Patrick McGilligan, Man of Commonwealth', *Journal of Imperial and Commonwealth Political History*, vol. 8, no. 8. (October 1979).

Harrison, Richard S., *Irish Anti-War Movements, 1824–1974* (Dublin, 1986).

Hartley, Stephen, *The Irish Question as a Problem in British Foreign Policy, 1914–18* (London, 1987).

Higgins, James, *The Irish Government Difficulty, Considered as a Race Question* (Manchester, 1867).

Hilliker, John, *Canada's Department of External Affairs, Volume 1: The Early Years, 1909–1946* (Montréal, 1990).

Hodson, H. V., 'Éire and the British Commonwealth', *Foreign Affairs*, vol. 16. No. 3 (April, 1938), pp. 525–36.

Hogan, James, *Ireland in the European System* (London, 1920).

Horgan, John, *Seán Lemass, the Enigmatic Patriot* (Dublin, 1997).

Horgan, John J., 'The World Polity of President Wilson', *Studies*, vol. 7 (Dec. 1918), pp. 553–63.

Horgan, John J., Ireland and World Contract', *Studies*, vol. 8, no. 29. (Mar. 1919), pp. 35–45.

Horgan, John J., *Parnell to Pearse* (Dublin, 1949).

International Labour Organisation, *Edward Phelan and the ILO, The Life and Views of an International Social Actor* (Geneva, 2009).

Irish Republican Association of South Africa, *The Irish in South Africa 1920–21* (Cape Town, 1921).

Jaspe, Alvaro, '"Cautela, seguir mudo." Madrid's Diplomatic Response to the Emergence of the Irish Free State 1918–1931', *Estudios Irlandeses*, Issue 3 (2008), pp. 121–31.

Karsh, Efraim, *Neutrality and Small States* (London, 1988).

Keatinge, Patrick, *The Formulation of Irish Foreign Policy* (Dublin, 1973).

Keatinge, Patrick, *A Place Among the Nations: Issues of Irish Foreign Policy* (Dublin, 1978).

Kelly, M. J., *The Fenian Ideal and Irish Nationalism* (Woodbridge, 2006).

Kennedy, Michael, '"Candour and Chicanery": The Irish Free State and the Geneva Protocol, 1924–25', *Irish Studies in International Affairs*, vol. 29, no. 115 (May 1995).

Kennedy, Michael, '"Principle Well-Seasoned with the Sauce of Realism": Seán Lester, Joseph Walshe and the definition of the Irish Free State's Policy Towards Manchuria', *Irish Studies in International Affairs*, vol. 6 (1995), pp. 79–94.

Kennedy, Michael, *Ireland and the League of Nations, 1919–1946, International Relations, Diplomacy and Politics* (Dublin, 1996).

Kennedy, Michael and Skelly, Joseph Morrison (eds), *Irish Foreign Policy, 1919–1966, from Independence to Internationalism* (Dublin, 2000).

Kenny, P. D., *Five Years of Irish Freedom* (London, 1927).

Keogh, Dermot, *The Vatican, the Bishops and Irish Politics, 1919–39* (Cambridge, 1986).

Keogh, Dermot, *Ireland and Europe, 1919–48: A Diplomatic and Political History* (Dublin, 1988); revised edition, *Ireland and Europe, 1919–1989* (Cork & Dublin, 1990).

Keogh, Dermot, *Ireland and the Vatican, The Politics and Diplomacy of Church-State Relations, 1922–1960* (Cork, 1995).

Keogh, Dermot, *Jews in Twentieth-Century Ireland: Refugees, Anti-Semitism and the Holocaust* (Cork, 1998).

Keown, Gerard, 'Taking the World Stage: Creating an Irish Foreign Policy in the 1920s' in Michael Kennedy and Joseph Morrison Skelly (eds), *Irish Foreign Policy, 1919–1966, from Independence to Internationalism* (Dublin, 2000), pp. 25–43.

Keown, Gerard, 'The Irish Race Conference, 1922, reconsidered', *Irish Historical Studies*, xxxii, no. 127 (May, 2001), pp. 365–76.

Keown, Gerard, 'Seán Lester: Journalist, Revolutionary, Diplomat, Statesman', *Irish Studies in International Affairs*, vol. 23 (2012), pp. 143–54.

Kettle, Tom, *The Irish Party and its Assailants: Its Policy Vindicated* (Dublin, 1907).

Kissane, Bill, *The Politics of the Irish Civil War* (Oxford, 2005).

Knowles, Sir Lees, *Irish Impressions* (London, 1918).

Kohn, Leo, *The Constitution of the Irish Free State* (London, 1932).

Laffan, Michael, *The Resurrection of Ireland, The Sinn Féin Party, 1916–1923* (Cambridge, 1999).

Litvack, Leon and Graham, Colin (eds), *Ireland and Europe in the Nineteenth Century* (Dublin, 2006).

Longford, Earl of, and O'Neill, T. P., *Eamon de Valera* (London, 1970).

Lynd, Robert, *If the Germans Conquered Ireland and Other Essays* (Dublin, 1917).

Lyons, G. A., *Some Recollections of Griffith and his Times* (Dublin, 1923).

MacNeill, Eoin, 'Ireland's Place Among the Nations' in Eoin MacNeill and William Moore, *Representative Irishmen and International Resurrection* (Dublin, 1918).

McCartan, Patrick, *With de Valera in America* (Dublin, 1932).

McCarthy, John P., *Kevin O'Higgins, Builder of the Irish State* (Dublin, 2006).

McCullagh, Francis, 'The Baltic States from an Irish Point of View', *Studies*, no. 11 (Mar. 1922), pp. 29–44; (June 1922), pp. 186–98; (Sept. 1922), pp. 400–8; No. 12 (Mar. 1923), pp. 7–25.

McGarry, Fearghal and McConnel James (eds), *The Black Hand of Republicanism, Fenianism in Modern Ireland* (Dublin, 2009).

McKenna Kathleen, Napoli, 'The Irish Bulletin', *Capuchin Annual* (1970), pp. 526–8.

McMahon, Deirdre, *Republicans and Imperialists, Anglo-Irish Relations in the 1930s* (New Haven & London, 1984).

McMahon, Deirdre, 'Ireland and the Empire-Commonwealth, 1900–1948' in Judith M. Brown and Wm. Roger Louis (eds), *The Oxford History of the British Empire: The Twentieth Century* (Oxford, 1999).

McMahon, Paul, *British Spies and Irish Rebels, British Intelligence and Ireland, 1916–1945* (Woodbridge, 2008).

Maguire, John Francis, *The Irish in America* (London, 1868).

Maguire, Maria, *A Bibliography of Published Works on Irish Foreign Relations, 1921–78* (Dublin, 1981).

Maguire, Martin, *The Civil Service and the Revolution in Ireland, 1912–38, 'Shaking the Blood-stained Hand of Mr Collins'* (Manchester, 2008).

Mahon, Tom and Gillogly, James A., *Decoding the IRA* (Dublin, 2008).

Manela, Erez, *The Wilsonian Moment, Self-determination and the International Origins of Anticolonial Nationalism* (Oxford, 2007).

Mansergh, Nicholas, *The Irish Free State, Its Government and Politics* (London, 1934).

Marks, Sally, *The Ebbing of European Ascendancy, an International History of the World, 1914–1945* (London, 2002).

Matthews, Ann, *Renegades, Irish Republican Women 1900–1922* (Dublin, 2010).

Meleady, Dermot, *John Redmond, The National Leader* (Dublin, 2014).

Mitchel, John, *Jail Journal*, (Dublin, 1915).

Mitchel, John, *Ireland, France and Prussia* (Dublin, 1918).

Mitchell, Arthur, *Revolutionary Government in Ireland: Dáil Éireann 1919–1922* (Dublin, 1995).

Montegut, Emile, *John Mitchel, A study of Irish nationalism*, (Dublin, 1915), p. 11. (Originally published as 'An exile of Young Ireland' in *Revue des Deux Mondes*, (Paris, 1855)).

Murphy, Brian P., *John Chartres, Mystery Man of the Treaty* (Dublin, 1995).

Nolan, Aengus, *Joseph Walshe, Irish Foreign Policy, 1922–1946* (Dublin, 2008).

O'Connor, Emmet, *Reds and the Green, Ireland, Russia and the Communist Internationals, 1919–43* (Dublin, 2004).

O'Donnell, Elliott, *The Irish Abroad* (London, 1915).

O'Driscoll, Mervyn, *Ireland, Germany and the Nazis, Politics and Diplomacy, 1919–1939* (Dublin, 2004).

O'Halpin, Eunan, *Defending Ireland, The Irish State and its Enemies Since 1922* (Oxford, 1999).

O'Halpin, Eunan, *Spying on Ireland, British Intelligence and Irish Neutrality During the Second World War* (Oxford, 2008).

O'Hegarty, P. S., *Sinn Féin, an Illumination* (Dublin & London, 1919).

O'Hegarty, P. S., 'The Significance of Woodrow Wilson', *Studies*, no. 13 (Mar. 1924), pp. 129–30.

O'Hegarty, P. S., *The Victory of Sinn Féin* (Dublin, 1924).

O'Higgins, Kevin, *The New De Valera* (Dublin, 1922).

O'Higgins, Kevin, *L'Irlande d'Aujourd'hui* (Brussels, 1925).

O'Kelly, J. J., *The Sinn Féin Outlook* (Dublin 1930).

O'Kelly, J. J., *The Republic of Ireland Vindicated* (Dublin 1931).

O'Kelly, Seán T., *Sinn Féin and the Peace Conference* (Dublin, 1919).

O'Kelly, Seán T., *Ireland and India* (New York, 1925).

O'Leary, John, *Recollections of Fenians and Fenianism* (London, 1896).

O'Malley, Kate, *Ireland, India and Empire: Indo-Irish Radical Connections, 1919–64* (Manchester, 2008).

O'Riain, W. P., *Lessons from Modern Language Movements* (Dublin, 1902).

O'Riordan, E. J., *Modern Irish Trade and Industry* (London, 1920).

O'Shea, John Augustus, *Leaves from the Life of a Special Correspondent* (London, 1885).

O'Sullivan, M. D., 'Eight Years of Irish Home Rule', *Quarterly Review*, no. 504 (April 1930), pp. 230–49.

Pearse, Pádraig, *Three Lectures on Gaelic Topics* (Dublin, 1913).

Pearse, Pádraig, The Sovereign People, *Tracts for the Times* No. 13 (Dublin, 1916).

Pearse, Pádraig, *The Story of a Success* (Dublin & London, 1917).

Pedersen, Susan, 'Review Essay: Back to the League of Nations', *American Historical Review* (October, 2007), pp. 1091–117.

Phelan, E. J., 'Ireland and the International Labour Organisation', *Studies*, vol. 15 part 1 (Mar. 1926), pp. 1–18; part 2 (Sept. 1926), pp. 381–98.

Pope-Hennessy, Col. R., *The Irish Dominion* (London, 1919).

Redmond, John, *The Home Rule Bill* (Dublin, 1912).

Redmond, John, *The Justice of Home Rule* (Dublin, 1912).

Redmond-Howard, L. G., *Ireland, the Peace Conference and the League of Nations* (Dublin, 1918).

Regnault, Raymond, *Le Courroux nationaliste en Irlande* (Paris, 1932).

Riste, Olav, *Norway's Foreign Relations—a History* (Oslo, 2005).

Russell, George (Æ), *Thoughts for a Convention, memorandum on the State of Ireland* (Dublin & London, 1917).

Russell, George (Æ), *The Inner and the Outer Ireland* (London, 1921).

Russell, George (Æ), *Ireland and the Empire at the Court of International Conscience* (Dublin, 1921).

Russell, George (Æ), 'Twenty-five Years of Irish Nationality', *Foreign Affairs*, vol. 7, no. 2 (Jan. 1929), pp. 204–20.

Russell, T. D., *Is Ireland a Dying Nation* (Dublin, 1906).

Ryan, John, 'The New Era in Spain', *Studies*, vol. 13, no. 51 (Sept. 1924), pp. 467–75.

Salmon, Trevor, *Unneutral Ireland: An Ambivalent and Unique Security Policy* (Oxford, 1989).

Samuels, Arthur Warren, *Home Rule: Fenian Home Rule: Home Rule All Round: What do they mean?* (Dublin, n.d.).

Shaw, George Bernard, *The League of Nations, Fabian Tract No. 226* (London, Jan. 1919).

Sheehy Skeffington, Hanna, *Impressions of Sinn Féin in America* (Dublin, 1919).

Sinn Féin, *Sinn Féin Economic Programme* (Dublin, n.d.).

Sinn Féin, *Sinn Féin in Tabloid Form, Sinn Féin Tracts no. 1.* (Dublin, 1917).

Sinn Féin, *The Small Nations, Sinn Féin Tracts no. 5.* (Dublin, 1917).

Sinn Féin, *The Constructive Work of Dáil Éireann No. 2.* (Dublin, 1921).

Sluga, Glenda, *Internationalism in the Age of Nationalism* (Philadelphia, 2013).

Smiddy, T., 'The Position of the Irish Free State in the British Commonwealth of Nations', in *Harris Foundation Lectures* (Chicago, 1927).

Spedding, Rosamund, *The Call of Democracy: A Study of the Irish Question* (Dublin, 1919).

Steiner, Zara, *The Lights that Failed, European International History, 1919–1933* (Oxford, 2005).

Stephens, James, *On the Capacity of Ireland to Exist as an Independent State* (Dublin, 1862).

Sullivan, A. M., *The Story of Ireland* (Dublin, 1880).

Sullivan, T. D., *Recollections of Troubled Times in Irish Politics* (Dublin, 1905).

Tonra, Ben, *Global Citizen and European Republic: Irish Foreign Policy in Transition* (Manchester, 2012).

Treguiéz, Louis (Yann Goblet), *L'Irlande dans la crise universelle* (Paris, 1917).

Waller, Bolton C., *Hibernia, or the Future of Ireland* (London, 1928).

Waller, Bolton C., *Ireland and the League of Nations* (Dublin, 1928).

Walters, F. P., *A History of the League of Nations* (Oxford, 1952).

Wells, Warre B., *An Irish Apologia* (Dublin & London, 1917).

Wells, Warre B. and Marlowe, N. (J. M. Hone), *The Irish Convention and Sinn Féin* (Dublin & London, 1918).

Whelan, Bernadette, *United States Foreign Policy and Ireland, From Empire to Independence, 1913–29* (Dublin, 2006).

Yearwood, Peter, *Guarantee of Peace, The League of Nations in British Policy, 1914–1925* (Oxford, 2009).

Young, Peter, 'Defence and the New Irish State', *Irish Sword*, vol. 19, nos. 75, 76 (1993–4).

Index